DOWNFALL

DOWNFALL

DOWNFALL

Putin, Prigozhin, and the fight for the future of Russia

ANNA ARUTUNYAN
& MARK GALEOTTI

EBURY PRESS

UK | USA | Canada | Ireland | Australia
India | New Zealand | South Africa

Ebury Press is part of the Penguin Random House group of companies
whose addresses can be found at global.penguinrandomhouse.com

Penguin Random House UK
One Embassy Gardens, 8 Viaduct Gardens, London SW11 7BW

penguin.co.uk
global.penguinrandomhouse.com

Penguin
Random House
UK

First published by Ebury Press in 2024
This edition published by Ebury Press in 2025
1

Typeset by Jouve (UK), Milton Keynes

Printed and bound in India by Replika Press Pvt. Ltd.

The authorised representative in the EEA is Penguin Random House Ireland,
Morrison Chambers, 32 Nassau Street, Dublin D02 YH68

A CIP catalogue record for this book is available from the British Library

ISBN 9781529927382

Contents

A Note from the Authors   *vii*

Chapter 1: Thug   1

Chapter 2: Entrepreneur   17

Chapter 3: Chef   35

Chapter 4: Minigarch   53

Chapter 5: Trollmaster   75

Chapter 6: Condottiere   101

Chapter 7: Scavenger   129

Chapter 8: Warlord   147

Chapter 9: Rebel   165

Chapter 10: Ghost   193

Epilogue   215

Notes   *223*

Index   *252*

A Note from the Authors

This is a book about one man, but at the same time about the world he inhabited and, in his own ways, shaped. Yevgeny Prigozhin first acquired infamy for the overhyped role of his trolls during the 2016 US presidential election, then for his Wagner mercenary army. When we first started considering this project, neither of us was sure that he, as a person, deserved a book, especially as so much about his life, routines and family remained a closely, ever ferociously guarded secret. The story goes, for example, that one journalist who contacted Prigozhin's press representatives because she wished to write a fairly vanilla 'day in the life' story about his eldest daughter Polina was told, first, that if she tried, they would get her sacked; then that her emails would be hacked and her secrets leaked; and finally, when she had the temerity to suggest that hers was really not that intrusive a suggestion, that her car would be run off the road and that she would be lucky not to be raped. She dropped the idea.

However, our feeling was that he represented an archetype of the Putin regime, whom we could use to explore some of our respective interests. Anna has long been tracking the way it outsources not just catering and cleaning, but statecraft and warfare. Having run into Russian mercenaries and militias in the undeclared war in the Donbas since it began in 2014, and watched how various tails could begin to wag the Kremlin dog (you can read more about this in her *Hybrid Warriors*), she thought that Prigozhin's career through businessman to trollmaster to mercenary entrepreneur seemed a perfect example. This overlaps heavily with Mark's view of Putin's Russia (as explored in his *We Need to Talk about Putin*) as a modern state ruled by a medieval court, in which a class of jealous 'adhocrats' compete for the monarch's favour, desperately aware of how precarious their position can be. Our notion, then, was that a book about Prigozhin could just as much be about all those other adhocrats and the system they had to navigate.

Of course, fate will have its fun with authors, and less than a month after we signed our contract to write the book, Prigozhin staged his abortive June 2023 mutiny and then, exactly two months later, died in a plane crash that we can pretty confidently consider a Kremlin hit. It made the writing process a little more frantic than it might otherwise have been, but at least it saved us having to write one of those final chapters full of conditionalities and speculations. More to the point, it confirmed our belief that this system, having successfully kept Putin directly and indirectly in power for 23 years, is now showing its age. It depended on economic expansion, to keep elites and masses bought off, and a monarch with the energy and attention to keep on top of the internecine conflicts in his court. With Russia now locked in a vicious and debilitating war in Ukraine, with its economy increasingly consumed by that conflict, and with a septuagenarian Putin seeming increasingly detached from court and country alike, the strains and stresses are showing – and Prigozhin's mutiny was as much a symptom of this crisis as the desperate gamble of one man who felt he had nothing to lose. Nor just a symptom: it has also exacerbated it, demonstrating the moral bankruptcy of the Kremlin, the new tsar's own limitations, and the degree to which the security forces, once assumed to be the backstop of the system, are growing disenchanted. A thug, an opportunist, a profiteer and a master of war criminals, Prigozhin may yet go down in history as the man who kicked the pebble that eventually became the rockfall which buried Putin's regime.

We have to thank Robyn Drury at Ebury not just for taking on the book in the first place, but recognising that Prigozhin's death did not mean the end of this book's relevance. Beyond that, there are particular individuals whose help and work we wish to acknowledge, such as the assiduous researchers of Wagner, John Lechner and Jack Margolin, and the former mercenary Marat Gabidullin. Perhaps even more so, the intrepid Russian journalists who dared to dig into Prigozhin's life and crimes, despite the very real risks they faced in doing so. It continues to be an inspiration that, even as Putin's regime becomes increasingly intolerant and authoritarian, there are still so many Russians willing to shine a light into its many dark corners.

AA and MG, March 2024

CHAPTER 1
Thug

It was a beautiful overcoat: fine wool fabric, a touch of fox, newly bought. Even for the clientele of the Okean restaurant on the bank of the Neva River – and few in Soviet Leningrad could regularly afford to dine out, let alone at Okean – it shouted wealth and prestige. I am of the upper caste, the fine-dressed lady signalled, and I have access to things you lowlifes can only dream of, things money (rubles, at least) cannot buy.

Zhenya was drunk and down on his luck. There he was, sitting with three of his friends: the toughened, ambitious female ex-convict Valentina, the older ex-convict Alexei and the underage tearaway Vladislav, with nothing to chew on but his own frustration, as his latest heists had gone badly. Why not go after this one, wasn't she asking for it? The four of them followed her home in a taxi and then stalked her on foot. In the darkness of a dank alley, they accosted her and Valentina asked if she had any cigarettes. As she began reaching for her pack, Zhenya grabbed her from behind in a stranglehold. Even though Valentina threatened her with a knife, the woman screamed. So Zhenya just squeezed harder, until she lost consciousness.[1] Vladislav, eager to prove himself, pulled off her boots, while Zhenya grabbed her earrings.

Hearing the police approaching, the four thieves fled, leaving the woman lying unconscious in an abandoned lot. But Vladislav, the slowest, was arrested. The Soviet police, the *militsia*, were not always the most efficient, but they were methodical. It wasn't long before they knew who his associates were, and in a country where everyone had their *propiska* residence registration on file, it soon followed that the others were taken, too. And if the last time Zhenya had been caught for burglary, he had got away with a suspended sentence, this time the law wouldn't be so lenient.[2]

The Outsider

It didn't have to be like this. Zhenya – Yevgeny Viktorovich Prigozhin – was born in 1961 into a typical, middle-class Soviet intelligentsia family, his mother Violetta a doctor and his father Viktor, who died early, the nephew of a famous engineer who mined uranium in Ukraine.[3] 'My mum worked in the hospital, but not in any senior role,' Prigozhin would recall years later. 'Also, we had a grandmother to take care of. So we all fed ourselves, including our sick grandmother, on one ruble fifty kopecks a day.'[4] While prone to embellishment later on, especially when playing down any sense of a comfortable childhood, he does not seem to be exaggerating in this case. In the worker's state, many white-collar specialists were generally paid less than their blue-collar counterparts, and a doctor's salary averaged just 100 to 150 rubles a month (£65–£100, according to the laughably unrealistic official exchange rate, but close to an average manual worker's salary in the UK), well below the 200-ruble average income, and just a fraction of what the highest earners in the Soviet system made. Skilled industrial workers, senior military officials and professors could bring home up to 1,800 a month in some cases.[5] Still, in the 1960s, it was perfectly possible to feed a family of three on one and a half rubles a day. Staples including bread, grain, cheese and milk were cheap, while poultry and beef, and even vegetables such as tomatoes and cucumbers, were readily available. Subsidised housing, however cramped, meant that you had a guaranteed roof over your head, and it was exceedingly difficult to get fired from your job.

Zhenya Prigozhin, in other words, lived no worse than the overwhelming majority of Soviet citizens, and as a doctor, his mother had both a certain prestige and, truth be told, more opportunities for some off-the-books earning than most, taking a payment here to expedite a treatment, earning a favour there by signing someone's son off as medically exempt from national service. This was *blat*, the economy of favours, and integral to Soviet life as the centrally planned economy continued to fail to deliver the plenty that successive Communist Party leaders had promised. Soon, his mother remarried. Zhenya's new stepfather was a ski instructor named Samuil

Zharkoi. There are some suggestions that he may have had a somewhat heavy-handed parenting style, yet he did pull strings to enrol the boy in the elite Leningrad Sports Boarding School No. 62, to train as a cross-country skier.

But something cracked and, after graduation in 1977, Zhenya got mixed up with the wrong crowd. The problem was not poverty, or coming from a broken home, or any of the other clichés often mobilised to explain how youngsters turn to a life of crime. The problem was that he was surrounded by criminals who enjoyed a standard of living he felt he never could achieve just by playing the game. 'There was a highly visible class of the elite, which consisted of children of high-ranking Party bosses, diplomats, department store directors, or any significant post in the food supply chain,' a Russian entrepreneur of Prigozhin's generation would recall. 'That elite class had everything, and doctor families did not. Those people flaunted their wealth. They dressed better. They had cars, clothes. But corruption was widespread, and you couldn't get a cushy job like that without first embezzling and then bribing your way to the top.'[6]

Yet even if you were willing, you still had to know the right people. Soviet society was not only riven by economic inequalities, there were also divisions of class and caste that, perversely, worked *against* the intelligentsia. Members of the Soviet intelligentsia imposed a certain moral and intellectual code on themselves and especially on their children. 'An *intelligent* [member of the intelligentsia] simply *cannot* get a blue-collar job,' the entrepreneur said. There were no legal or practical bars. Rather, although blue-collar jobs tended to pay better, there were rigid social constraints. A well-educated boy from an intelligentsia family was expected to stay within his class, and not just by his own family. In theory, there was nothing stopping him from becoming a janitor or a roofer but, if he did, he was stranding himself between his old class and his new one. At best, he would be considered an oddity and a source of fun by his blue-collar colleagues, at worst ostracised and bullied. He would be unlikely to rise through the ranks, and equally unlikely to be able to switch back into a white-collar profession. This was the irony of Soviet socialism: it created new class divisions and snobberies at least as rigid and oppressive as the bourgeois societies it affected to despise.

For someone as clever and ambitious as Zhenya, an elite school that trained athletes who went on to compete in the Olympics seemed like the best ticket, until it wasn't. Maybe it was the competitive pressure, maybe it was the lack of any material incentive, knowing that no matter how much you achieved, you'd never be able to afford the kind of clothes that *those* people wore. Or maybe it was simpler: he was good – 'he wasn't just athletic, he was also well-read', a schoolmate would recall – but he turned out not quite to be good enough.[7] He would later claim that he dropped out of school – and lost the chance to be a professional sportsman – because of an injury, but there seems no evidence to support this; it was more likely, rather, that Zhenya was simply doing what he did throughout his life and refusing to acknowledge any failures.

He was smart enough to be able to dream of a specialist career, but not so smart or intellectually disciplined that a top university would welcome him, especially at a time when there were quotas limiting how many students of Jewish heritage (his father came from a Jewish family) would be accepted. He was athletic enough to be able to dream of the fame and comfort of life as a top-tier sportsman, but not quite enough to attain it. He was ambitious, but the system seemed to offer him no opportunities to match. Besides, everybody was breaking the law, so why not him? Whether out of anger, or disillusion, or simple acquisitiveness, Zhenya turned to crime. Soon after graduating from school, after a brief stint as a physical education trainer, he was arrested for petty theft and on 29 November 1979 convicted in Leningrad's Kuibyshev District Court. As he was still just 18 years old, though, he was sentenced merely to two years' probation.

Nonetheless, Soviet authorities had a great deal of say where people got to live and work, and this was especially true of a convicted felon. The court ordered Zhenya to move to the nearby provincial capital of Novgorod, where he was assigned a cot in a dorm and work in a chemical plant. For a boy from a 'good family', it must have been a demoralising blow. On offer was a potentially redemptive path: do his work, keep his head down, save up some money and later get into a decent university and back on the straight and narrow. But according to friends and acquaintances, 'Jacko', as he would soon come to be known, did not do straight and narrow. The teenager had an impulsivity and what one of his gangmates would call an 'inner cruelty' that supercharged his ambition.[8] He fled back to Leningrad where, if he had already been labelled a thief, he was determined to be a good one.

Jacko made friends with a former convict four years his senior, Alexei Bushman, and quickly became the de facto leader of a small gang of thieves, even though several were older and more experienced in the ways of the underworld. Throughout his life, people would comment on his uncanny ability to dominate any group of which he was a part. For instance, in the holding cell into which he was briefly locked for his very first theft, the 18-year-old novice managed to intimidate a room full of experienced criminals into submission after they had tried to bully him. It was a formative lesson: Zhenya had found a way to channel his drive and ambition into something that could actually pay. In a year or so of robbing apartments, it was Jacko who picked the targets and led the heists. Their loot – crystal vases and china, a leather steering-wheel cover, a set of ballpoint pens – may not sound like much, but as scarce 'deficit' items they were exceedingly valuable: all told, they were worth about a year's salary on the black market.[9] But even more importantly, for a boy like Zhenya, they were status symbols. His zeal may have driven the heists, but it ultimately didn't keep him free. Days after their violent robbery of the woman in the expensive coat on 20 March

1980, he was arrested and this time jailed not just for fraud and robbery but also for violating the terms of his parole. The Soviet courts took a dim view of recidivists. On 6 October 1981, he was sentenced to 13 years in a high-security correctional labour colony.

Reform

One didn't listen to the ponderous speeches of the Communist Party's general secretaries if one could avoid it. With their repetitive, obsessive citations of Leninist doctrine, their obligatory quotations from past Party congresses, and their dogmatic proclamations of the obvious filled with meaningless factoids, they were not just tedious, they seemed to have little connection with the realities of Soviet life. But on 17 March 1985, the newly appointed general secretary, an energetic and (relatively) young man who talked dangerously straight, came to Leningrad to give a speech. After some ritual praise of his predecessor, he began talking of the need for a 'decisive turn' in policy, of the need to 'speed up the country's social and economic development'. It was unheard of – you couldn't simply complain about standards of living like that. 'Everyone in the Soviet Union was glued to their television screens that day,' *The Times*'s Moscow correspondent Louise Branson would recall. 'For the first time, the Soviet leader talked like a simple normal person.'[10]

The very word that Mikhail Gorbachev used in passing, *perestroika*, literally rebuilding, might be a staple of any normal, elected Western politician promising structural change, but in the Soviet context, where difficult things were just not said openly, and where challenging dogma was so existentially dangerous, it was revolutionary. Gorbachev was just beginning his own journey, which would start with his believing that the system was fundamentally redeemable, just needing some housekeeping and modernisation, and end with him all but turning against the Party and ultimately signing the Soviet Union out of existence. In the process, the economy would effectively collapse and the 'fraternal bonds' holding this multi-ethnic empire together fray and break. At first, though, this was a time of excitement and growing optimism.

Gorbachev would preach *glasnost*, loosely translated as 'speaking up': a more honest reappraisal of the country's blood-soaked past and its dysfunctional present. In time, this would spin out of control as there were just too many skeletons in the Party's closet for this to be manageable. In the early days, though, it promised a new era, one in which people were citizens and not subjects. Previously banned books appeared on the shelves, and people who had once derided Soviet newspapers as little more than badly printed toilet paper lined up to read them in their thousands, such that copies had to be displayed on stands in the streets since they sold out so quickly.

Gorbachev also hoped to tap public enthusiasm to reform the moribund economy. Just as *glasnost* encouraged civic agency, *perestroika* would see efforts to harness entrepreneurialism. Through small businesses called *kooperativy*, cooperatives, the idea was that people would find that hard work and enterprise would be rewarded – legally. For many, it was, but reform would increasingly expose fundamental contradictions in the system. How could private business and the planned economy truly coexist? How could a Party that had presided over industrial-scale murder and repression claim legitimacy? How could a reform programme promising to work within Soviet rule of law cope when the logic of those reforms undermined or dismantled that very system of legality?

Gorbachev came to power hoping to preserve the system through reform; instead, he destroyed it. The optimism of the early years would give way to anger and misery. The cooperative movement was largely strangled by bureaucratic obstructionism and predatory officials. Party conservatives increasingly openly conspired against Gorbachev, and would eventually even launch an abortive coup against him in August 1991. The economy lurched into crisis: by the later 1980s, sausages, grain and butter were being rationed in most of the country and even the spartan simplicity of Zhenya's childhood seemed like a lost time of plenty. Nonetheless, the public energy and enthusiasm Gorbachev had unleashed would not disappear. Instead, people turned to new causes, from anti-Soviet nationalism to religion, from get-rich-quick schemes to an emerging ecological movement.

Life in the Zone

Zhenya saw none of those things, though. At least not in real life. He didn't line up to read the newspapers pasted up on public noticeboards, he didn't take part in the demonstrations, and he certainly didn't have a chance to set up a *kooperativ* as soon as the Law on Cooperatives was passed in 1988, like his friends on the outside were doing. Until his early release in 1990, when the Soviet Union was already in its death throes, he was 'sitting' in Russian parlance, stuck behind barbed wire in what was known as the Zone, the Soviet penal camp system.

Old hands in the criminal subculture of the *vorovskoi mir*, the 'thieves' world', would claim that their real life was that lived inside the Zone. Rather than the prisons of the West, the Soviets – and the Russians after them – largely sent their criminals to penal colonies. There, living in crowded barracks blocks, the inmates largely kept their own code exalting thuggish machismo and made their own rules, exploiting and abusing those who broke them out of ignorance or defiance.[11] A newcomer to a barracks might find a clean white towel laid down like a doormat, for example. The temptation might be to step over, but those in the know would calmly wipe their feet on it, demonstrating that they felt at home. Tests like these determined who got a decent bunk and who was relegated to the coldest or hottest corners; who could sleep sure in the knowledge that their meagre possessions would not be stolen; who would be forced to do the worst jobs.

The most unfortunate risked being 'lowered', or being made into *petukhi*, 'roosters' – euphemisms for being sexually exploited by other male prisoners and in the process turned into outcasts. At the end of 2022, when Prigozhin was at the peak of his power, two self-styled criminal godfathers going by the underworld nicknames Grisha Moskovsky and Sasha Kurara claimed in videos released on social media that Prigozhin had been 'lowered', and forced sexually to gratify them and other inmates.[12] It seems most likely that this was a smear campaign organised by his enemies, precisely to undermine his reputation as a tough guy. There had, after all, been no suggestion of this in the previous decades, and many of the details simply did not fit. Nonetheless, the very fact that his rivals targeted his macho prison reputation demonstrates how important this was to his later image, and how it became an asset rather than a stigma.

After all, contrary to Moskovsky and Kurara's claims, Zhenya seems to have thrived in the Zone. He had knocked about with ex-cons enough to have picked up the basics of the criminals' code, and that 'inner cruelty' stood him in good stead. He may not have enjoyed his time in the notoriously austere Soviet penal system, but he certainly immersed himself in the ways of the *vorovskoi mir*. Indeed, the first thing Zhenya did in jail was get a tattoo of a woman across his back, done by a convict tattoo artist or *kolshchik* ('pricker'), using a makeshift needle and ink mixed from rubber, soot and urine.

He was so proud of it that he even showed it off to the judge who handed down his sentence.[13]

The perpetual wannabe had finally found his place. Indeed, the prison system in which he would spend the next nine years offered not only its own opportunities for him to be schooled in the hard rules of the *vorovskoi mir*, but also to discover his entrepreneurial talent. At first, by his own account, he was unruly and recalcitrant, in and out of solitary, losing part of a finger in unknown circumstances (he was happy for people to assume it was the result of some violent altercation, but others have suggested an industrial accident). He seems to have come to realise that there was little to be gained in trying to buck the system, though, and rather more from working with it. He applied for vocational courses, read everything he could lay his hands on (in the free time he did not spend working out, for example, he was reading, recalled one fellow prisoner[14]), and then applied successfully for a transfer to a timber-logging labour colony, AN-24/34 in the Republic of Komi. The work there would be physically gruelling, but it also offered greater freedom of opportunity, which is likely to have been part of his calculation. Equally happy to reward an apparently reformed character and also to find workers able to handle the hard work of logging, the authorities obliged. There, he soon set up a small business, presiding over inmates who would craft souvenirs out of offcuts from the workshops or pilfered materials, to sell on the outside. What they earned was trivial by most standards, but a small fortune for those otherwise eking by on token prison allowances.

To be able to get away with this, he could not just rely on his own force of character. Zhenya needed the blessing of the two rival sources of power in the colony: the senior *vor* ('thief') and the camp authorities. At that time, most of the high-security colonies were so-called 'black', rather than 'red', in that the real power inside rested with the career criminals rather than the prison officers. Nonetheless, there was no way an enterprise of the scale of Prigozhin's could have been maintained, much less the knickknacks smuggled outside for sale, without the connivance also of the guards, as they still controlled passage into and out of the colony. Zhenya seems to have had no problem navigating this complex informal political environment, another talent that would serve him well in his later career. As one businessman who worked with him in the 1990s recalled, 'he always looked for people higher up to befriend. And he was good at it.'[15]

So this was Yevgeny Prigozhin on the eve of the collapse of the Soviet Union at the end of 1991 and the emergence of a crisis-ridden new Russia. His had not been a hard childhood, at least not by Soviet standards, and it certainly was not the case that he had lacked the chance for a normal, decent life. Yet there always seems to have been a tension between his ambitions and his opportunities – until he found himself in the Zone. There, so many of the characteristics that would shape his later life came into their own. His capacity to bully and intimidate, a vice on the outside, became not just a survival skill but a source of authority in the colony. The entrepreneurial instincts and capacity to balance multiple businesses that would allow him to build his Concord Management and Consulting group, spanning everything from catering at St Petersburg's schools to running the Wagner mercenary group in Africa, first really began to be evident in his capacity to build a business empire behind bars.

On one level, when he stepped out of the colony a free man in 1990, wearing the old suit he had worn when convicted, nine years previously, and carrying a small bundle of possessions and a travel warrant home, he was a man out of time. The 1980s had transformed the Soviet Union, empowered a new generation and brought free enterprise out of the black market and into the open. The old unspoken rules of Soviet society – *ne ver', ne boisya, ne prosi*, do not trust, do not fear, do not ask – were seemingly banished. Yet they had been central to life inside the Zone, where the values and instincts of the 1970s still held sway.

On another, though, Prigozhin was a man already prepared for the coming decade. The end of the Soviet Union ushered in a time of troubles, in which a handful would become vastly rich while most went hungry, in which organised and disorganised crime alike would prey on the emerging capitalist market, and in which the old rules no longer applied while the new ones were yet to be made. Mercedes-Benz would sell more bulletproof limousines in 1990s Russia than in the rest of the world put together and if in Soviet times everyone had spare rubles because there was nothing in the shops to buy, now everything was available, but no one had any money. Ambition, enterprise, cunning and a willingness to use violence and threats would be essential to prospering in this brave new world, and Zhenya had them all.

Then again, there was another man who had missed out on the early promise and optimism of *perestroika*, returning to a country of failed ideals and broken promises, where brute force ruled both the streets and the halls of power. This was a middle-ranking, middle-achieving KGB officer by the name of Vladimir Putin, who had spent the period 1985–90 in East Germany. Returning to a Motherland in crisis and trying to make their way, both of them had to hone the new skills that were in demand, each in their own way, and they were destined to meet and have their fates intertwined.

CHAPTER 2
Entrepreneur

When is a banana not a banana – or at least not just a banana? When it is quite literally the taste of a world that had been so long denied to most Soviet citizens. In 1990, as the Soviet Union was opening up, many of the creature comforts that Westerners took for granted were coveted as exotic luxuries by people accustomed to deficits, and who saw them more on screen than in real life. Hamburgers, denim jeans, bananas – these simple things were in such high demand that people queued up for miles for McDonald's, and street-corner rubbish bins were buried deep in banana peels. All this pent-up, unmet demand offered enormous business opportunities for anyone with the hustle and entrepreneurship to make and move product.

Someone like Yevgeny Viktorovich Prigozhin. Later in his life, after he had become rich, got himself at least part of a university education, and was rubbing shoulders with statesmen and dignitaries, he would recall of the days when he just got out of prison: 'It so happened in our country that many were imprisoned. For them it became a serious school of life. This did not break many, but on the contrary, they became real men and patriots.'[1] It is no coincidence that the criminal slang for prison is *akademiya*. For so many inmates, this is where they learned more than just the ways and language of the underworld. Who needed university when you had just graduated from prison, which taught you all you needed to know about an economy where rules had been replaced by force?

Hot-dog Millionaire

Fresh out of prison with nothing much to do, but apparently eager to clean up his act, 30-year-old Yevgeny initially followed his mother's example and enrolled at the Leningrad Chemical and Pharmaceutical College. Who knows what might have happened had he simply become a pharmacist, but he soon dropped out, although not too soon to have caught the eye of Lyubov Kryazheva, an attractive younger student who, despite his criminal record and the nine-year difference in their age, would marry him in 1991.

Yevgeny was in a hurry, doubly so once he was married. He first took a job at a car dealership. There he sold patched-up Zhigulis, the archetypal boxy Soviet car, a tacky duplicate of a 1960s Fiat design, out of a ramshackle lot on Prospekt Energetikov, a brutalist multi-lane highway in the east of the city. Like so many others at the time, though, he also had a second job, teaming up with his stepfather to make some quick money. They set up a *kooperativ* and opened some kiosks on Apraksin Dvor, known as Aprashka, one of the burgeoning and notoriously dodgy open markets of Leningrad (or St Petersburg, as the city was once again officially named from 6 September 1991). There, he started selling hot dogs: again, what may sound a pretty banal delicacy, but at the time an iconic taste of the West, taking the *sosiski* sausages that had long been a Soviet staple, but now serving them in a bun with ketchup and mustard, just like in the movies. Later on, Prigozhin would claim that his was the first hot-dog stand in the city – likely an exaggeration, but it is fair to say that he was selling a still-rare commodity. 'It's a shame they didn't have advertising pamphlets back then,' he would recall. 'We would mix mustard in my kitchen, that's where my mother would also count the cash. Each month I made about a thousand dollars, which was mountains of rubles. It was hard to count.'[2]

That was no slur on his mother's mathematical abilities. The ruble, which the state had for so long artificially pegged at parity to the dollar, was beginning its long, painful slide towards its real market value. At the time, a thousand dollars would have been worth anything between 1,800 rubles at the official rate and perhaps 20,000 rubles on the street. Meanwhile, although there were 100-ruble banknotes in circulation, the overwhelming majority of the cash in question would have been grubby 1-, 3- and 5-ruble notes. No wonder these earnings were hard to count and bulky to keep, at a time when no one trusted the banks of an increasingly bankrupt

Soviet state. When a disgruntled buyer found that the Zhiguli he had purchased through the dealership didn't actually work, he tracked down the seller – a certain Yevgeny – who agreed, grudgingly, to refund him half the cost. When the buyer came to Prigozhin's apartment, he was amazed to see him retrieving the money from a huge safe stuffed with piles of cash.[3]

This may have sounded like easy money, and for the Western free-market economists watching from afar and the young, liberal intellectuals advising Gorbachev, all this emerging capitalism was indeed beautiful to behold. But that was as long as you were far enough away from Aprashka not to hear the gunshots. Like most retail hubs in Soviet cities, and Moscow and Leningrad in particular, these open markets were fast becoming centres of criminality. While making money may have been easy, keeping it (and your life) was anything but. According to Prigozhin himself, like all *kooperativs*, he had to pay $100 per kiosk per month – equivalent roughly to the average Soviet salary – to the gangs running the market protection rackets, which in this case was a branch of the Malyshevskaya gang, the second most powerful in St Petersburg. But the school of life that was prison taught him to navigate those dangerous streets so well that, soon enough, Zhenya found bigger fish to fry, and dealing with a gangster's runner, his *shestyorka*, suddenly became less appealing than dealing with his bosses. His experiences in prison, his newfound wealth and his natural entrepreneurialism had all prepared him for this moment. What he needed, though, was a patron, someone who could steer his way the lucrative new business opportunities generated by the transition from the planned state economy to the free market.

The Man in Grey

In 1970, when Zhenya Prigozhin was just nine, before he was even thinking of becoming a thug, just across town from his school, a scrawny, light-haired 17-year-old showed up at the Main Directorate of the KGB for Leningrad and the Leningrad Region, asking for a job. He was an odd mix of bland and street, already a veteran of many a brawl. Unlike Zhenya, he 'wasn't a hoodlum himself but was constantly hanging out with them', as a childhood friend recalled: he could mix it with the best of them, but could see beyond the apartment-courtyard hangouts, a bottle of cheap booze being passed from hand to hand.[4] This combination of apparent toughness, wits and determination sufficiently impressed the duty officer interviewing him that he suggested the young man get a law degree and try his luck again. Which is exactly what the young man did. He enrolled at the Leningrad State University and studied hard, focusing in particular on the laws and norms that regulate how governments trade with each other. There was officially no capitalism in the Soviet Union then, but in practice everyone also played the black market: you had to, to survive. There certainly was an economy, trading something you have for something that you want, from goods to favours. The young man was growing up in a poor, working-class neighbourhood of a Leningrad still recovering from the devastation and mass starvation of the Second World War blockade, when the city was besieged and battered for 872 days. Vladimir, Vova for short, didn't have a lot, but, unsurprisingly, he wanted more and was determined to get it. By taking business law, the wannabe spy (or secret policeman) found himself in a faculty that attracted young, liberal, pro-Western intellectuals who were aware that the Soviet economy simply wasn't working because there were fundamental contradictions between the rigid ideology that the government sought to enforce through its laws and the way commerce actually worked on the ground. This was, after all, a time when *blat* – meaning pull, or favours – was as much a currency as those over-valued rubles, and when even Putin's family had from time to time to turn *na levo*, 'to the left', as resorting to the black market was known.

Many of these young liberals would in the 1980s go on to work in the new, reformist government under Gorbachev and then post-Soviet Russia's first president, Boris Yeltsin, but meanwhile most wouldn't let their respect for the Western business law model get in the way of breaking their own country's laws when they wanted to enrich themselves. Vladimir Putin looked up to these new thought leaders. In 1975, he successfully defended his thesis, 'The Most Favoured Nation Principle in International Law', focusing on a norm that would become the bedrock of the World Trade Organization: if a WTO member grants one country a special favour, then it has to do the same for all members.[5] The young man, coming from an essentially proletarian family with no particular assets, status or *blat*, may have quite appreciated the thought of a level playing field. After all, by dint of hard work he had found himself at one of the Soviet Union's most prestigious universities. Most of his peers came from *nomenklatura* families, those who had already made it into the Party and the state's elite, confident in the privileged lives that awaited them. Vladimir Vladimirovich, like Yevgeny Viktorovich, was an outsider, and was going to have to work and fight for what he wanted.

Putin did work hard, both at his studies and in conforming to his new milieu. He joined the Communist Party, which was essentially a prerequisite to any serious career, not least in the KGB, and did the basic reserve officer training, which was the price for avoiding national service. Upon graduation, the young man did indeed get to join the KGB and, after some training, began working in counterintelligence. This was apparently something of a disappointment to someone who had set his eyes on the agency's elite First Chief Directorate, the intelligence officers working abroad, but he set about his duties, monitoring consular officials, foreigners and anyone who interacted with foreigners. His was a routine of by-the-book interviews to find any traces of espionage or sedition in the rare, though usually innocuous, interactions that

Soviet citizens had with foreigners, and the 'prophylactic chats' the KGB used to intimidate those who might be getting too close to the line. He was a small, grey man with cold eyes who liked beer and making friends, especially when there was a material incentive. Bland and forgettable, he could nonetheless be amicable and even open: one of his colleagues in the KGB recalled him as projecting an image of an easy-going kind of chap, the sort to swing his arms casually as he walked the corridors of the Lubyanka, the service's headquarters.[6]

Some say that even though he worked for the KGB, he developed a perverse kind of affection for some of the dissidents to whom he sometimes had to talk, and ultimately had to suppress. While he couldn't openly say anything so subversive, he would, for example, share his admiration for Alexander Solzhenitsyn over a beer in the kitchen.[7] It was not that he was a liberal so much as that even he recognised that the whole Soviet system was not just corrupt, but crumbling – and the institution he had worked so hard to join, the 'Sword and Shield of the Communist Party' as the KGB styled itself, was engaged in an exercise in futility.

However, the moment when it became possible to talk openly about all these things outside of one's kitchen, when a new Party leadership under Mikhail Gorbachev was sparking hope of reform, of actually building something in which it was worth believing, that was when the young man was sent off to serve in Dresden, East Germany, one of the backwaters of the Warsaw Pact.

While it had better beer than back home, he missed out entirely on the optimism, change and hope that his country experienced in those brief five years. Instead, he spent his time collecting newspaper clippings and holding meetings as a KGB liaison officer, little more than a glorified clerk.[8]

After returning from Dresden in 1990, watching an empire he had sworn to protect crumble, 38-year-old Vladimir Putin left the KGB. But he had few job prospects, by his own account getting by as a taxi driver as he watched others begin to get rich cannibalising the scraps of a bankrupt country. In 1991, though, he got a job working for Anatoly Sobchak, one of his professors from his university days, who had become mayor of Leningrad. Putin soon rose to become deputy mayor, heading the External Affairs Committee, which curated business and sought to attract foreign investment to the city. Crucially, he also chaired the Supervisory Council for Casinos and Gambling Business, which ensured that the city government had a controlling share in every new casino.

Today, the humble beginnings of the man who would eventually rise to the apex of Russian state power have been woven into spectacular conspiracies. All along, these stories read, the ambitious bureaucrat and his corrupt friends were channelling money into special and secret accounts so that one day they could rebuild the Soviet Union and finally accomplish their dream of revenge and world domination. It's a compelling story, but a closer look at the real experiences of those who actually served in the KGB shows a sadder, more mundane picture of disillusionment, cynicism and a struggle to rebuild their lives when the system to which they were committed collapsed. Like everyone else, they were using every contact, skill and opportunity they had to get through today and make some money tomorrow.

The Administrative Entrepreneur

Vova was a social climber who craved to be part of an elite both for its prestige and its material perks. But virtually overnight, the elite he had joined had been stripped of any status, any meaning. No wonder corruption became ubiquitous: in the absence of values, what other motivation was there but money? 'We considered ourselves an elite force,' a disillusioned Federal Security Service (FSB) captain lamented about the early 1990s. '"What are we, cops, to take bribes?" we used to say. First, we began noticing that our generals were living beyond their means. We thought they were behaving strangely, but they were just running businesses.'[9]

Another KGB officer who continued working for the agency after it became the FSB, recalled how the idealistic purity that first drew him into the service disappeared after 1990. 'When I started working in the KGB the difference [from today] was that we didn't mix [personal gain with legal responsibility]. People went there – and I know this about myself and my colleagues

– for the sake of an idea. The idea of the government, of government law and order. But now there is no central idea in Russia. However bad the idea that Russia used to have, it was still there. Now, there is nothing. What is it that we are trying to attain? Personal profit? But then where are the boundaries?'[10]

Prigozhin had learned to break or ignore the boundaries of law and custom through disillusion and prison, and he became an entrepreneur in business. For Putin, equally disillusioned by the lack of direction, the answer was administrative entrepreneurism, using his office not simply to extort bribes but in effect to create business monopolies. Under the guise of 'bringing order to St Petersburg's gambling business', as he put it, in effect he went into the business himself. His committee didn't own any casinos, but through a separate company controlled 51 per cent of the shares in any within the city, in the name of the local government, the FSB and the tax police. As shareholders, they (the exact word Vladimir Putin used is 'the government') were to profit from the dividends.

Of course, on paper, they never did. Putin claimed that the gambling establishments were 'laughing at us and showing us losses'.[11] In practice, the casinos were making money hand over fist, and so too were those they had to pay off. Money flowed into Vova's coffers and those of his friends: that was the way of thousands of KGB officers like him, who monetised their clout, their connections and their authority. 'We, the patriots of the KGB, were moving millions and millions of dollars into bank vaults,' admitted one KGB officer. 'And along those same channels also moved money from organised crime, to the point that I would not be able to tell which monies belonged to the KGB and which to the mafia. In response to my timid questions, they responded: just move the damn money. And I did.' The practice, at least in part, originally followed a Party Central Committee decree from 1990 authorising a sort of rainy day 'cash box' for future political operations.[12] But after 1991, whatever designs the Communist Party may or may not have had for this fund were rendered moot, because the governing structures of that Party were dissolved and the only man who knew for sure where all the money was, Central Committee treasurer Nikolai Kruchina, fortuitously fell out of a window. That collective *obshchak* – a word borrowed from criminal slang for a gang's common kitty – was not used to fund some nefarious and ambitious political conspiracy so much as plundered, largely by the very KGB officers who had assembled it.

But what about those, like Putin, who had not been involved in this high-level embezzlement? Instead, they were able to exploit the symbiotic relationship that developed very early between the newly emerging private business enterprises (like Prigozhin's) and the thousands of KGB officers (like Putin), who proved instrumental for their connections and their muscle. One had or could make the money; the other could offer access and security. Both ended up empowering each other, but at the cost of enabling and perpetuating the lawlessness that had pushed them into each other's arms in the first place. As marriages went, it certainly had not been made in heaven.

When Zhenya Met Vova

Prigozhin himself claimed first to have met Vladimir Putin when the new president dined at his restaurant together with Japanese prime minister Yoshiro Mori in 2000.[13] The evidence suggests closer and less legitimate ties nearly a decade earlier, though. Around that time, Prigozhin, by then swimming in loose cash that he was eager to invest, made friends with a former classmate from the sports boarding school, a businessman named Boris Spektor. He had already established a reputation for his commercial acumen and boasted influential connections. One of these was his Jewish-Georgian partner, Mikhail Mirilashvili, who by then already had the kind of connections needed to make real money in the city. Another was the up-and-coming entrepreneur Igor Gorbenko. Spektor, Mirilashvili and Gorbenko had opened Konti, the first casino in the city.

According to company records, Spektor and Gorbenko cut Prigozhin in on the action: he would become a director of several firms, including the Spektr Joint Stock Company and Contrast Consulting, both of which were involved in the gambling business.[14] They seem to have been impressed. 'Prigozhin – he's a go-getter,' a businessman friend recalled. 'He's also a Jew, which probably played a role in Spektor and Mirilashvili taking him on.'[15] In fact, they were instrumental in starting him along the path that would earn him the misleading nickname 'Putin's Chef'. In 1993, Spektor made Prigozhin a manager of, and 15 per cent shareholder in, Contrast Ltd, a new chain of grocery stores. Once again, these entrepreneurs were capitalising on one of the most basic and most repressed demands of the final Soviet generation: the demand for food. This suited Prigozhin, as his first child had just been born, and Polina would prove to have something of a sickly childhood. Although in his world, child-rearing was strictly woman's work, he needed a stable source of income while Lyubov ran the home and looked after their daughter. Nonetheless, it was clear even at the time that he saw this just as a stepping stone.

For a while, Contrast would be a runaway success, as it offered a range and choice of goods near enough unmatched in St Petersburg. Within a few years, its competitors were catching up but, by then, Prigozhin already had a new venture in mind.[16] In 1995, he opened a wine bar, but he had grander ambitions and, as will be discussed below, Prigozhin opened his first restaurant the next year, aptly titled Staraya Tamozhnya (Old Customs House), hinting at the Soviet and Russian state's most lucrative – and, frankly, corrupt – institution. At first, for all the foie gras, fresh oysters and strippers that the restaurant had to offer, it still had a difficult time attracting customers. It was almost too ostentatious for its times. But soon business picked up as it became a place to be seen, and before his term in office ended in 1996, Anatoly Sobchak showed up at the establishment together with Vladimir Putin.[17]

Though that is the most widely cited legend, it is unlikely that the restaurant really was the place where Zhenya and Vova first met. Gambling was legal but obtaining a coveted gaming licence required personal ties with key people in City Hall who needed to approve it. Above all, that meant Putin, and Gorbenko had so successfully cultivated him that he became deputy director and then director of Neva-Chance, the company through which the city's Supervisory Council for Casinos and Gambling Business oversaw the gaming industry and took its cut. Zhenya the go-getter, the social climber who knew valuable people when he saw them, was not in a position to go straight to the top: he wasn't yet rich, powerful or influential enough to get through the door. His restaurants would become one way for him to make the connections he needed but, in the meantime, he looked to cultivate people further down the food chain. 'Prigozhin gradually gained Putin's trust,' a friend from the 1990s recalls, 'first by building a relationship with his personal driver, Viktor Zolotov.'[18] Zolotov was more than just Putin's driver: he would become one of his bodyguards and a judo sparring partner, making him an invaluable contact. Zhenya was thus able to get to Vova thanks to his friendship with Zolotov, one that would last three decades, long after the latter had become a general and commander of the powerful National Guard.

In those early days, though, it wasn't just Zolotov who helped Zhenya establish his links to Vova. Zolotov and the rest of the protection officers guarding Putin, Sobchak and other senior city officials worked for a private security company called Baltik-Eskort. It had been founded by a former police captain with KGB links called Roman Tsepov. He acquired a reputation as a go-between, brokering deals between City Hall – which in this context meant Putin – and St Petersburg's powerful underworld. Indeed, his funeral in 2004 was quite telling. Having had a potentially incautious cup of tea with former colleagues from the FSB, Tsepov soon sickened and died, showing symptoms uncannily similar to those of Aleksander Litvinenko, the defector who was murdered in London with radioactive polonium in a cup of tea offered by a former FSB officer.[19] Tsepov's funeral was attended not only by an array of security veterans, including Zolotov, but also Vladimir Kumarin, known as St Petersburg's 'night governor' for his status as the leading figure in the city's Tambovskaya organised crime network.[20]

The widespread assumption is that Tsepov knew too much about Putin's old crime connections and the profits he made from them, and so he was a loose end that needed conclusively to be tied up.

As one source who knew his circle noted,

usually Putin's acquaintances, who were involved in crime in the past, understood this. Those of them who remembered meeting the president and tried to use it ended up either in a cemetery, like security guard Roman Tsepov, or in prison, like the leader of the Tambov group, Vladimir Kumarin.[21]

In any case, back in the 1990s, Tsepov played a crucial role not just in protecting the young deputy mayor but also in expediting his various dubious enterprises. His company even ended up providing security for Neva-Chance. That made him useful to Prigozhin who, according to mutual friends, was able to charm Tsepov with his jokes and his picaresque prison stories, and quickly established himself as something of a 'court jester' at City Hall.

It would be more than a decade before this bald, jovial, profane restaurant server (for he never felt it beneath him to personally serve the dignitaries who honoured his establishments – a habit that Putin reputedly valued) would become truly conspicuous. Nonetheless, so long as they know their place, the grey bureaucrat who never became the super-spy of his dreams does seem to have had a soft spot for the real 'hoodlums' as an adult, just as he had as a teenager. He would show unexpected indulgence to figures ranging from the eventual governor of turbulent Chechnya, Ramzan Kadyrov, a former guerrilla who pummelled one of his own ministers in a boxing ring as a punishment, to Prigozhin, the tattooed ex-con turned restaurateur. At a dinner at the presidential residence in

St Petersburg in 2011, a waiter was seen bending over to place a napkin on Vladimir Putin's lap. 'Thanks, Zhenya,' he said, confusing the reporters present. 'How're you doing?'[22] Who was this guy, that the president addressed him by his first name only?

CHAPTER 3

Chef

The nineteenth-century revolutionary thinker, Alexander Herzen, recalls that his family had a serf, a bonded peasant, virtually a land slave, who happened to be an excellent cook. One of the more forward-thinking, liberal members of his family, a senator, took such a liking to the budding chef that he got him an apprenticeship working in the kitchen of Emperor Alexander I himself, and then a position at the prestigious English Club in Moscow. The chef's career – despite his being a serf – took off and soon he was making enough money to live like an aristocrat. However, 'with the noose of serfdom still round his neck, he could never sleep easy or enjoy his position'. He tried to buy his freedom, offering the senator 5,000 rubles, perhaps a hundred times a typical serf's sale price. His benefactor, the senator, was proud of his possession and refused, instead promising manumission for free in his will. So the serf was rich and free in practice – but not by law or in his heart. He lived in the milieu of the rich and privileged, but would never feel like he was anyone's equal, and assumed that everyone would look at him as a serf. In the end, he drank away all his possessions, his job and an advantageous marriage, and the senator had to take him back in, out of pity. Herzen described his childhood impressions of the man: 'I saw then what concentrated hatred and malice against the masters lay in the heart of a serf.'[1]

Russian folklore is filled with such tales of a lowly serf rising to serve the tsar. While these fairy tales usually have happy endings, as Herzen's account suggests, the real ones were fraught with tragedy and danger: it is rare that social climbers ever feel at home among the elites, who will eternally regard them as suspect outsiders, even as they take advantage of them. There are, of course, exceptions: Vladimir Putin's grandfather, Spiridon, spent five years training as a chef in the kitchens of pre-revolutionary St Petersburg before going on to cook for Vladimir Lenin, Joseph Stalin and subsequent general secretaries. He lived to the ripe old age of 86, although then again, if the old man did feel any class resentment, we would have no way of telling. Maybe it was for this reason – his grandfather's self-propelled rise to the kitchens of the tsars – that Putin took a liking to the gregarious businessman placing a napkin on his lap. At least, Prigozhin seemed to think so: 'Vladimir Putin saw how I turned a kiosk into a business,' he would boast years later, long before the resentment started to set in that would overflow and lead to his downfall. 'He saw how I do not hesitate personally to bring a plate to crowned heads, because they came to visit me. And I tried my best.'[2]

But while Prigozhin would later earn the moniker of 'Putin's chef', the truth was that he never was anyone's chef. He was not a cook but an entrepreneur and opportunist. His role – and his rise – was thanks to his acquiring another, equally important function: as a convener, of sorts, of a rising new elite, the kind of people who would eventually forge Putin's Russia, the land where Prigozhin would rise to the top, and then come tumbling down.

Restaurateur

With his grocery-store chain having expanded to ten shops, their wide variety of products drawing customers from all over the city, it was time to diversify. First, he set up the wine shop and bar imaginatively named Wine Club, but it was serendipity that launched Prigozhin into the upscale restaurant business. His business partner in Contrast, Kirill Ziminov, one day got a call from an acquaintance in the restaurant business who held the lease for an old warehouse with which he really didn't know what to do. It turned out to be on the ground floor of the Kunstkamera, the baroque eighteenth-century museum on University Embankment, facing the Winter Palace. Something about its vaulted brickwork attracted Prigozhin, who saw this not only as an opportunity to make money, but also to move up in the world from being a glorified grocer, and he decided to open a restaurant there. Spektor and Mirilashvili stumped up a quarter of a million dollars, and Prigozhin mustered $100,000 of his own, and with that, Staraya Tamozhnya was opened in 1996, St Petersburg's first truly top-drawer restaurant.

With its spruced-up antique architecture and bare red-brick walls, it truly stood out with a distinct sort of class at a time when other developers were still obsessed with bling, glitz and making cheap things look expensive. Whether by luck or judgement, Prigozhin was just ahead of the curve, as Russia's new rich began to crave a certain faux traditionalism, cosplaying the aristocratic lifestyles of the nineteenth century. While it would take some time for its reputation to spread, within five months it had covered the $350,000 initial investment and began bringing in real money.[3] Tony Gear, an Englishman whom Prigozhin had lured over from Hotel Europe to manage the restaurant, recalled: 'People started to travel more, and Prigozhin realised that there wasn't a single real haute cuisine restaurant. He just decided to do that.'[4] Prigozhin involved himself in every meticulous detail: from the plush chairs to a special projector that would show the cleaners even the finest dust on the floor.

He may not have been a chef, but a restaurant of this class required a particular know-how: cheaply obtaining high-quality and rare food, and selling it expensively. This was a job for a wheeler-dealer, and Prigozhin delivered. Oysters and fresh seafood would seem to be the least of his problems in a port city like St Petersburg, but it was imports that were the most lucrative, especially as one could charge extra for something that was in practice cheaper and easier to get from abroad than domestically. The snobbish new elite assumed foreign was superior to domestic, just as they assumed pricier was necessarily better: showing off one's success with performative displays of consumption was very much the done thing at the time, and a wallet-busting meal was a status symbol on a par with the Rolex or Patek Philippe watch and the imported limousine. So the oysters, for example, came from Brittany, not because they were necessarily tastier than those harvested in the Black Sea or the Pacific Far East, as they had been since Soviet times, but because they were *imported*. Nonetheless, Russia still had its share of elite luxury foodstuffs: *oladyi* (a type of traditional thick Russian pancake, different from *blini* or crêpes) with sturgeon caviar from Astrakhan, Kamchatka crab salad, oysters baked with smoked duck, and the fragrant porcini mushrooms for which Russian forests were known – all this fused seamlessly with the most coveted French delicacies and the finest imported wines.

Staraya Tamozhnya was at the forefront of the revival of Russian cuisine, a certain culinary nationalism that sought to differentiate itself from Soviet cuisine – which had been shaped more by deficit, cheap state-produced staples (think of such delights as canned cod liver and meat in gelatine) and the need to fill stomachs efficiently rather than by tradition or creativity. But its success reflected Prigozhin's particular acumen not just as a businessman who effectively established the logistics of obtaining quality ingredients, but also one who navigated that otherworld equally well – the world of deficit, corruption and underpaid civil servants trying to get their cut at the first sight of any expensive, glittering new venture.

From the *kooperativs* that sprung up under Gorbachev's liberalisation, to any food establishments well into the Putin era, restaurants were all subject to arbitrary checks from various inspectorates ostensibly trying to ensure hygiene and fire-safety compliance, but in reality simply trying to make a buck and find someone they could shake down. High net-worth establishments such as Staraya Tamozhnya in particular were vulnerable not just to racketeers demanding protection money, but to this far more mundane, and far more ubiquitous, semi-legal racket. It took a particular skill to distinguish those whom one could afford to brush off from those who needed to be paid off, lest they cause real damage. The best response to such predators was to have a strong, high *krysha*, or 'roof' – in other words, protection. And the best *krysha* in 1990s St Petersburg was City Hall. Fortuitously, the kind of people Prigozhin needed to ensure that business ran smoothly – not just mayors and celebrities but more so the well-connected middling civil servants, like Vladimir Putin, who actually handled disputes and contracts – were precisely the ones who liked to patronise Staraya Tamozhnya. Gear recalled, 'I first met Vladimir Putin when he came here with Mister Sobchak', the mayor of St Petersburg.[5]

Haute and Bas Cuisine

If he was going to grow his business and expand, Prigozhin had to continue to diversify. He opened three more restaurants with more 'democratic' prices to target the new, growing middle class: the Jewish-themed Sem Sorok (7/40, also the name of a popular 1992 comedy film about Soviet immigrants heading to the United States), and two Russian-cuisine ones, Stroganovsky Dvor (the Stroganov Courtyard, with a groaning buffet under a huge tent) and Russky Kitch (Russian Kitsch, whose décor was everything the name suggested, and which would, in due course, go upmarket and offer herring in gold leaf, and foie gras with gingerbread).

It was the budding fast-food sector that promised the most profits, though, and fortunately Prigozhin already had a foot in the door, even if he had dreams beyond a handful of street-market hot-dog stands. He already had the skills and know-how for mass production and distribution, and initial capital wasn't so much of a problem anymore either. But to establish a chain that could compete with McDonald's and the other big foreign fast-food franchises that were colonising Russia meant getting into real estate, both for outlets and for warehouses. That took connections: a project of such strategic proportions needed serious political support, and here Prigozhin's careful cultivation of contacts bore fruit. In 1996, the structures of power in St Petersburg had changed. The position of mayor was replaced with a governor, and Sobchak narrowly failed to win re-election, being ousted by one of his former deputies, Vladimir Yakovlev. Fortunately for Prigozhin, Yakovlev was one of his most regular customers, one whom Prigozhin had always been keen to serve personally. Doing so paid off: the governor signed over all the necessary land for a budding enterprise named by Prigozhin himself: BlinDonald's – a riff on the Russian pancake staple, *bliny*, but also cheekily on the slang use of *blin* as an expression meaning something like damn, so that this could also be read as DamnDonalds![6]

The chain eventually opened in 2002 and, having acquired a name for the surpassing blandness and cheapness of its fare, closed down in 2012, although the lessons learned in feeding many badly for little would be transferred to Prigozhin's subsequent contract catering firms. In any case, in the late 1990s the real opportunities for him were still at the other end of the market. It was his next fancy restaurant that really took off and consolidated his position not as a member of the rising new Russian elite, but as their chosen serf-chef. All things French were the cynosure in a city still balancing an imperial past with a decrepit present, and Prigozhin had been impressed with the boat restaurants he had seen on the Parisian Seine during a trip abroad. So he and Ziminov hunted down a sad and rusting party boat that had been a floating disco, *Moskva-177*, and snapped it up for $50,000. They then spent almost ten times as much remodelling it throughout, and in 1997 launched it as the boat-restaurant New

Island. Although it would later float along the Neva, the wide river that winds through St Petersburg, at first it was simply moored in the shadow of the iron-domed, nine-teenth-century St Isaac's Cathedral. The most expensive restaurant in the city, with its own separate truffle menu, it quickly became its most exclusive, too.[7] In those days of the fabled 'New Russians' who went after anything that screamed affluence – from oversized maroon suits to imported Amaretto liqueur – making something more expensive than it needed to be was part of a widespread and depressingly effective business strategy. As one joke went, a New Russian shows off his new watch to a friend. 'How much did you pay for it?' the friend asks. 'Two hundred bucks, why?' 'You fool – they're selling them for $500 just around the corner.'

It was this approach, perhaps, that elevated the venue and started bringing in the kind of new friends whom Prigozhin wanted to court. For him, this was a deep source of pride and he cultivated these relationships with relish, making a point of coming out of the kitchen and talking to customers whenever he could, and especially when the status of the customers warranted it.[8] Prigozhin would turn out to have no real sense of how to deal with peers, and could be a terror to his underlings – once, for example, he had one of his kitchen team taken to the cellar and beaten so badly that he was hospitalised for two months after one of his A-list customers complained about the quality of the tomatoes on their plate. However, he could also be charming, attentive, even witty with his social superiors when he wanted to cultivate them, and so the rising stars of 1990s St Petersburg, from entertainers and businesspeople to officials and diplomats, came to his restaurants.

Prigozhin's Salon

In Staraya Tamozhnya's VIP room – aptly named the Presidential Hall – there was, at least until the day of his death, a painting depicting Prigozhin, Gear and two other, unidentified people dressed in the style of nineteenth-century gentlemen dining around a table. Gear is the one serving this time, while Prigozhin, dressed in a frock coat, is sitting regally, eyeing a glass of brandy on the table.[9] Prigozhin himself was tight-lipped about his relations with the powerful people who frequented his restaurants. The same was true of those about him. Gear, when asked what Putin and Prigozhin talked about at Staraya Tamozhnya, disclaimed any knowledge, saying, 'I'm not interested in politics. We can talk about beef tartare, or football. Yes, I think they did [meet and talk], but I was too busy to notice.'[10] But that painting speaks mountains of the fantasy that Prigozhin entertained of himself: a gentleman presiding over a salon of distinguished men and women.

More by accident than design, that is what he turned out to be. In the early and mid-1990s, there was no sense that the indispensable yet unremarkable grey deputy mayor would become president of the Russian

Federation, and in the process drag his friends, business partners and cronies to the heart of the state. Nor was there any secret plan, so much as networking and opportunistic deal-making in a time when nothing was certain but everything was up for grabs. In those days, while Putin himself might have been moderately useful to a businessman like Prigozhin, he was far less influential than others who frequented the establishment, such as Anatoly Sobchak or his successor, Vladimir Yakovlev.

They were just two of the big names who patronised Staraya Tamozhnya and then, when it took off, New Island. The floating restaurant was considered even more attractive to distinguished elites – even international ones. And Prigozhin, in his rare interviews, was proud to namedrop the dignitaries he had the honour of serving. 'Putin came there with Japanese Prime Minister Mori, then with Bush. And before that, Sergei Stepashin' – who at the time was prime minister – 'met with the President of the International Monetary Fund and it just so happened that in my presence Yeltsin called Stepashin and said "Seryozha, don't come back without a loan."'[11]

Rumours circulated of tables bugged and *kompromat* – compromising materials – gathered, but the truth was rather more prosaic, in that a favoured waiter appears to have been charged with serving VIP customers and sending Prigozhin reports of what he overheard. According to hacked emails, this rarely turned out to be explosive stuff, whether it was that Putin advised Venezuela's

Hugo Chávez to stop trying to bring the whole economy under state control ('Hugo, I love you very much, but stop nationalising companies, you will only make things worse') or that he told Italy's Silvio Berlusconi that he didn't read the newspapers ('so that his opinion and future decisions do not become dependent on the opinions of journalists and editors').[12]

Nonetheless, this former thug and convict found himself rubbing shoulders almost every day with powerful and famous people, and took pride in it. In a five-page résumé culled from the hacked emails of Capital Legal Services, a Russian law firm that represented him, Prigozhin lists no fewer than 70 crowned heads and elected leaders for whom he had catered, from the now-king of England, who was then Prince Charles, and Prime Minister Tony Blair, to the flamboyant Berlusconi (one cannot help but think he and Prigozhin would have got along) and Saudi Arabia's King Salman.[13] Indeed, he had a track record not simply of boasting about his contacts, but also letting the stories grow in the telling. He struck up an unlikely seeming friendship with Mstislav Rostropovich, for example, and in 2001, when the famous cellist hosted the queen of Spain at his home in St Petersburg, it was Prigozhin who handled the catering. Next year, Rostropovich invited him and his wife to London to attend a gala concert by the London Symphony Orchestra to celebrate the cellist's seventy-fifth birthday.[14] That much is on record, but in Prigozhin's own telling, the two events combined and expanded into a tale of smoking banned cigars and hobnobbing with the king of Spain at Buckingham Palace.[15]

It's not likely that Prigozhin was confused: he just understood the power of a good story, and especially one that combined the appeals of snobbery with a hint of bad-boy transgression. Just as during his time in prison, though, he appreciated that he had to show he knew his place in the hierarchies of power and money. There has been much confusion about the nature of Russian political corruption, confounding foreign policymakers and businessmen, who often assume it works just like corruption in Western democracies. In the environment that was quickly taking hold after the collapse of the Soviet Union – where Soviet rule of law had been obliterated and a new system had not yet been built – it was not that money could buy you power so much as that power got you money. Even the oil tycoon Mikhail Khodorkovsky, Russia's richest man who nonetheless went to jail for trying to challenge the system, knew that you accrued and held your wealth at the pleasure of the tsar because, ultimately, he was the one who held the final monopoly on the use of force.[16]

Prigozhin, who had learned this on the streets of Leningrad and in prison, knew the unspoken rules of the game, the *ponyatiya*, and especially when to keep his mouth shut. Discretion was key if he was to enjoy his privileges, and while he liked to drop names, he knew when to stop. Cosying up to figures like Zolotov, Yakovlev or even Putin – especially Putin – had its perks, but in his case those perks worked as long as he didn't get too close or learn too much (another good reason not to bug his restaurants). Instead, his role was more like that of the quiet gentleman presiding over a salon in the painting. His restaurants, offering the right mix of snobbish elegance and discretion, became one of the crucibles of a new elite. The kind of people who socialised at that salon, be it Staraya Tamozhnya or New Island, formed a *tusovka* – the slang of the day for a tight clique of like-minded people – of politicians, security officials and simply friends who would go on to make up the core of Vladimir Putin's government.

The Rise of the Tusovka

It is impossible to overstate the degree to which power became personalised under Putin. When he became president at the end of 1999, he began to appoint his friends and former colleagues to key positions throughout the system, putting a premium on loyalty above competence. These were law-school classmates from Leningrad State University, former KGB officers with whom Putin had served in Leningrad and Dresden, and officials from Sobchak's administration. Among the latter was Igor Sechin, a linguist from Leningrad State University who became Putin's chief of staff (and literal bag-carrier) at City Hall and went on to become his one of most powerful allies both as an oligarch and Kremlin official, a man so dangerous he came to be known as 'Darth Vader'. There was the future stand-in president, Dmitry Medvedev, back then a liberal, who was another of Sobchak's former students. There were KGB officers like Nikolai Patrushev, who had worked with the future president in Leningrad in the 1970s, and would go on to become secretary of the powerful Security Council and in effect Putin's national security adviser. If Patrushev was from the first a hawk, there were also many liberals like Alexei Kudrin, chair of City Hall's Economic and Finance Committee, who would go on to become Putin's most trusted economic adviser despite fundamental political disagreements that would later see him stepping down from government. Also working at City Hall alongside Putin would be future oligarchs like Alexei Miller, who would later head Gazprom, the government's gas monopoly, and Nikolai Shamalov, the dentist who became a tycoon and, for a while, the father-in-law of one of Putin's daughters.[17]

When Sobchak lost the election to Yakovlev in the summer of 1996, the *tusovka* took care of its own. Putin was offered a job in the Presidential Property Management Department, perhaps one of the most corrupt offices in Moscow, thanks to the fact that it serviced all the material and logistical needs of the sprawling Presidential Administration, from food, transport and vacations to financial accounting and procurement. From there he went on to work in the Presidential Administration itself, and then the FSB, the successor to the KGB. While he would bring his friends with him once he gained power as president, the idea of Putin presiding over a powerful clan in the 1990s is a caricature – the *tusovka* was made up of capable, entrepreneurial men who found their own ways into the halls of power. Kudrin, for instance, was in the Presidential Administration before Putin, thanks to his ties to another liberal friend, Anatoly Chubais.[18]

In any case, it wasn't just City Hall. There was the judo circle: men like the Rotenberg brothers, who would become billionaires under Putin, trained alongside the future president in their teenage years. There was even a holiday circle. In November 1996, a group of officials and businessmen who had dachas – summer houses – on a prestigious lakeshore near St Petersburg decided to form a cooperative, which became known as Ozero, so that they could build a gated community of expensive villas. The head of the cooperative was Vladimir Smirnov, a businessman who would act as Putin's proxy in a number of German joint ventures and who later headed the St Petersburg Fuel Company. Another member was Yuri Kovalchuk, a banker who would go on to become one of Putin's closest confidants. While Putin was not the head of the cooperative, when he became president, all of its members would go on to hold top government posts.

There is, of course, no paper trail placing all of these characters together in Staraya Tamozhnya or New Island. There wouldn't be. The point is that in the late 1990s and early 2000s, the personalistic court of a new tsar was emerging in St Petersburg. These people socialised together, conducted legal and illegal business together, and dined together in the same trusted establishments. Their nexus, though he didn't know it back then, was Yevgeny Prigozhin. Two and a half decades later, when he found himself trying to orchestrate a coup against his rival, Defence Minister Sergei Shoigu, he had good reason to believe he was well versed in the various Kremlin clans and factions. Serving their wine and memorising the way they liked their steak prepared, he had come to know the likes of Zolotov and Sechin intimately. Indeed, he had thought they were willing to throw in their lot with him.[19] Why did he get it so wrong? Perhaps his real problem was that he had never served a meal to Shoigu. Arguably the only member of Putin's inner circle not to have come from this *tusovka*, Shoigu was a heavyweight political veteran who nonetheless really got to know the president and win his trust in the later 2000s. He was a subtle and dangerous political operator who ultimately would outmanoeuvre and outgun 'Putin's chef'.

Nonetheless, Prigozhin could rightly claim to have played a role as midwife to the emergence of a new elite, which formed amidst the late-night toasts at his restaurants, as much as in the backroom deals of St Petersburg's City Hall or in dachas along the banks of Lake Komsomolskoye. Elites evolve over time, though, and as Prigozhin leveraged his entrepreneurial acumen and political connections to move into ever-more serious business, he seems not to have realised that he was no longer everyone's favourite facilitator but a player in his own right – and players need allies and acquire enemies.

Prigozhin would find himself much more capable at accumulating the latter than the former. Above all, he never made the crucial jump from servant of the tsar to friend. Just like Herzen's cautionary tale, the serf-chef could be feted, enriched and even admired – but he would never be more than a serf.

CHAPTER 4
Minigarch

In a framed picture in Prigozhin's office, Zhenya is show-ing Vova some shiny new equipment at the 2010 opening of one of his factories.[1] The photograph is a typical fixture for any businessman eager to boast his connec-tions and proud to stand next to celebrities. But it's also a picture worth much more than a thousand words. In the televised visit, Putin, then technically prime minister as part of a game of political musical chairs to get around constitutional term limits, is depicted as a benevolent micromanager, ensuring everything is up to standard. 'Is that soup?' he asks Zhenya, pointing at one of the vacuum packs. 'Yes, that's borsht,' Zhenya replies, and eagerly points to another offering. 'And that's cream of wheat porridge. You want to try it?'

'Later,' says the prime minister. And then he turned to his chief sanitary inspector, Gennady Onishchenko, and asked what he thought.

'I'm very pleased!' the official beamed. Adding, in what would prove a prophetic aside, 'You can feed prison-ers, the army, hospitals and children with this.'[2]

Below the picture, there is an autograph from Putin. Russian businesses tend to take Putin very seriously: a year after his visit in 2009, for instance, the Pikalyovo Cement Factory was still keeping on display the chair on which Putin had sat, emblazoned with his name tag. There is good reason for this: long after the lawless 1990s, these ostensibly private businesses still very often owed their sustenance, their funding and their protection not so much to the government, but to the patronage of specific people within it – and most of the time to Vladimir Putin personally.

The Rise of the Minigarchs

This was very much part of the process of the creation of a new elite. The original oligarchs had been creatures of the 1990s, the Yeltsin era: bankers and businessmen who accumulated fantastic wealth, largely through the rigged privatisation campaigns that saw the assets of the Soviet state sold off for kopeks on the ruble, and often to those who already had the money, muscle or connections to keep their rivals at bay. This relative handful of men were as politically powerful as they were obscenely rich. It was largely thanks to them that Boris Yeltsin beat off a renewed challenge from the Communists in the far-from-honest 1996 presidential elections, and many of them were supportive of the decision to elevate the little-known Vladimir Putin as his successor in 1999, thinking he would be a biddable instrument of their will. Of course, they were wrong.

Even before his election, when asked in a radio interview how he felt about the oligarchs, he said that if one meant those who fused power and money, well, 'there will be no oligarchs of this kind as a class'.[3] His backers did not seem to have taken him seriously, but Putin quickly disabused them. In July 2000, he summoned 21 senior business leaders to a meeting in the Kremlin where he promised not to look too deeply into where people's wealth had come from, so long as they henceforth stayed out of politics. He offered to 'make our relationship civilised and transparent', but arguably it was rather more transparent than civilised.[4] Two of the most politically active oligarchs, media tycoons Vladimir Gusinsky and Boris Berezovsky, were forced out of the country, but the most striking example of this 'transparency' was the treatment meted out to Mikhail Khodorkovsky, Russia's richest man. He continued to bankroll opposition politicians and speak out against corruption and so, in 2003, security officers stormed his private jet during a refuelling stop in Novosibirsk and arrested him at gunpoint. His oil empire, Yukos, was broken up and largely handed to Igor Sechin, Putin's former assistant in St Petersburg, and Khodorkovsky himself was sentenced to nine years in a penal colony on fraud and tax-evasion charges.

The other oligarchs chose to accept their new status: they were no longer masters of the (Russian) universe so much as Putin's managers, allowed to retain their fortunes and business empires so long as they knew their place. Meanwhile, Putin's closest friends and allies were themselves becoming phenomenally rich, phenomenally quickly. As already mentioned, Sechin became, as head of the Rosneft petrochemicals empire, in effect the shadow minister of oil. The Rotenberg brothers, Putin's childhood friends and judo sparring partners, became billionaires largely on the back of their construction companies, which built everything from arenas for the Sochi Winter Olympics to the Crimea bridge. Fellow KGB officer Sergei Chemezov ended up running Rostec, the giant state defence–industrial conglomerate. The list goes on: it was a good time to be Putin's friend.

Prigozhin was no oligarch. Indeed, with his wealth estimated at just 6.4 billion rubles, or $106 million, in 2015, he was not even a billionaire in anything other than ruble terms.[5] And yet, the prime minister himself had brought a delegation of officials to the opening of his factory. This was not just a favour for an old St Petersburg contact, it reflected the way that this new elite was being formed: the real backbone of the Putin system was and still is made up not by the handful of billionaires comfortable in the president's favour, but the mere multi-millionaires, the 'minigarchs' who have done very well but know that – unlike Putin's handful of genuine friends – they cannot just rely on the tsar's goodwill. As one consultant who worked with them in the mid-2010s put it, 'they need to keep proving that they are loyal and useful, and they are all competing against each other so they can never just sit back and enjoy life'.[6] Prigozhin would become one of these rich but insecure minigarchs, able to leverage his

Kremlin connection to turn restaurants into a massive catering business and more, but always conscious that what the tsar gave, he could always take away.

Party Like a Russian

Back in 1996, before Putin's favour was the only real currency of success, Prigozhin was already thinking strategically about building a food empire that went beyond just a couple of shops and restaurants. That year, he founded Concord Catering.[7] The name was suggested by Gear, who wanted to steer him away from the fancy French words that were all the vogue in St Petersburg in those days. For Zhenya, Concord appealed because it meant harmony and agreement.[8] After all, the real success of his restaurants was not so much the rubles they earned but the way they became a space in which hard-nosed men could broker their own kind of harmony and agreement. He had been able to bring the most influential people in St Petersburg together, but now was the time to take advantage of that, because he knew that he couldn't build the empire he wanted without their patronage, and he realised that this was a moment to expand.

In 1998, Lyubov had given birth to their second child, a son, Pavel. Although Prigozhin would use his various female relatives, from his mother Violetta through to his daughters – for in 2005, his second daughter, Veronika, would be born – as convenient proxies to front many of his companies, ultimately, he clearly felt that business was a man's world. (Indeed, a European court would agree when, in 2023, it lifted sanctions on Violetta, accepting that whatever her ostensible interest, in practice she had no control over the companies she 'owned'.) When Prigozhin died, it turned out that his will bequeathed near enough his entire commercial holding to the then 25-year-old Pavel. Now that he had an heir, his business empire could become a dynasty.

While establishing the logistics of his fast-food chain, BlinDonald's, Prigozhin had set up a catering service infrastructure. BlinDonald's never really took off, not least because each restaurant had its own food standard, so that customers couldn't really rely on the same level of quality. Unlike McDonald's key selling point – its consistency – BlinDonald's was hit or miss, and frankly more often a miss. So, by 2009, he started closing them down, but the structures that he had created to service the chain turned out to have another use, one that proved far more lucrative.

In the summer of 2001, a year after becoming president, Vladimir Putin was basking in finally having made it into the club of serious men. He loved lavishly to wine and dine the heads of state who visited Moscow, demonstrating to them that Russia was open and ready for business. When US president Bill Clinton visited in 2000, Putin saw it as an opportunity to showcase his largesse: he treated him to an informal dinner of boiled boar and goose, proudly gave him a tour of the Kremlin, and brought the country's best jazz musicians to play before him. Party like a Russian indeed.[9]

By that point, thanks to connections forged at New Island, Concord was emerging as a high-end catering solution for Russia's most powerful men. Prigozhin's partner, Ziminov, was well connected to St Petersburg's deputy governor for external affairs, Gennady Tkachev. There were deals to be made, and ultimately, thanks to Ziminov's facilitation, Tkachev threw Concord some of the city's choiciest catering contracts. Official forums, meetings, banquets – Prigozhin's food was becoming a fixture of them all. It was no wonder, then, that the next time Vladimir Putin needed to show off his country's opulence, he turned to Zhenya.

For a state visit by French president Jacques Chirac and his wife in the summer of 2001, the itinerary called for an exquisite dinner and a chance to show off St Petersburg during its white nights of almost 24-hour-daylight, thanks to its northern location. New Island, now operating as a moving restaurant boat, offered exactly what was needed. It was there that Prigozhin, unexpectedly, found himself personally serving Putin and Chirac. Instead of business, the guests had a leisurely sightseeing dinner, with Ziminov acting as their impromptu tour guide and Prigozhin pouring their wine. They ate duck liver pâté and gingerbread, served with prunes and an aged port-wine caramel, followed by black caviar on ice, and then a beef fillet with black truffles, served with fresh morels and young carrots boiled in rowan broth, and concluding with a raspberry millefeuille as dessert.[10] It was precisely the blend of Russian tradition and European standards that Putin wanted to symbolise his emerging nation, and if Zhenya had managed to impress the foreign president, then he had certainly managed to impress his own. In 2002, Putin took George Bush to dinner at New Island, and in 2003 he celebrated his birthday there. With guests like these, one hardly needed a marketing department.

To truly grow in Russia those days, one needed not just the permission of the government but its enthusiastic support. Prigozhin had to convince Putin that their interests were one and the same. 'When I decided to launch a [processed food plant] on an industrial scale,' Prigozhin recalled, 'I proposed to [then St Petersburg governor Valentina] Matvienko, but she refused. I went to [deputy governor Alexander] Beglov, he went to [prime minister Dmitry] Medvedev, and he went to Putin. This didn't happen yesterday. We included school meals in the national project. Vneshtorgbank provided a loan.'[11]

So the final permission came from the Kremlin. Vneshtorgbank, later renamed VTB, was a majority state-owned commercial bank. State-funded institutions – like schools – provided Concord with its most lucrative contracts. One could fairly ask: who was feeding whom?

Feeding the Nation

In 2008, Vladimir Putin decided to respect the term limits imposed by the Constitution, and stepped down from the presidency. It was a tough decision: popular support was robust enough, and his parliament by that point was sufficiently docile that he could have easily passed the necessary amendments extending the limit beyond two four-year terms. Indeed, he would do just that over a decade later. But at the time, Putin may have been contemplating stepping back from politics and in any case was keen to court Western business, with Russia an eager contender to join the very same World Trade Organization on which the president had written his undergraduate thesis. It was a time when Sergei Naryshkin, then deputy prime minister (and later hawkish spy chief), would hold meetings with Western investors and ask, 'how else may we be of service to you?'[12] Demonstrating all the trappings of a law-abiding democracy was key to projecting the image that would get Putin the kind of international standing he craved – even if the reality was that it was a 'managed' democracy at best, where the Presidential Administration dictated the makeup of parliament and, increasingly, how each party should vote.

But Putin was in no position actually to trust the democratic process and rule of law – who knew what would happen to him, his friends, his wealth and, yes, the country if Russia were suddenly to succumb to the kind of parliamentary chaos – full of fistfights and scandals – that defined the legislative process just across the border in Ukraine? So instead of ceding power entirely, he stepped down to the office of prime minister, promoting his friend from the St Petersburg days, Dmitry Medvedev, to be his proxy president. The liberal lawyer, who had a fondness for British classic rock and innovative technology – who, indeed, was one of the first Russian officials to get himself a Twitter account – easily won the presidency in 2008.

With Putin carefully watching over his shoulder, Medvedev launched a liberalisation campaign intended to modernise Russia and foster better economic and political ties with the West. At the same time, though, Putin was keenly aware of the need to balance this new pivot with the more statist and nationalist elements within the government elites. By choosing Medvedev, after all, he had passed over the hardline defence minister, Sergei Ivanov, disappointing not just him, but the security community that backed him. Moreover, there were growing financial troubles at home: Russia was hit hard by the financial crisis of 2008, poorly managed Soviet-era factories were on the verge of bankruptcy, and there was the risk of mass unemployment and, with that, plummeting approval ratings. Putin would have to mitigate his pro-market pivot with some populist assurances. While Medvedev swanned around in Western capitals and tweeted selfies, Putin played the hard-nosed *khozyayin*, or boss, at home, haranguing oligarchs as though they were errant schoolboys and micromanaging the economy.

In one of his most famous performances, the angry tsar ordered a meeting with the head of the steel company Mechel, which had been accused of selling more cheaply to foreign buyers than domestic ones. When the head of the company, Igor Zyuzin, sent word that he could not join the meeting, Putin, flashing with anger before the cameras, threatened a criminal case. 'We'll have to send a doctor to him to clear up all these problems ... And a prosecutor.'[13] The value of Mechel's shares plummeted by almost 40 per cent overnight.[14] In 2009, visiting the town of Pikalyovo after underpaid local workers blocked a highway in protest, Putin verbally thrashed the billionaire Oleg Deripaska for mismanagement of the local cement factory, in front of his company bosses, town residents and TV cameras. At the end of the tirade, he ordered a sulking Deripaska to walk across the room, bend over and sign an agreement to restart the factories. 'Now give me my pen back,' Putin said, in a final humiliation for the oligarch.[15]

Putin may have been on a populist roll, but his man-of-the-people performances only highlighted what any average Russian knew all too well. The Soviet Union's social safety net had been shabby and dysfunctional, but at least it had existed. In Russia, thanks to the shock therapy reforms of the 1990s, it all but collapsed. The Yeltsin government often had barely enough money to function, hence the bargain-basement sale of Soviet companies that created the new class of oligarchs, and while the free-market ideologues of the time believed that private business would invest in infrastructure, even in the oil boom of the 2000s, that clearly wasn't about to happen. Yet what Yeltsin's administration could get away with, a government swimming in oil revenues could not.

Putin had to at least give the appearance of trying to rebuild the social safety net.

So in 2005, he created the so-called National Priority Projects, with a commitment to build affordable housing, hospitals, clinics and schools. Putin pledged $1 billion – raised by leaning on Russian oligarchs to contribute – towards rebuilding and equipping hospitals under the Health National Project alone. The commission overseeing these projects bustled with activity but by 2009 they had ground to a halt. Putin was prepared to invest – but only so long as he and his friends could benefit. Instead Putin opted – as he often did when it came to something actually worth doing well, but which bore a cost he wasn't prepared to pay, whether it was democracy or reform – for performance over substance, embezzlement over levelling up. In 2010, investigative journalists discovered that money had been siphoned off from these National Priority Projects to build Putin a palace at Cape Idokopas in southern Russia, complete with gold-plated disco and underground ice rink. It emerged that under the programme, suppliers were charging hospitals three times what the equipment they were selling was worth. Under a scheme overseen by one of Putin's friends from the Ozero cooperative, Nikolai Shamalov, the extra cash was squirreled away into Swiss bank accounts. While Dmitry Medvedev decried the scheme as 'cynical, loutish theft', some of those funds ended up paying for Putin's lavish residence.[16]

Indeed, for Putin, leaning on oligarchs to do what the state promised to do was turning into a very appealing strategy. It made him look tough and powerful, a benevolent ruler who thought of his people – and if the private sector failed to deliver, he could always blame the fat cats, swooping in to make himself look even tougher. Some heads would roll, but he would always emerge as the good tsar among the bad boyars, as the ancient Russian nobility was known. Either way, this would pave the way for a massive expansion in the outsourcing of all kinds of government services, including catering contracts for everything from schools to the army, and create an opportunity for a well-connected minigarch with an existing infrastructure and friends in high places.

'How May I Be of Service?'

'I launched not a kitchen factory, but an industry,' Prigozhin boasted in 2011, while milking the publicity from Putin's visit to his new factory. 'I have a tried and tested public catering philosophy that is new for the country. So there will be a lot of factories – we are buying land near Krasnodar, half of them have already been built near Moscow, Tambov and Altai are in our plans.'[17] He had started his catering supply empire first with the patronage of successive governors of St Petersburg, Yakovlev and Beglov, and sweetheart deals for the city's school food contracts. Yet while he almost certainly paid bribes and called in favours from his new friends there, at least at first, he also seemed eager to provide a good service. In 2011, an experiment to supply 14 schools in

St Petersburg began. According to the head of the city administration's social nutrition department, there were no problems, and beyond a few complaints from parents that Concord skimped on salt or sugar, the food complied with all the appropriate standards. Furthermore, the city saved money. Next year, though, Prigozhin opted not to bother bidding for the contract again, to the surprise of the official, who noted that 'they had every chance of winning, but they didn't [apply], apparently for some reason of their own'.[18]

The point was that Prigozhin had ambitions beyond catering for a few schools in a single city. He probably didn't make much money with that pilot project, but that wasn't the goal. Indeed, that 'exemplary' factory Putin inspected was all but mothballed by the end of 2011, having done its job. Rather, he was willing to treat it as a loss leader, a chance to prove that he could handle substantial government contracts. After all, by the time Putin visited that factory in 2010, Prigozhin had already built the foundations of a business empire that would expand well beyond food, with stakes in development, construction and even cleaning. He had founded Concord Management and Consulting LLC in 1995, and this would remain the main holding company for his various businesses (including the Wagner mercenary army) to his death, even if for tax reasons his mother Violetta was the registered owner between 2011 and 2017. Concord controlled a bewildering and ever-changing array of companies, from Moskovsky Shkolnik

('Moscow Schoolchild') to M-Invest and Meroe Gold, the latter two later coming under Western sanctions for their role in funding mercenary operations through exploiting Sudan's mineral resources.[19] Indeed, their ostensible ownership was also often hard to pin down, as Prigozhin used his family constantly to switch the formal ownership of properties and companies, all the while actually remaining in charge. For example, the Credo rental agency was registered to his wife, Lyubov, until 2019 when it was transferred to their older daughter, Polina, even though she seemed more interested in show jumping. Between 2012 and her short-lived marriage in 2014, she had managed a horse-breeding venture in Germany. Likewise, her even more horse-mad sister Veronika – who intersperses a fairly successful presence on the competitive equestrian circuit with the luxury lifestyle of the pampered daughter of a rich Russian, including regular trips to Dubai – showed no particular interest in hotel management, but was formally registered as owner of St Petersburg's Red Stars Hotel when she was just 17.[20] Prigozhin paradoxically combined a desire to build a grandiose narrative of business success with an habitual need to try to keep his empire's expansion unclear in its detail and extent.

Central to this expansion would be the patronage of powerful men and powerful institutions. Having originally partnered with the entrepreneur Mikhail Mirilashvili, in 2000–1, Prigozhin was trying to distance himself from potentially problematic associations. It was an acrimonious process, and for a time Prigozhin and Ziminov had to be shadowed around the clock by armed bodyguards, but eventually a deal was struck that saw Mirilashvili bought off with ownership of the restaurant 7/40 – probably just in time, as in 2001 he was arrested on kidnapping charges.[21] This helped cauterise one particular potential obstacle to Prigozhin's being considered respectable in Putin's Russia: it was not so much that people were expected not to have dealt with gangsters in the 1990s – near enough everyone did – it was rather than you had to appear to have moved on.

It was also time for Prigozhin to jettison Ziminov, whom he seems to have increasingly felt was too small-time in his ambitions. Ziminov agreed to sell up his share in their joint venture for a million dollars, but was going to end up another one of the angry and disappointed figures Prigozhin would leave in his wake. He received a first payment of $600,000 and was promised the rest soon, after he stepped down. This Ziminov duly did, but as soon as Prigozhin had full control of the companies, he simply transferred all the assets to new corporate vessels and liquidated the original ones, leaving Ziminov with nothing. He turned to the St Petersburg Prosecutor's Office, claiming fraud, but in near record time – just five days – the case was closed on the grounds of a 'lack of evidence of a crime.' Once again, having great contacts in the city turned to be a valuable advantage for Prigozhin.[22]

Going National

By the later 2000s, though, Prigozhin was actively seeking to move beyond St Petersburg. In 2009, mysteriously bypassing state tenders, he scored another grand opportunity, opening Office 1237, an exclusive restaurant on the twelfth floor of Moscow's White House, the official seat of the prime minister and the cabinet. It was open only to officials and their guests, with a special VIP room for ministers and sweeping views over west-central Moscow. Like Staraya Tamozhnya and New Island, it offered untold opportunities for access. Considering the paranoia and conspiracy theories constantly bubbling just under the surface of modern Russian politics, it is unsurprising that for some, the concern was again that Prigozhin was not just feeding high-level officials, but bugging them. 'With any restaurant in the White House, there's always a question of who installs the wiretap,' a government source told Russian investigative reporters.[23]

However, this seems to have been nothing more than another wild rumour, not least because the White House is regularly swept for bugs by the technical specialists of the Federal Protection Service, and it would have been suicidal for someone like Prigozhin to have been caught in such a clumsy operation. Rather, this was a case of his exporting his old model to a new city, creating a fashionable and exclusive venue that powerful men would seek to patronise – to prove just how rich and powerful they were – and in the process give him new opportunities to make contacts. Which he did, not least with deputy prime minister, and soon to be mayor of Moscow, Sergei Sobyanin. In December 2012, Concord secured a three-year contract to cater for schools and colleges in Moscow's South-Eastern and Northern districts, worth more than 3 billion rubles per year. However, Prigozhin – as Onishchenko had foreshadowed – was looking to even larger captive markets. 'Our plans are the army,' Prigozhin said in 2011. 'That's over half a million people. The police – two million.'[24] Traditionally, soldiers had largely done their own cooking, but as the military was looking to move away from bare-bones Red Army practices to attract more volunteers, the decision had been made to outsource catering. By 2012, Concord had managed to establish a virtual monopoly on catering contracts for the Defence Ministry – pushing out all but 8 per cent of the smaller firms that constituted the competition.[25]

Still, this was just the beginning. Concord moved into all kinds of new activities, from property development to advertising, again often operating through a variety of thinly disguised front companies. The chichi gated estates of North Versailles and Lakhta Park in St Petersburg, for example, were technically owned by Lyubov, although Pavel Prigozhin acquired the title to the Lyakhta Plaza development in 2020. In 2016, the company Megaline, 50 per cent owned by Concord, was awarded the lion's share of the Defence Ministry's construction contracts, after Concord's own lawyers had helped draft amendments to the requisite laws that would allow Megaline to qualify for the competition.[26] Until 2013, Megaline was owned by Prigozhin and his mother Violetta, but then in 2015, half of its shares were transferred to the imaginatively named company Business Project, which owned Prigozhin's yacht and private plane. Through these shell games, even if the final beneficiary always turned out to be Concord and Prigozhin, the true extent of his business empire could be concealed, and it became easier essentially to monopolise contract awards by putting up several of his companies in a pretence of competition. As a result, one study suggested that, by 2019, the various companies of Prigozhin's growing empire had been awarded at least 5,393 government contracts worth a total of almost 210 billion rubles, which, at the time, was worth around $10 billion.[27]

All this was ambitious enough for a billionaire – but Prigozhin, at best, was a minigarch. It could not have been done without the connivance or at least assent of the Kremlin. Putin may have liked his service at Staraya Tamozhnya, but you couldn't really ask Zhenya Prigozhin to build schools and hospitals across an impoverished region (as the oligarch Roman Abramovich did in Arctic Chukotka) or facilitate connections to foreign government (as banker Piotr Aven was requested to do when Donald Trump won the US presidency[28]). Nor was he one of Putin's real friends: Zhenya did not holiday with Vova, the way Defence Minister Shoigu did, nor did he attend the president's personal 'Night League' ice-hockey games the way crony-oligarchs such as the Rotenberg brothers so often did. Although Putin was friendly enough when they met, this was always in the context of official events, and often with the overtones of sly malice with which Putin habitually keeps his underlings in their place. In October 2011, for example, he was walking through St Petersburg's Konstantinovsky Palace, having both won re-election and also being about to sign a free trade deal between eight post-Soviet countries. He was in a good mood when he encountered Prigozhin who, true to form, was handling the catering. Nonetheless, Putin was not above a little jab: 'Nice hairstyle,' he said in passing, pointing at the businessman's smooth dome just in case there was any ambiguity about his point.[29] What could Zhenya do but smile?

Even when Prigozhin tried to assert for himself the perquisites of the oligarchs and aristocrats of Putin's circle, he faced pushback. Most Russians, for example, particularly resented the way the rich and powerful seemed to feel that traffic rules were for the little people, fitting flashing blue emergency lights on to their cars to claim priority. This even led to the rise of a civil society movement, the 'Society of Blue Buckets', who fixed blue children's buckets on to their car roofs during rolling protests. As a result, by 2011, there was something of a crackdown, but figures such as Sechin continued to get away with their use. Ignoring the rules became a way of trying performatively to demonstrate one's importance. In May 2016, an armoured BMW 760 limousine, closely followed by a Nissan Patrol SUV, ran through a traffic checkpoint in central St Petersburg, using the so-called 'quack', a distinctive 'get out of my way' horn used by emergency vehicles. There followed a high-speed chase, which concluded at Prigozhin's offices; he got out of the limo and entered the building, but a bad-tempered stand-off ensued as security officers piled out of the SUV and the offices, to be met by police and the Federal Security Service's Grom ('Thunder') counter-terrorist team.[30] Eventually, the matter was resolved, but one of Prigozhin's team was given a two-year suspended sentence as a symbolic warning.[31] Prigozhin was being reminded that he was no Sechin. He could never take his position for granted, and when it came to winning and keeping contracts, in many ways he had to cut corners to maintain a competitive edge.

Still, so far he was managing to get away not just with the obvious padding of contracts, but also often shoddy service. There were stories of weevils in the bread and plastic in the buckwheat porridge, of mini-scule portions and 'stews' that were little more than water, bones and fat. Even as late as 2018, it emerged that his catering services were responsible for a range of sick-nesses in Moscow's schools and kindergartens, and, in 2019, the court ordered Concord to pay compensation to the parents of children who had suffered from dysentery as a result. Likewise, in 2022 alone, the Defence Ministry would open 560 lawsuits against the Concord group for allegedly supplying the army with poor-quality, rotten and infected food.[32] Yet while customers began to grumble and investigative reporters wrote exposés of Concord's corrupt practices and poor service – especially in the newspaper *Novaya Gazeta*, which Prigozhin would come to see as something of a personal enemy – he continued to get contracts and rake in the money. Merely knowing your place while you pour the president's wine, while a valuable skill, could not be leveraged for billions of dollars in government contracts. What did a former thug and ambitious businessman have to offer, that he was being given such preferential treatment? More to the point, how can one draw a connection between Prigozhin's annoyance at having his business malpractices exposed and the potential upending of the US electoral system?

CHAPTER 5

Trollmaster

There was something special about 26 February 2012, a frigid day blessed by a gentle, pure, brilliantly white snow-fall. That day, more than 30,000 Muscovites took part in a political flashmob in which they pledged to come out to the Garden Ring – a giant thoroughfare girdling central Moscow – and hold hands in solidarity. What was special about it wasn't just the snow, the white ribbons and roses brandished by the participants, but the hope that, together, they could stand up for free and fair elections in Russia, for honesty, for integrity. This fragile hope still existed despite the apparent hopelessness of the moment: in a week's time, after all, Vladimir Putin was due to be elected president, and these protesters knew full well there was nothing they could really do to change this. All they could do was come out and speak their mind.

In the afternoon, tens of thousands joined hands along that 15km circle as cars honked and passers-by cheered. Regardless of how many people actually took part – according to police it was 11,000, but the organisers said it would take 34,000 people to close the circle, and by all accounts it was closed – it seemed like the whole city supported them.[1] Taxi drivers tied white ribbons to their car aerials, residents hung banners out of their windows, and volunteers set up stands along the perimeter of the road handing out free hot tea and biscuits to the participants, as they blew into their gloved hands for warmth.[2]

One of those stands was not quite like all the others. Like so many, it was organised by a businessman who wanted to do right by his conscience and support what he believed to be a just cause. But the man behind this particular stand was Dmitry Koshara, development director of Concord Catering, one of Prigozhin's longest-standing sidekicks.[3] And he and his boss were working for a somewhat different cause, and one in which Prigozhin would find himself able to enjoy his greatest and most dangerous vice: revenge.

The Revenge of the 'Best and the Most Productive'

On 23 September 2011, as Putin and his stand-in president, Dmitry Medvedev, took the stage in front of a cheering auditorium full of United Russia party members, he finally pronounced, as he humbly accepted Medvedev's formal nomination for president: 'I would like to say directly that the agreement about what should be done, what we should be doing – that we reached a long time ago, several years ago.'[4] The reality is more complicated, but the fundamental political shift that it reflects is central to the reasons behind the exponential rise of Prigozhin's empire from 2012. It was a time when the Kremlin abandoned liberalisation and turned to rely on those who saw their fortunes in peddling patriotism in return for Kremlin favour. It was a time of disappointment, betrayal and revenge – on the part of various sectors of society, on the part of Putin, and on the part of Prigozhin himself, who found his voice amid this new, thuggish populism.

In his first two presidential terms, 2000–8, Vladimir Putin had been all things to all Russians. His first deputy chief of staff, Vladislav Surkov, who had trained to be a theatre director, was the architect of Putin's 'managed democracy', granting him all the performative perks of a democracy without any of its constraints. Surkov set up what was in effect a fake democracy, where ostensibly 'opposition' parties such as the Communists and ultra-nationalist Liberal Democrats engaged in stage-managed spats with United Russia to create the illusion of real politics. Likewise, Putin's early years offered something to every stratum of society, from the elite's new opportunities for embezzlement to steady improvements in the standard of living of blue-collar Russians. Throughout Medvedev's regency, Putin likely intended to remain in a powerful role simply to protect himself, his family and his assets. After all, in a system like this, where the law always takes second place to political power, to abandon high office is to become potentially vulnerable. However, the question of what exactly this would mean, whether a return to the presidency or a move to some honorific 'father of the nation' role remained open until around the summer of 2011. Ultimately, Putin convinced himself that he was indispensable. In part, this was ego, fanned by cronies who feared for their futures under a new boss. It also reflected Medvedev's more emollient foreign policy, as he pursued a 'reset' with the West, and at one point even publicly disagreed with Putin over NATO policy towards Libya. This broke a central element of their pact, that Putin would continue to shape foreign and security policy.

But the bigger problem was that Medvedev's liberalisation campaign started to acquire a little too much momentum for Putin's comfort and, more to the point, for many of his cronies and confidants, who began whispering in his ear about the need for him to retake power. Medvedev was inadvertently exposing deep fissures in Russia's economy and political system. Although largely superficial, his anti-corruption campaign and drive to reform the economy further began to create a demand for real change, and liberals in the government started taking his messages rather too literally. Deputy Prime Minister and Minister for Finance Alexei Kudrin was becoming increasingly outspoken, at some instances openly clashing with the president over fiscal policies. A liberal wing began emerging within United Russia, even while Putin was still the party's leader. Most of all, Russia's growing middle class, which had come to enjoy growing standards of living thanks to more than a decade of high oil prices and relative political stability, started exhibiting signs of a healthy sense of entitlement. Having the economic means, they now started to expect political representation.

When Putin announced that he would be returning to the presidency, it triggered a shock and disappointment so powerful that it impelled the liberals into action. 'It felt like we were duped and betrayed for believing Medvedev,' said a retired official who had worked in the government IT sector, close to the reformist technocrats. 'I felt personally humiliated.'[5] Taking the parliamentary elections as a rallying point, these middle-class, metropolitan liberals began holding increasingly large protests demanding free and fair elections. Their numbers included prominent parliamentarians such as anti-corruption campaigner Gennady Gudkov, and other well-established members of the government elites, like Kudrin himself.

Elections in December 2011 saw United Russia predictably win a majority of seats, but even though the level of vote rigging was probably no worse than in the past, it galvanised the liberal opposition, which began holding large rallies, especially in Moscow, protesting the results and demanding a free and fair presidential vote. The emerging leader of this movement was a Western-educated blogger and anti-corruption activist, Alexei Navalny. A charismatic, even if at times also nationalist voice, he declared war against 'the party of crooks and thieves' – Putin's United Russia and his corrupt cronies. Largely unspoken at this stage was the degree to which this was also becoming something of a class war, reflecting a widening divide between the educated middle class and not just the elite, but also the blue-collar majority, and those whose livelihood meant depending on government money.

Certainly Putin's political machine exploited these nascent divisions. While the initial protest movement included a wide swathe of social and political actors – from nationalists and anarchists, to trade unionists and conservative monarchists – the Kremlin sought to isolate the liberal-left segment from the conservative right, cracking down on the one while trying to co-opt the other. It launched a propaganda campaign painting the protesters, and Navalny in particular, as part of a Western-sponsored plot to destabilise Russia. Most importantly, in what would become a cornerstone of his policies for years to come, Putin found a convenient scapegoat in US secretary of state Hillary Clinton, who had criticised the parliamentary elections for voting irregularities. 'She set the tone for certain activists inside our country, sent a signal, and they heard the signal,' Putin said in December 2011. 'And with the support of the State Department, they began to act ... [Western governments] felt they had leverage inside our country.'[6]

As tens of thousands of protesters gathered in venues such as Moscow's Bolotnaya Square, to be met by thousands of riot-armoured policemen, Putin went on to war footing. Surkov had spoken out in support of the protesters, saying, 'the best part of our society, or rather the most productive part, is demanding respect', but in any case, there was no more room for his too-clever political theatre.[7] He was replaced by the more heavy-handed and traditional-minded Vyacheslav Volodin, who began to mobilise the regime's base. These included the so-called *byudzhetniki*, those working directly or indirectly for the state and thus able to be leant on, but also more conservative working-class constituencies. Factory workers from UralVagonZavod, the country's largest tank manufacturer, even offered to come to Moscow to 'sort out' the protests. If the best and most productive part had betrayed Putin, it was time to build a new base.

Volodin also turned to the army of pro-Kremlin youth movements Surkov had built. *Nashi* ('Ours'), for example, was something like a cross between the Soviet *Komsomol* (Young Communist League) and the YMCA, and it bussed teenagers from the provinces to beat drums for Putin on Moscow's Triumfalnaya and Bolotnaya squares for a few hundred rubles apiece. In what was a cynical caricature of the reality, the Kremlin ruthlessly spun this as class war: an entitled and unpatriotic creative class pitted against the honest and upright children of disenfranchised factory workers from the rust belt. For many of the latter, politicised pro-Kremlin youth organisations were among the only career ladders to which they had access. When a young student from Ivanovo Region was asked why she supported Putin and United Russia, her clumsy response – 'United Russia has made a lot of achievements. They boosted the economy ... and we started dressing more better [*sic*]' – was mocked by many within the protest class as a symbol of everything wrong with the 'backward masses' forming Putin's base. In their ridicule of her bad grammar, they ignored her limited opportunities: her mother a textile worker, her father a driver, she lived in a dorm room with four other girls, studying to be an accountant. When the opportunity arose, she joined the 'Steel' youth organisation, because how else could she aspire to the lifestyle enjoyed by so many of the protesters? As one woman who joined *Nashi* put it, 'Putin gave us the path for self-realisation.'[8]

Long before Hillary Clinton brushed away half of America as 'deplorable' for voting for Donald Trump, a similar drama pitting the haves against the have-nots was playing out in Russia. Yevgeny Prigozhin, for all his middling origins and his education, had already come to realise that his criminal record, his lack of cultural pretensions, and his thuggish looks and manner meant that, no matter how good his oysters, he would never be good enough for the snobs of Moscow and St Petersburg. He saw his chance in this moment and didn't need to be prompted or paid to take it. Putin was giving him a path for self-realisation too – and a new opportunity not just for revenge but to make himself useful, lucratively so.

Tit for Tat

Throughout 2012, strange things began to happen at the editorial offices of the newspapers and magazines *Forbes*

Russia, *Argumenty i Fakty*, *Novaya Gazeta* and *Moskovsky Komsomolets*. Suspiciously eager people began showing up at their offices looking for a job; shadowy clients would place lengthy interviews with random businessmen who would then deny they had ever spoken to them; investigative journalists would be offered money to write hit jobs on supposedly corrupt entrepreneurs. Meanwhile, an obscure St Petersburg-based outlet, *Gazeta o Gazetakh* (Newspaper about Newspapers) began printing exposés about reporters working at these papers, accusing them of corruption, defamation and writing hit jobs for hire.

At first, it was hard to place what exactly these publications had in common. *Novaya Gazeta* endorsed the anti-Kremlin protests and while *Forbes Russia* produced serious investigative reporting often critical of the Kremlin, it also aspired to Western-style impartiality. Conversely, both *Argumenty i Fakty* and *Moskovsky Komsomolets* were tabloids hardly associated with the opposition, and although they occasionally criticised the Kremlin, they were generally loyal to the state, even if privately owned. What they all had in common was that at one time or another they all had run detailed exposés of Prigozhin's businesses, raising accusations about rotten food and special treatment from the Kremlin.

Prigozhin's bête noire, *Novaya Gazeta*, was a particular target. In 2011, it wrote about the poisoning that left 207 students at an Emergencies Ministry institute in the Urals in critical condition after they had eaten food provided by MedStroi, a subsidiary of Concord Catering ostensibly founded by Prigozhin's mother, Violetta.[9] It was *Novaya*, too, that uncovered one of Prigozhin's provocations. According to documents its journalists downloaded from Concord Catering's servers in 2012, that February Prigozhin had had his director for development, Dmitry Koshara, worm his way into the protest movement. 'Offered free catering services,' Koshara reported back in one of the leaked messages. 'They are happy. In general, it turned out to be very easy to infiltrate the organising committee; they are still collecting donations through social networks and will be happy for any help.'[10] Using a hidden camera, Koshara filmed himself and his assistant handing over 10,000 rubles to an opposition organiser, who was under the impression he was dealing with a protest-minded businessman who just wanted to help. The footage Koshara and his team gathered would be used both to create a database of activists and also for a film discrediting the opposition that aired on the Kremlin-controlled NTV channel that winter. Called *Anatomy of a Protest*, it showed activists allegedly paying people to turn up at rallies and even made broad hints that they were backed by the CIA. Prigozhin not only helped create the film, he financed it and signed off on the final edit before it was shown.[11] *Novaya Gazeta* pulled no punches going after Prigozhin personally as a result, and while the muckraking was entirely deserved, it takes a thick skin to withstand the ire of *Novaya*'s hardened reporters. But a thick skin – nor letting go of a grudge – had never really been among Prigozhin's strengths.

Rather, he struck back. First, one of his chief PR operatives, Andrei Mikhailov, tried to set up a reporter for taking off-the-books payments so that they could be exposed in *Gazeta o Gazetakh*.[12] When this provocation didn't work, Mikhailov sent a certain Maria Kuprashevich to infiltrate the *Novaya Gazeta* editorial office, posing as an intern. The advertising department hired her, but was able to out her before she could gather any dirt on them or do any other mischief. She was exposed as a provocateur and labelled 'Masha Hari', after the German spy, in a lengthy report that could have hardly soothed Prigozhin's already wounded ego.[13]

The provocations would soon escalate to those of a more kinetic nature. According to his own account, Valery Amelchenko, a former convict who then worked security for Prigozhin, arranged physical attacks on his boss's rivals and critics, even being behind the killing of an oppositionist blogger. Denis Korotkov, the reporter for *Novaya Gazeta* who actually interviewed Amelchenko, was in response sent a funeral wreath with a note calling him a traitor, while his newsroom received a gift basket with a severed ram's head.[14]

Provocations like this were expensive, but that didn't deter Prigozhin. He had long maintained a ruthless security service, to match his brutal methods. When a chair at one of Putin's palaces was damaged during a catered function, 11 waiters were forced to undergo polygraph tests to determine if they were responsible.[15] However, what later became clear was how far his PR department was likewise built not so much to spread good news about him as to go after his detractors. How do we know? Prigozhin's characteristically thuggish approach to human resources often backfired. One night in 2017, Mikhailov himself was taken to a forest by a team from Prigozhin's security department, threatened and beaten, to get him to give up his share in what would become Prigozhin's media holding. In revenge, Mikhailov went to *Novaya Gazeta* – the same newspaper he had tried to infiltrate five years earlier – and recounted the whole story of how he had been hired in 2012 as a black PR technologist by Prigozhin's chief of security, Yevgeny Gulyayev. The initial aim had been to discredit Prigozhin's former business partner Boris Ziminov, but by then Prigozhin had made a lot more enemies, simply too many for Gulyayev to handle alone. Prigozhin was so excited to get someone like Mikhailov on board that he gave him $22,000 in cash just to publish four issues of *Gazeta o Gazetakh* exposing his enemies.[16]

Even that had not been Prigozhin's first venture into the worlds of online fakes and political spin. As far back as 2009, he had brought together a small team of trolls and hackers to meddle in St Petersburg's local elections in favour of candidates under his thumb, a very small-scale precursor to his infamous Internet Research Agency.[17] There is also some evidence in the next couple of years of stories being planted online defaming his critics. In other words, a powerful arm was being built within Prigozhin's empire, complete with PR spin-doctors, agents provocateurs (one of Mikhailov's first tasks was to stage a food poisoning, which he insists was fake, at a public event catered by a rival business – just to film attendees vomiting on their white tablecloths) and social media trolls, all to mess with anyone who came after Prigozhin in word or deed. The specialists were well-paid, and the PR department was highly motivated – after all, what could be more inspiring than revenge?

Friends of the Kremlin

Around the same time as *Anatomy of a Protest* was being made in 2012, and as the Kremlin was just getting around to harnessing the power of social media in fighting the opposition, Prigozhin had a meeting with Vyacheslav Volodin, the political technologist who had just replaced Surkov. The political boss complained that his pro-Kremlin bloggers 'were fucking him over and giving him inflated figures', according to a Concord employee. He wondered if Prigozhin, who already commanded a well-trained, professional army of trolls, had any advice. Prigozhin, according to that employee, offered to deploy his own network of bloggers and offered 'fucking great' results.[18]

By the summer of the following year, advertising notices were offering jobs to young people paying up to 30,000 rubles (about $1,000) a month to sit in a 'gorgeous office' in St Petersburg's Olgino district writing comments and blog posts on an assortment of websites. Journalists would later discover a whole building devoted to this new enterprise, with sections for bloggers, cartoonists, journalists and commentators, registered to a limited liability company called the Internet Research Agency. Back then, there was nothing linking the agency to Concord or Prigozhin. Instead, it was technically run by a number of veteran political organisers from several pro-Kremlin youth movements like *Nashi* and United Russia's Young Guard.[19]

Employees wrote blog posts and comments for hire, mostly of a political nature, but at times simply to draw traffic to a particular website. Screenshots from the troll farm showed texts criticising the United States and Navalny, alongside pedestrian insights about how Russian filmmaking was rising from its knees and surpassing Western culture, which was succumbing to materialism and degeneracy as opposed to Russia's looming spiritual revival. Working 12-hour shifts every other day, they operated to strict quotas, with a blogger, for example, expected to write at least ten posts of 750-plus words across three accounts or identities: this was black PR on an industrial scale. It was also still a very personal venture, though. In 2014, Prigozhin's daughter Polina married the young businessman Alexander Sklyarov. It was as extravagant a wedding as one might expect, held in St Petersburg's Konstantinovsky Hall, decorated with a million fresh flowers, and the trolls were enlisted to ensure that everyone knew that Prigozhin was not just a doting father, but a rich one.[20]

From the beginning, however, this Internet Research Agency represented something much bigger. Prigozhin may have started building his PR machine to defend himself and his business empire, but he soon came to realise that narratives, opinion and spin were going to be valuable new commodities in the (dis)information age. According to Yevgeny Zubarev, a top manager at Patriot Media, 2011 was the year when it became 'strategically important to sow doubt about opposition journalists who were rocking the boat'.[21] However, especially in those early days, Prigozhin was neither tasked by the government nor even being directly paid for these smears. Instead, he and his social media specialists seem genuinely to have believed that what they were doing was right, as Navalny and the opposition were 'seriously trying to destroy our country', in Zubarev's words.[22] Even Mikhailov, not someone with any reason to cover for Prigozhin after what happened to him in that wood, concurred: 'This is the idea of Yevgeny Viktorovich Prigozhin himself … I read that this is an order from the Kremlin, "homework" that Prigozhin performed in exchange for billions in government contracts. Based on what I saw and heard, I'm certain that he did not receive "instructions" from anyone, did not consult with anyone and did not ask permission.'[23]

Of course, Prigozhin was not naive. He may have started his black PR operations to avenge himself on those who challenged him and out of a genuine sense that a bunch of effete creatives were leading the country astray, but he was always the entrepreneur looking for new ways to monetise being useful to the Kremlin. He gambled that his attacks on the liberals would be rewarded, and increasingly this did indeed pay off. The Kremlin become a useful client for the IRA and Patriot Media. On its behalf, they spread anti-Ukrainian narratives in the West after the 2014 'Revolution of Dignity' that toppled a friendly president in Kyiv, and pro-regime stories about the Assad dictatorship in Syria. At home, they continued to demonise opposition figures as traitors and hypocrites. By 2018, in time for the next presidential election, Prigozhin's media arm numbered 16 news portals attracting as many as 30 million monthly visitors in total, with a yearly budget of $4.7 million.[24] However, already Prigozhin's role as trollmaster had become an international story, as he stood accused of tilting the balance in one of the most seismic global events of the decade: the US presidential elections of 2016.

Making Hillary Squirm

If there was another man besides Prigozhin who couldn't let go of a grudge, then it was Vladimir Putin. When the middle class rose up against him in 2011, he not only promoted the idea that this was all the work of Hillary Clinton, he seemed to have convinced himself of it. The corollary was that a West which had long tried to thwart Russia's attempts to assert what he saw as its rightful status as a global power, not least by fomenting 'colour revolutions' against friendly regimes, was now actively coming for him. What followed domestically was not just a policy shift, but the beginnings of a witch hunt. The Kremlin introduced ever-tighter controls over foreign-funded political movements and media; parliament went into a legislative frenzy, churning out laws crippling NGOs, independent politicians and journalists. The narrative of an external enemy responsible for domestic strife is a powerful one, and it is easy to see how a whole slew of officials and budding entrepreneurs whose livelihood depended on the state and whose corrupt way of life was challenged by the protests bought into this narrative with gusto. It wasn't just a matter of patriotism, of defending slighted honour, but, as a cat will lay dead mice at the doorstep of its master, of expecting certain perks in return. Of course, from the first there had been meetings between Prigozhin and Volodin and other senior officials. There had been suggestions and requests that sometimes turned into actual commissions. Much of the time, though, the initiative still came from Prigozhin, with the anticipation or expectation that his actions would be rewarded.

In February 2018, as America still struggled to come to grips with Donald Trump's election in 2016, Special Counsel Robert Mueller indicted 13 Russians working for the Internet Research Agency who had allegedly tried to influence the presidential election. At the heart of the influence campaign were 3,500 Facebook ads placed by the IRA focusing on race, policing, immigration and other divisive issues. These were, arguably, a drop in the toxic ocean of existing American social media hysteria, but, just as it was for Putin, pinning domestic strife on an external enemy was too tempting for the DC establishment. The IRA's objectives, the Mueller investigation concluded, were to 'sow discord in the US political system, including the 2016 presidential elections' and 'included supporting the presidential campaign of then-candidate Donald J. Trump and disparaging Hillary Clinton'.[25] As other, separate Russian influence operations emerged, including a hack of the Democratic National Convention servers by groups tied to Russian intelligence, panic spread in the United States about a coordinated campaign from Moscow to destroy its political system.

Later, it would emerge that about a hundred trolls worked in the American Department of the St Petersburg factory, churning out about a thousand posts a week and setting up dozens of Facebook communities. Far from being single-mindedly dedicated to the downfall of American democracy, some of them even used their fake online personae to talk an unwitting US citizen into posing in front of the White House on 29 May 2016, with a sign reading, 'Happy 55th Birthday Dear Boss.'[26] The boss in question was, of course, Prigozhin. Although by the 2016 elections, the IRA's budget was at least equivalent to $1 million a month, most of this went on salaries and facilities, not on Facebook advertising and the like, and this was dwarfed by the $6.5 billion spent in all the legal campaigning in that year's presidential and congressional races combined by Democrats, Republicans, lobbyists and special interest groups.[27]

The idea that Prigozhin's trolls were specifically charged with garnering support for Trump – popular in an American media horrified at the time that half the country could elect such a president and eager to find a scapegoat – doesn't really stand up to evidence. Most of the troll factory's content had little to do with backing a specific candidate or side. One IRA-created community staged a Black Lives Matter flashmob, simply for the sake of testing out whether social media commentators in St Petersburg could get people to a rally in Charleston, and others exploited existing scandals associated with Trump. The content was much more about exploiting hot-button issues in the United States – the same toxic, populist narratives that have long been the staple of demagogues. It was no wonder that they often aligned with Trump's narratives but according to one employee at the troll factory, this was 'correlation', and not support. 'There was no objective to "support Trump." All current problems [that were being criticised] were directly related to the actions of the ruling party at that time [the Democrats]. Hillary [Clinton] is their representative, which means she is to blame,' according to another employee. Indeed, Clinton figured in the troll posts far more often than Trump did.[28]

After all, it was not just that she had become their bête noire, the Russian leadership was convinced she would win, and that she would bend all America's resources to toppling Putin. To a considerable degree, this was mirror-imaging: they thought US democracy was as 'managed' as Russia's. As a Foreign Ministry staffer confidently told us a few months before, 'the American establishment will not allow a Trump to be elected'.[29] The aim seems to have been to support any and all divisive causes and actors across the political spectrum (indeed, at one point they managed to spark simultaneous pro- and anti-Trump demonstrations in New York), not just to make Clinton squirm, but to try to ensure that her presidency would be so consumed with domestic crises that it lacked the opportunity to look towards Moscow.

'There was no massive campaign,' another Russian government official told us. 'Disparate activities of this or that activist, or special services group, or businessmen and entrepreneurs – these people are always active in fields like this. It's what they do. It doesn't mean that they are part of some grandiose plan to instigate regime change in the United States … We have a lot of strange people, in Moscow and abroad, who call themselves agents of the Kremlin. They are trying to earn money or political capital that way.'[30]

What were Prigozhin's true motivations in unleashing a dark PR campaign that would, inadvertently, assume such global significance? Was he indeed tasked by the Kremlin, even though his operatives, and he himself, scrambled to deny it? Or was he one of those 'strange people', doing this out of patriotism, or to guarantee the millions of dollars in government contracts that were coming his way? It is impossible to know for sure: Prigozhin largely avoided interviews at the time and would only admit to founding the Internet Research Agency – proudly at that – after Russia's full-scale invasion of Ukraine in 2022. But given what we do know, it was likely a combination of all of these things: an entrepreneur with a budding PR force and a wounded, aggressive ego looked to please a Kremlin that was in the market for any help it could get, as long as it could disown the help at its pleasure. He clearly enjoyed the notoriety, expressing himself 'not at all bothered' by being indicted by the Mueller inquiry in 2018: 'the Americans are really impressionable people, they see what they want to see. If they want to see the devil, let them see him.'[31] This was classic Prigozhin: making a play of denying any involvement, but with a knowing nod and a wink, and still using the opportunity to promote himself. After all, the furore in America had been very good for him, making an often amateurish and ineffective online campaign seem like some Machiavellian masterstroke. The more reviled Prigozhin was in Washington, the higher his stock in Moscow.

Prigozhin the Motion Picture

After all, Prigozhin was always careful to curate his image at home. Although he was notorious for largely avoiding interviews unless he absolutely needed them to secure a contract or make a political attack, he did have that very active and even aggressive press team doing their best to hype his triumphs and conceal his failures. As his ambitions grew, though, so too would his media profile. First, his social media would become an increasingly important channel for him to share his thoughts – and often his complaints – with the world. In due course, though, he would even go on to back and essentially shape fully eight films that advanced his political and personal agendas, manufacturing a whole mythology around his operations. He first dabbled by financially backing the 2019 film *Rzhev* (released in the West as *Unknown Battle*), about the eponymous bloody battles that took place during the Second World War. Hardly coincidentally, the film and the book on which it was based both mentioned his grandfather, Yevgeny Ilyich Prigozhin.[32] What may have started simply as a vanity project (which nonetheless earned him profit and a producer's credit) then became a branding opportunity. From 2020, a string of pyrotechnic action films emerged exalting the operations of his Wagner mercenary company, which had been formed in 2014, in Ukraine and above all Africa.

First came *Turist* (*The Tourist*, 2021), following heroic Russian mercenaries – Wagner is not mentioned by name – in the Central African Republic, defending locals against villainous rebels backed by France and the USA. 'Americans say they fight for democracy,' one of the mercenaries pointedly says, but 'Russians fight for justice.' In many ways, it would be harder to find a better encapsulation of Putin's own view. In short order, there followed *Solntsepyok* (*Blazing Sun*, 2021) and *Granit* (2021), in what was an impressive display of speed, if not necessarily quality. *Solntsepyok* is set in Luhansk in 2014 after Prigozhin's men had begun serving in Russia's undeclared war against Ukraine, while *Granit* covers Wagner's operations in Mozambique, although whereas in reality that deployment was an embarrassing failure, this displays his mercenaries as successful warrior-humanitarians. Like *Turist*, *Granit* was produced by Aurum, a company of which Prigozhin was a major shareholder. Then came *Luchshiye v Adu* (*The Best in Hell*, 2022), a raw depiction of urban warfare in Ukraine co-authored by Alexander Nagin, a serving Wagner fighter, and in which the mercenary group's role in that year's invasion was explicit.[33]

As if all that were not enough, Prigozhin's people also distributed two films, *Shugalei* (2020) and *Shugalei 2* (2020), highly fictionalised accounts of Maxim Shugalei, a political technologist and operator who runs the Prigozhin-backed Foundation for the Defence of National Values and who is under sanctions in Ukraine for being an ally of his.[34] Shugalei was detained in Libya in 2019, accused of being a Russian spy, but the films present him instead as seeking to unravel CIA-backed networks of corruption and subversion. While the two *Shugaleis* are rather more questionable (and frankly, dull), the Wagner-related films are tolerable B-movie actioners, if one disregards the realities behind the screen, and their role was, in classic Prigozhin style, both to make money and also to paint the right picture of true Russian patriots making the world a better place with fist, guile and Kalashnikov. They were also extended recruitment adverts, especially as the trollmaster made sure his social media operators' dark arts boosted this venture. Established film critic Anton Dolin, for example, was surprised to discover he had apparently penned very favourable reviews of both *Rzhev* and *The Tourist*, while, in other cases, a suspicious number of fawningly positive comments appeared about Prigozhin's Wagner films on Russian social media platforms and websites.[35] Prigozhin was not simply inventing an agenda, he was creating both a fictional backstory and a mythologised historical record.

Arguably this was most visible in *16-i* (*16th*, 2021), a departure from the rest of his oeuvre by being a rather clumsy attempt at humorous political satire with a heavy dose of slapstick. A mismatched bunch of young Russians looking to earn some money end up inadvertently swinging the 2016 presidential election Donald Trump's way, while two-dimensional American spooks take everything at face value and cannot conceive of anything but a subtle Russian conspiracy. Much like Prigozhin, the film is vulgar, heavy-handed, yet also quite carefully calibrated to win over the (undiscriminating) audience. Again, the trolls did their bit to make the film a sensation. Hacked social media accounts were used to claim that the Angelika Film Center in New York was raided by police when it tried to show *16th*, and these fake stories were duly recycled on Prigozhin's media outlets under breathless headlines such as 'New York Police Disrupted the Premiere of Prigozhin's Film'.[36] The cinema itself denied that any of the story was true.

Was Prigozhin really trying to distance himself from the whole presidential election scandal? Of course not, quite the opposite: he wanted it both ways, to make his jabs at the Americans for their supposed Russophobic paranoias, while continuing to keep himself associated with this alleged success. He may actually have had no or very limited role in Trump's victory, but so long as his enemies were willing to ascribe him with such Mephistophelian powers, he was happy to take fullest advantage of this. Prigozhin had become the trollmaster first to punish his detractors, then to express his own particular kind of Russian patriotism, and finally as a business. Having become an informational hitman for hire – and in the process further deepening his dependence on Kremlin contracts and goodwill – perhaps the transition to mercenary captain was rather less of a leap.

CHAPTER 6

Condottiere

They were covered up by the suit he was wearing, but the man standing in front of Prigozhin had SS tattoos on his shoulders and a Nazi eagle on his chest. It was spring 2014, and Dmitry Utkin had until last year been the lieutenant colonel commanding the 2nd Special Forces Brigade's 700th Detachment, but his career had hit something of a ceiling. He had not been selected to study at a higher level at a military academy, generally a precondition for rising to full colonel and beyond, and in any case, the special forces are quite light in senior officers compared with the top-heavy regular army. Nor was he apparently in line for a transfer to the regular military or the paratroopers, two other time-honoured ways for ambitious Spetsnaz to get a colonel's third star. So, he left the military for private security and became a prime mover behind an abortive early attempt to deploy mercenaries into Syria. He was just the man Prigozhin would soon come to need – a field commander looking for a new berth, who didn't mind getting his hands dirty and who, according to his ex-wife, never really adapted to peacetime: 'he wanted a military career as a combat officer, not to wear out the seats of his pants sitting in some HQ somewhere'.[1]

The two were introduced by Alexei Dyumin, the former deputy head of the Presidential Security Service, whose claim to fame was having once successfully defended a peacefully sleeping president from a bear eager to enter his residence.[2] But that spring, Dyumin had a different mission: popular protests in neighbouring Ukraine had toppled the government of Kremlin ally Viktor Yanukovych, and Moscow was in the process of a military–political operation to secure the Crimean Peninsula and wrest it from the hands of a new, pro-Western government. Dyumin, as head of the Special Operations Forces Command (KSSO) – the 'polite people' without insignia covertly deployed to the peninsula – was looking for additional muscle, in the form of mercenary groups that the Kremlin could deny. Thousands of Russian volunteers had flocked to Crimea and eastern Ukraine to join the separatist militias sprouting there out of their own initiative, but while these were useful, the Kremlin was aware that it needed forces that were competent, deniable and controllable.

Prigozhin was apparently in the Donbas that spring, scouting for new opportunities. According to Marat Gabidullin, a mercenary who joined Wagner and worked as Prigozhin's aide until falling out with him in 2018, he had travelled to the Luhansk Region, where, just as in neighbouring Donetsk, pro-Russian separatists would take over the regional administration building and proclaim an independent republic. With Kyiv's control over the area shaky, and law enforcement conflicted about which side to take, the unrest left a good chunk of the local economy – particularly coal and minerals – up for grabs. Prigozhin was eager to snap up what he could. Meanwhile, the Russian Ministry of Defence (MoD), and military intelligence (GRU[3]) in particular, was looking for something better than the often-unruly volunteer militias that had flocked to join separatists in the Donetsk Region.[4] Under normal circumstances, Dyumin, his hands full with the KSSO's operations, would have had no reason to meet Prigozhin, and apparently did not even know Utkin personally. Nor would the businessman have had any particular interest in sitting down with a washed-out ex-commando. But there and then, the Kremlin's political goals and Prigozhin's business ambitions were unexpectedly aligning.

Rival Narratives

There is no official order, decree or record for the creation of the Wagner Private Military Company (PMC). As of writing, the very existence of private military companies in Russia is still illegal. Under Article 359 of the Criminal Code, mercenary work remains punishable by seven years in prison, while recruiting, training and financing mercenaries can land a Russian citizen in jail for 15 years. So how was it, exactly, that a restaurateur, a businessman close to the president himself, wound up doing just that? And why?

Prigozhin, as ever, would spin a narrative that made him master of his own fate when he finally took ownership of his role as warlord in September 2022. By his account, he made his decision in spring 2014, when

> Russia jumped on the last train and managed to block the arrival of the Ukrainian army into Crimea. I, like many other businessmen ... tried to recruit a group to go and protect Russians. I flew to an old training ground and did it all myself: cleaned old weapons, sorted out [kit], and found specialists. On 1 May 2014, a group of patriots was born, which later acquired the name Wagner. And now the time of revelation has come. These guys, the heroes who defended the Syrian people, other peoples of the Arab countries, destitute Africans and Latin Americans, have become one of the pillars of our Motherland.[5]

Prigozhin's claim to having been driven by patriotism is not exactly untrue, merely not the whole truth. Marat Gabidullin – who, admittedly, joined Prigozhin's team only in 2015 – stresses the financial over the patriotic dimension, but otherwise accepts his former boss's line. He said Wagner was 'the personal initiative of Prigozhin himself ... He had the acumen to achieve for himself the role of sole curator of this project.'[6] Yet it seems that there was a third element: the Kremlin's own calculations.

There is, after all, some evidence that at first Prigozhin had not been that interested but, in the words of a former Presidential Administration staffer, the government 'knew what Prigozhin wanted, and that gave them all the leverage they needed'.[7]

Certainly at the time, all kinds of forces were emerging in the Donbas, from militarised gangs of local thugs to Cossack volunteers. After Putin had seized the strategically vital Crimean Peninsula in February 2014, protests against Kyiv broke out in parts of eastern Ukraine. In part out of genuine patriotism, in part at the quiet behest of the Kremlin, many Russian adventurers and entrepreneurs supported these uprisings.[8] While Prigozhin claims that this is when Wagner came into existence, the first public accounts of it being on the ground date back to 2015, and there is no evidence that he was one of the figures involved in the Crimean operation. Instead, he would find himself involved in a process that dates back to calculations made before the Ukrainian revolution, the Crimean annexation and the Donbas war.

Covert War

The Kremlin and the Defence Ministry under Putin had long been enamoured of privatising expensive state functions in the name of efficiency (and, a cynic might suggest, handing lucrative contracts to cronies and favourites). It was partly to that end, after all, that, in 2007, Putin appointed a civilian former tax minister,

Anatoly Serdyukov, as his defence minister. Serdyukov was another of the 'Petersburgers' from the president's home city, and he quickly colonised the upper reaches of the ministry with his own people, again disproportionately from St Petersburg. Once again, Prigozhin's habit of making connections who might come in useful paid off, as he knew several and, through them, got to woo Colonel General Dmitry Bulgakov. For all his heavyset bearing and fondness for wearing his field-grey dress uniform, Bulgakov was a storekeeper more than a soldier, and from 2008 the deputy minister of defence and chief of logistics. He was to be crucial for Prigozhin's efforts to win lucrative contracts feeding, housing and otherwise servicing the military, but also acted as his eyes and ears in the Defence Ministry's sprawling main building on Frunze Embankment, alerting him to new opportunities.[9] When Prigozhin's phone records for an eight-month period between late 2013 and early 2014 were leaked, for example, they showed that he had spoken with the defence minister just twice – but 31 times with Bulgakov.[10]

There had long been talk of creating private military companies just like the Americans' or the British, but serious discussion only began in 2010. Eeben Barlow, founder of the South African military company Executive Outcomes, had spoken at the St Petersburg Economic Forum about the kind of things that excited the Kremlin and the General Staff: how the military can build ties with the private sector and how the projection of power could be privatised. There was also a closed presentation especially for the military. Although to this day official sources remain reticent, General Nikolai Makarov, then the chief of the General Staff, was reportedly enthused.[11] The right kind of PMC could, it was reasoned, be a cost-effective tool for Russia, were it to want to run political–military operations beyond its immediate strategic neighbourhood.

But 2010 was not the time to ruffle anyone's feathers. Russia was quickly recovering its economic standing after the 2008 financial crisis, and was re-establishing relationships with the West and, with that, its global influence. Rather, it was in 2012 that everything changed, and the Kremlin began considering another important advantage of PMCs: their deniability. As Putin's system really began to move into a wartime footing after the Bolotnaya protests, Russia's strategy became dominated by a paranoid attribution of every domestic ill to an all-powerful Western foe bent on weakening Russia. As far as the Kremlin was concerned, Western meddling could mean that, in the words of the new chief of General Staff, Valery Gerasimov, 'a perfectly thriving state can, in a matter of days … become a victim of foreign intervention, and sink to a web of chaos, humanitarian catastrophe and civil war. The very "rules of war" have changed.'[12] Naturally, Putin felt he had to step up to the challenge and push back against a West that had finally showed its true colours. What better way than ape what he believed the Americans had been doing so well, for so long? True to form, though, Putin was still strangely loath to appear

autocratic. He needed to appear merely to be accommo-
dating the people's will. When a parliamentarian asked
him a clearly planted question on private military companies as a means of furthering Russia's influence abroad
in April 2012, Putin affected to be won over by the idea:
'I think that it really is an instrument of realising national
interests without the direct participation of the government. You're absolutely right.'[13]

In 2012, the first such PMC was established, the
Slavonic Corps. Vadim Gusev and Yevgeny Sidorov, two
managers from the established private security company,
Moran Security Group, created a new firm, technically
registered in Hong Kong.[14] Officially meant just to
guard oil fields, its foray into Syria proved as disastrous
as it was brief. After a skirmish in November 2013, the
Slavonic Corps was forced to return to Moscow. There,
in an act of characteristic Kremlin double standards
and ingratitude, Gusev and Sidorov were arrested by the
FSB on charges of mercenary activity.[15] The Slavonic
Corps had been a failure – and Utkin had been part of
this debacle – but the Kremlin still thought that a tame
PMC could be a useful deniable instrument of power
projection, whether in the Middle East or Africa. It was
just that finding the right organiser who could handle
both the military and entrepreneurial challenges the job
entailed, and was trusted enough yet not too close to
the Kremlin, was proving a challenge. Prigozhin may
even have been felt out for this role in 2013, but was
not interested.

Everything changed with the Ukrainian 'Revolution of Dignity' in the winter of 2013–14. As far as Putin was concerned, the United States was on the march. The popular protests that toppled the government of Kremlin-backed president Viktor Yanukovych were, he was convinced, not just encouraged but directed from Washington. Spring 2014 saw eastern Ukraine gripped by a scrappy, disconnected conflict as local militias hostile to the new government in Kyiv, a handful of out-and-out pro-Russian forces and a miscellany of Russian national-ist volunteers clashed with loyalist forces. At the time, the Kremlin had no specific and coherent goals and strategy towards the Donbas. Policy was being driven, to a large degree, by a limited cohort of pro-Russian Ukrainians and Russian nationalists who believed that the 'liberation' of the Donetsk and Luhansk regions was strategically neces-sary if Russia wanted to hold Crimea. The Kremlin did not disagree, but it was reluctant to deploy regular troops, even while it soon began to harbour a deep distrust of the self-driven separatists and their enthusiastic Russian backers. Initially, the Kremlin did not even want formally to recognise the new separatist pseudo-states. Although by summer 2014 it had opted to deploy limited contin-gents of its own troops when it was clear that the only alternative was to allow the rebels to be defeated, the Kremlin still wanted to keep its involvement as limited, and as able to be disavowed, as possible.

Suddenly, a PMC had a new and urgent role closer to home. According to sources in the Defence Ministry,

Prigozhin was chosen by the Kremlin because he was both 'a man of initiative' who 'knows how to get what he wants', as well as close enough to Putin to be considered reliable, but not so close as to be too powerful, and too obviously a Kremlin proxy. The interesting thing is that, according to these sources, he was apparently initially reluctant, with one person involved in the original discussions recalling that 'it immediately seemed to me that Prigozhin didn't like this whole idea with PMCs at all'.[16] He was a businessman, why would he want also to become what in Renaissance Italy would be called a *condottiere*, a mercenary captain? What seems likely is that all the stories are true, in their own ways. The Kremlin wanted someone to set up a new PMC for deployment in the Donbas, and chose Prigozhin. Genuinely fired up by the muscular nationalism of the moment, but also well aware that he was not in a position to deny the Kremlin, Prigozhin ultimately opted to volunteer himself before he was volunteered.

He was not everyone's choice, though. When Sergei Shoigu replaced Anatoly Serdyukov as defence minister in 2012, he had been wary of Prigozhin and gave orders to members of his team to avoid contact with him.[17] (Although by all accounts, Bulgakov ignored this stricture.) This hostility may have been about politics and personality, but also profit: the incoming minister, like any senior Russian official, was looking for his share. Originally, this concerned Prigozhin's catering contracts, but Wagner would become another bone of contention. 'Shoigu's main complaint against Prigozhin,' Gabidullin claims, 'the main reason for the hostility, was that the [Wagner] money did not go through the Defence Ministry. He had no contact with this money and couldn't take a cut.' Instead, the money came directly from the Kremlin, through a series of front companies. 'It was like in that movie, *Casino*,' Gabidullin continued. 'They come in, go to the closet, open it, load the money into bags, everyone else looks away and pretends not to notice anything. And it's the same here. A certain circle of people come to the bank with a power of attorney, load up with money, and leave.'[18]

Adhocracy in Action

This was why Prigozhin was suddenly shopping for a field commander – and probably why Dyumin had played a key role in matchmaking. At the time, Dyumin was the head of the KSSO, but this was a temporary position, and his links with Putin, the security agencies and the Presidential Administration were crucial. Shoigu was sceptical that Prigozhin was the right person for the job, so someone else had to help find the caterer a right-hand man, and that role seems to have fallen to the half-soldier, half-security officer. Dyumin and Prigozhin had had no real contact beforehand, but the leaked phone logs showed that they spoke more than 25 times in the period leading up to Wagner's genesis.[19]

By 1 May 2014, then, Prigozhin had signed an agreement with Utkin, and his head of security, Yevgeny

Gulyayev, had already begun recruiting mercenaries,[20] all to create a private army to 'defend Donbas'.[21] This is, after all, how Putin's system works. To a considerable extent, it is a modern, bureaucratic state like so many others, its day-to-day actions defined by rules, laws, regulations and institutions. Atop it, though, is an almost medieval court, in which constantly competing factions and individuals are struggling for the most important currency of them all: Putin's favour.[22] That, in turn, can be converted into whatever else one could want: wealth, fame, power over one's enemies. Some grandees, like the Rotenberg brothers (Putin's childhood judo sparring partners who were, as of 2023, estimated to have assets worth $5 billion) or Security Council secretary Nikolai Patrushev (a colleague of Putin's in the KGB back in the 1970s and now in effect his national security adviser), are close enough to the president that they can count on his indulgence. Most others, like great white sharks, must keep swimming or drown, constantly demonstrating their loyalty and usefulness. Gabidullin, who had a ringside seat to Prigozhin's wheeling and dealing, described this 'desire to move closer to the source of public funds. Increase your well-being, squeeze through the dense crowd that has already surrounded the state trough, and get something for yourself.'

In this 'adhocracy' (where real power lies largely not in the formal structures but instead in personal relationships, and where individuals and institutions are often charged by the sovereign with responsibilities on an ad

hoc basis), whatever role people think they may be playing is constrained by and often clashes with their real role:
which is whatever Putin wants them to be, something that
may well change from day to day. Prigozhin was a serious
player in St Petersburg and in the catering industry, but
he was no oligarch – scarcely even a minigarch – and
certainly not a power in Putin's court. Ultimately, if the
Kremlin wanted him to be a *condottiere*, then he had little
scope to refuse, and good reasons to agree. After all, the
'adhocracy' works because of how many carrots are
bundled with the sticks. Prigozhin was not just getting a
chance to prove his patriotism, he was being paid hand-
somely through direct transfers and also mysteriously
overinflated government contracts for other services.
In due course, Wagner would even get its own base,
at Molkino in southern Russia, on the grounds of the
10th Spetsnaz Brigade's own encampment. Technically,
Prigozhin was breaking the law, but that didn't matter so
long as he was doing the Kremlin's business, and he was
being well-rewarded for his 'crime'.

Establishing the Orchestra

The earliest mention of mercenaries belonging to a
company specifically called Wagner appears in October
2015 – well over a year after they had begun their operations in eastern Ukraine. Before then, Wagner fighters
in the Donbas – unlike the various Russian volunteer
battalions who actively recruited anyone who wanted

to fight in defence of Russians in Ukraine and proudly advertised their roles – were practically non-existent on social media or in the press. Nonetheless, remnants of the Slavonic Corps, now under new commanders, cropped up in Crimea and then the Donbas.[23] 'Someone was shut down, and someone else was made an offer they couldn't refuse,' a Wagner fighter would recall years later.[24]

The curators behind this new mercenary experiment seemed to have learned lessons from the Slavonic Corps debacle. This new force was properly trained and armed – unlike its predecessor, which had been promised T-72 tanks and then provided with buses covered in iron plates[25] – and Utkin apparently knew his business.[26] But the unit he commanded was so secretive that there was no mention of it at the time. The first proper reports, as opposed to vague rumours, emerged in early 2016, when the St Petersburg-based *Fontanka* news outlet discovered secret decrees from the Presidential Administration issuing post-mortem awards to fighters killed in Ukraine and Syria.[27]

This would be Wagner, so named for the callsign used by Utkin, a man who, as one Russian newspaper report so coyly put it, was 'known for his commitment to the aesthetics and ideology of the Third Reich'.[28] (He would even sometimes greet Prigozhin with 'Heil Petrovich,' using his boss's codename.) Naming a mercenary army after the German composer may seem surreal, but it later led to a whole slew of supportive memes, with the force being referred to euphemistically as the 'orchestra'. The connection to Prigozhin would only emerge later, as reports of Utkin conferring with Gulyayev began to surface.[29] Even so, it would take another eight years for Prigozhin finally to admit what had already been becoming clear by 2015.

Wagner in the Donbas

If the Kremlin was going to underwrite the war in the Donbas, it would want to call the shots. Wagner would fight in a number of the crucial early battles of this undeclared war, including the summer 2014 seizure of Luhansk airport, where Utkin himself reportedly took a shrapnel wound to his liver, and the hard-fought recapture of the contested city of Debaltseve in January–February 2015.[30] However, Wagner's utility in the Donbas, in that regard, was less of a frontline fighting element so much as a 'mop up' force. They arrived in Donetsk and Luhansk in May 2014, around the time when other forces connected to the GRU were being deployed to restore order, as it became clear that the half-drunk, half-feral assortment of amateur militias had become a real problem for the Kremlin and needed to be reined in. The GRU-mustered Vostok Battalion, for example, rolled into the city of Donetsk on 29 May and proceeded to take over the separatists' headquarters as a symbolic show of Moscow's authority.[31]

Wagner's role was less overt and more violent. Among its missions was, apparently, taking out those separatist warlords who had become inconvenient for the Kremlin. In January 2015, for example, Alexander 'Batman' Bednov, the head of the 'Batman Battalion', was driving back to his base, accompanied by fully six bodyguards, when he was ambushed by assailants who apparently knew his route and the minibus in which he was travelling, which was raked with machine-gun fire. In May 2015, Alexei Mozgovoi, commander of the Prizrak, or Ghost Brigade, was also killed in an ambush. His motorcade was blasted by a bomb and then riddled with gunfire, killing him and his team.[32] In December 2015, Pavel 'Batya' Dremov, whose Cossack militia had carved out a fiefdom in Luhansk Region, was killed on his wedding day, when a bomb placed in his car exploded.[33] Although the self-styled 'prosecutor-general's office' of the Russia-backed separatist government in Luhansk (LNR) would claim that Bednov was killed by LNR forces after resisting arrest,[34] in most of these and similar cases, the blame was officially placed on mysteriously competent Ukrainian 'diversionary troops' who somehow managed to infiltrate, assassinate and escape without hindrance or even leaving any traces. Instead, many Russian nationalist sources – including field commander Igor Girkin (known by his callsign 'Strelkov') – claimed Wagner was behind these killings, eliminating commanders who were too ambitious and aggressive for the Kremlin's comfort.[35]

However, while many Wagner fighters were ideologically motivated to fight in the Donbas – 'Putin only impressed me when he took Crimea – I felt I had to [continue the work of defending Russians] and go to Donbas,' one confessed[36] – eastern Ukraine was merely a place where they demonstrated their efficacy, their capacity to apply violence while still shrouded in the fog of war and cloak of deniability. (A case in point: some claim that the allegations about Wagner's role in killing Bednov and the like was simply to mask the use of GRU Spetsnaz: like a classic Russian matryoshka doll, there always seems one more layer of conspiracy theory.[37]) This was what the Kremlin had wanted them to do, though, and they were rewarded. In the course of his whole regular military career Utkin, for example, had received only one of the significant Russian military awards, the Order of Courage. By the end of 2016, he had accumulated three more, and had been personally presented to Vladimir Putin in the Kremlin at the Day of Heroes of the Fatherland reception on 9 December 2016.[38] Utkin, along with Andrei Troshev (known by his callsign 'Sedoy', or 'Grey-hair'), Wagner's chief of staff, and Andrei 'Brodyaga' ('Vagabond') Bogatov, would soon also be made Heroes of the Russian Federation. Naturally, this reflected to Prigozhin's credit, even if it would only be much later that he would receive his own Hero of the Russian Federation medal. Having built up Wagner from a force of around 300 by summer 2014 to 700–1,000 a year later, though, he was now ready for something more extensive (and profitable), and it just so happened that the Kremlin had bigger plans for his private army.

The Syrian Concerto

In the summer of 2017, Alex (not his real name), who had once been wounded fighting alongside pro-Russian Ukrainian militias in the Donbas, found that he desperately needed employment. He heard a company was recruiting. Some of his friends from the 2014 insurgency had already joined up, many on patriotic, ideological grounds. Whatever this company was, it was offering far more than a contract with the regular military, but Alex didn't really care who they were. 'I just turned up in Molkino, and said hi, I'm here about finding a job. They gave me a job. They sent me to Syria, and gave me a machine gun.'

The Molkino base appeared sometime in mid-2015 and initially consisted of about 20 tents flying the Soviet flag, surrounded by barbed wire and including some residential barracks, a training complex and its own checkpoint. On paper, of course, it did not exist. The implication might be that the GRU was running its own private mercenary army, but to hear Alex describe it, that wasn't exactly how it worked: 'They stand separate … They don't talk to each other. And they don't like each other very much.'[39]

The GRU connection was higher up the chain of command. Having demonstrated its value in the Donbas, from 2015 Wagner was being actively supported and guided – 'curated' in the Russian jargon – by the GRU. Lt General Vladimir Alexeyev, deputy head of the GRU, was a former Spetsnaz commando, who had been appointed to his position before Shoigu and Gerasimov took over the military, and seems to have had little sympathy for his new masters. He was, however, the key figure in Russia's covert campaign against the West, including meddling in the 2016 US elections (which led to his being put under sanctions), and Major General Andrei Averianov, commander of Unit 29155, the GRU's assassination and sabotage team, reported directly to him.[40] He also became the coordinator of Russia's mercenary units, initially just Wagner but in due course a range of others, and his relationship with Prigozhin would later prove crucial.[41]

After all, the GRU had begun to play a more active role because, in the understated words of one security officer, 'the global situation has deteriorated'.[42] The Crimean annexation had led to Western sanctions, redoubled when pro-Russian fighters in the Donbas used a Russian-supplied missile to shoot down a Malaysian passenger airplane, MH17, thinking it a Ukrainian warplane. Meanwhile, Moscow felt that its international standing was under threat. In September 2015, Vladimir Putin agreed to help Syria's Bashar Assad put down a popular rebellion that had escalated into a full-blown civil war. The United States had long been providing some rebels training and equipment, and so this was a demonstration that Russia was prepared to fight proxy wars against the United States if necessary.

The Kremlin asserted that it could rely on airpower alone and not deploy ground troops. At least, not officially.

'I will not deny that there are units of our special operations forces working in Syria,' said the then-commander of Russian forces in Syria, General Alexander Dvornikov, in March 2016.[43] He was being disingenuous: there were many other Russian troops there, and they had been for months. The Kremlin had faced, after all, something of a dilemma. On the one hand, the Syrian military had been decimated and demoralised, and would need some muscle on the ground. On the other, this was not a popular war at home: having been sold an air operation that would not endanger Russian lives, the population would not be happy with casualties. Wagner was deployed to provide that muscle, a force that was deniable not so much to the West as to the Russian people. When reports started to circulate, the Defence Ministry would dismiss them as *vbros*, 'stuffing', perhaps better translated as 'stuff and nonsense'.

Of course, it was nothing of the sort. According to Wagner sources, it deployed to Syria even before the Russian military had set up its bases there in autumn 2015. At peak, some 2,500 Wagner mercenaries were stationed near Latakia and Aleppo, commanded by officers of the GRU and FSB special forces.[44] They would play a key role in a series of offensives, including the Palmyra operations of 2016 and 2017. From artillery spotters to assault troops, Wagner's well-armed and experienced mercenaries did much to help turn the tide of the war, even if Russian airpower was still the crucial element. As one US military observer later put it, 'had Wagner not helped stop the Syrian lines crumbling, arguably all the airpower in the world wouldn't have saved Damascus'.[45]

In the process, as Prigozhin became an occasional visitor to the Russian Group of Forces' forward base at Hmeimim, in western Syria, one heavyset, bald-headed thug met another. Colonel General Sergei Surovikin was one of the military's high-flyers. A career army officer, he was unexpectedly made the first outsider to head the Aerospace Forces at the end of 2017 and was widely tipped to be a future chief of the General Staff. Undoubtedly able, he was regarded as a hard man even by the standards of Russia's macho military culture. Back in 2004, one of his subordinates complained that Surovikin had assaulted him when he voted for the 'wrong' candidate and, later that year, Surovikin reamed out another of his juniors, a full colonel, with such vigour that he later committed suicide with his service pistol, in the general's own office.[46] Nonetheless, a mark of Surovikin's upward trajectory was that he served not one but two terms as commander of the Russian Group of Forces in Syria, in March–December 2017 and January–April 2019. Although his first tour in Syria coincided with a scaling down of MoD support for Wagner, this was ultimately decided in Moscow, not Hmeimim.

Surovikin first met Prigozhin at that time, and apparently they got on well. Certainly, under Surovikin's tenure the relationship between the regular military and the mercenaries worked a great deal more smoothly, and in 2017 the general was even made an 'honorary member' of Wagner.[47] Surovikin would get the gold star of a Hero of the Russian Federation medal after his first Syrian tour, and according to former Wagner mercenary Marat Gabidullin, he 'owed all the victories of the Russian army in Syria in 2017 to Prigozhin'.[48] Prigozhin, in turn, would later describe him as a 'legendary figure … born faithfully to serve his Motherland'.[49] This relationship may not have saved Wagner's position in Syria, but would prove fateful for both men later on.

After all, it was at that point that the true nature of Prigozhin's predicament started to come home – literally, in zinc coffins, and in his long-running and ultimately fatal feud with Defence Minister Sergei Shoigu. Wagner forces were retaking Syrian towns, but all the credit went to the Defence Ministry: as one former mercenary complained, 'First, Wagner's guys do their work, then Russian ground units come in, then the Arabs and the cameras.'[50] This was policy: Shoigu reportedly flatly stated that '*gopniks*' – a Russian term that somehow combines the qualities of thugs, muggers and trashy working-class 'chavs' – 'cannot go down in history'.[51] 'Everything was fine before [the Palmyra offensive of March 2016],' recalled one former Wagner fighter. 'We had army kit. When we took it the first time, the PMC had T-90 tanks, howitzers and BTRs [armoured personnel carriers]. But when Shoigu reported to the commander in chief that we took Palmyra, Prigozhin got upset. "It was us, not you, that took Palmyra!"'[52] Shoigu was reportedly so angered by Prigozhin's insolence that he ordered the ministry to stop supplying Wagner with weapons.

The Condottiere Betrayed

This is where the story again becomes Prigozhin's rather than Wagner's. What Prigozhin was forbidden from doing in public, he was expected to do in private for the good of the Motherland, and fat payments from the MoD budget. But this doesn't seem to have been enough for Prigozhin. It was too much to watch someone else take the credit for the achievements of his private army. Forced to pander to Putin, he took out his anger on his peers, alienating and creating enemies in the very institutions that were tasked with supplying him: the Defence Ministry and the GRU. Surovikin's successor in Hmeimim, Lt General Alexander Zhuravlyov, was quickly antagonised by Prigozhin's hectoring, something that would have serious implications later.[53] Once again, Prigozhin's anger at feeling excluded and taken for granted would push him into a dangerous overreach. After all, the Syrians were now in better shape, the Russian commanders in-theatre were heartily sick of the cocky and overpaid mercenaries (a Wagner fighter could be being paid twice as much as an experienced Spetsnaz), and Shoigu, confident in his personal friendship with Putin, saw no reason to put up with the complaints of a thuggish entrepreneur on the make.

By the time Alex arrived in Syria in 2017, the mutual resentments had become evident even to an outsider.

Wagner was now fighting with the bare minimum, operating hand-me-down vintage tanks and wielding older AK-47s instead of the more modern AK-74s they used to be issued. The MoD had cut them off, deciding that Wagner's services were no longer needed. Even the camp at Molkino was stripped of much of the kit that had previously been provided, and military trainers were withdrawn.[54] At the same time, Concord lost the lion's share of its Defence Ministry contracts for cleaning, catering and maintenance services. From a peak of 27 billion rubles in 2015, by 2017 it only held contracts worth less than a billion.[55] In part, this may have reflected a shutting off of covert funding for Wagner through these contracts, but it also suggested that Shoigu had decided that the Defence Ministry was no longer going to pay through the nose for substandard services and cockroach-infested food.

Yet Prigozhin was not off the hook. Perversely, Wagner had done too well, and the Kremlin decided that it needed to be kept in existence, a useful tool in the box for future deniable operations. A mercenary army is not cheap. Without indirect subsidy from the government, how could Prigozhin afford to maintain it? Here the entrepreneurial side of his nature kicked in, with an initiative that would prove at once disastrous in the short term but crucial in the long. At the end of 2016, Evro Polis, a company connected to Prigozhin's Concord Group, signed a five-year contract with the Syrian government to recapture rebel-held oil and gas fields. In return, the company would get a quarter of the consequent profits, plus reimbursement of the costs of the operation.[56] In January 2018, this was upgraded into a binding agreement.[57] For Prigozhin, it was a vast expansion of his business empire into oil. More to the point, it allowed him to do what the Kremlin was demanding, without bankrupting himself.

With the agreement made under the auspices of the Russian Energy Ministry, it was also a demonstration to Shoigu that Prigozhin could find his own way, without help from the MoD. Tensions with the military were near breaking point, though. By early February 2018, Syrian forces, backed by the Russians, and Kurdish rebels, backed by US troops, found themselves just a few miles from each other on opposite sides of the Euphrates River. To avoid accidental conflict, the Americans and the Russians were in constant contact. Yet something broke down. On 7 February 2018, a force of Syrians and Russians crossed the river and attacked an outpost on the way into the oil-rich, rebel-held province of Deir ez-Zor.[58] The Americans reached out to the Russian command centre at Hmeimim airbase: were these their troops? On being reassured on Zhuravlyov's orders that they were not, the US forces delivered what may have been a deliberate and performative exercise in overkill, hammering the attackers with everything from artillery and Reaper attack drones to helicopter gunships and massive B-52 bombers. Four hours later, the attackers had been decimated and routed, at the cost of just one rebel soldier's life. Some US reports suggested that between 200 and

300 Russians were killed,[59] and while this is likely an exaggeration – Russian sources put the figure at 15–20[60] – it was a shocking blow to the mercenaries. By mid-2018, most Wagner forces had been withdrawn from Syria, and although they would continue to contribute small numbers of veterans under contract to Damascus, especially trainers and specialists such as snipers and forward observer teams, they would never play as important a role in that war again.

Not only had the military neither protected nor warned Wagner, the Defence Ministry completely disavowed the Wagner fighters who died in the attack, claiming that no Russians had taken part: 'the cause of the incident were reconnaissance and search operations carried out by the Syrian militia which had not been agreed with the command of the Russian operational group'.[61] According to US intelligence reports, Prigozhin had been in close contact with senior Russian officials, including Presidential Administration head Anton Vaino, and had 'secured permission' to conduct an operation.[62] Prigozhin claimed he had also cleared this with the Defence Ministry, which had even promised air cover, but this was flatly rejected by insiders who were interviewed by *The Bell*, who said the military were 'simply dumfounded' by Wagner's foolhardiness.[63] Either way, the ministry had no qualms throwing Prigozhin and his army under the bus.

As Prigozhin describes it, Shoigu demonstratively ignored his questions and his demands for a meeting.

When he finally did get to speak with the minister, Shoigu 'calmly and arrogantly answered: "Did you want to play the hero? All the heroes are here now, in this room." Here he waved his hand at those around him in expensive suits. "And you just got your countries confused"'. The conversation ended there.[64] Of course, there are other accounts, with claims that, instead of 'expensive suits', the men whom Shoigu indicated were actually combat veterans in uniform, but Prigozhin was never one to let tedious facts get in the way of a good story or telling jab.

Putin's system relies on unspoken understandings – much like the criminal world in which Prigozhin was raised – including the simple bargain that means the patron owes his deniable vassals respect and protection in return for their homage and service. But Putin seemed to feel he was due loyalty without having to reciprocate. Prigozhin was reportedly furious at what he regarded as betrayal, both by Shoigu and Putin. Nonetheless, he was smart enough to accept the realities of the situation. Both were, to different degrees, off limits for the moment. Prigozhin needed to maintain a relationship with the Defence Ministry if Wagner were to continue to operate, and Putin was too powerful even for Prigozhin's well-developed sense of vendetta. What Prigozhin regarded as Shoigu's betrayal would not be forgiven or forgotten, but for now he could not afford to brood: if he was to retain the patronage of the Kremlin, he needed to find new worlds for Wagner to conquer and thus pay its way.

CHAPTER 7

Scavenger

In 2018, Yevgeny Prigozhin started turning up in very strange places. At the end of August, he boarded his private jet and landed in Khartoum, Sudan – and was seen strutting around as part of a Russian peacemaking delegation.[1] It was a success: the Russian Foreign Ministry boasted that it had managed to get rebel groups from the Central African Republic (CAR) to sign a declaration committing themselves to ending five years of civil war, a step that would lead up to the CAR government signing a peace accord with 14 rebel groups the following February.[2]

Then, in November, the Libyan military released a video showing Shoigu meeting the head of the Libyan National Army and the de facto head of Libya's government (one of them, at least), Khalifa Haftar. Standing to the side of the two generals shaking hands, and then sitting together with the entire Russian delegation at a conference table, Yevgeny Prigozhin stood out as the only man in a civilian suit amid a sea of uniforms.[3] Russia's military officials didn't deny his presence, but claimed he was there in his capacity as a caterer – an odd assertion given his prominent position at the conference table.[4]

The appearances whipped up a frenzy among Western diplomats and press corps, most particularly the French, who, on a wave of trendy decolonial politics, had withdrawn their own peacekeeping forces from the CAR in 2016. There he was again, though: 'Putin's chef', spreading Russia's malign tentacles all over the world in the Kremlin's deniable quest to sow trouble. Prigozhin, meanwhile, basked in the glory. On the record, he still had to deny his connection to Wagner, or even many of his own commercial interests on the African continent. But it must have felt great to play the peacekeeper in an area where Western powers had demonstrated their growing impotence, withdrawing from country after country, leaving them in a shambles as Russia stepped in to pick up the pieces. From Syria, to Libya, the CAR to Sudan, Prigozhin appeared to be at the forefront of making Russia great again.

Diamonds and Death

That patriotic glow, however, masked a great deal of chagrin. What to the rest of the world appeared to be a covert yet coordinated influence campaign – a conceit that flattered both Prigozhin and the Kremlin, and which both were thus loath to disavow – was in fact an improvised scramble by a privateer eager to make up losses suffered after being royally screwed by Moscow.

Meanwhile, Russia itself was looking for quick, easy and above all cheap victories that could be spun as evidence that it was still a player on the global stage, however much the West was trying to ostracise and isolate it after the annexation of Crimea, the shooting down of the airliner MH17 and the brutal intervention into Syria.

At first, Concord's pivot to Africa was about lucrative mining opportunities. Prigozhin had emerged on the Russian scene a bit too late to compete with more established oligarchs, who had cornered the country's own metals and minerals early on in the 1990s through corruption and influence. But Moscow's bid to reestablish ties on the African continent offered Prigozhin a chance to expand into a new market and take advantage of opportunities in places that better-established Western companies found too restive for comfort. In September 2017, thanks to the facilitation of Russian diplomats, representatives of a newly established Concord subsidiary called M-Invest travelled to the CAR at the invitation of its president, Faustin-Archange Touadéra, to discuss establishing a mining company in the minerals-rich country. The following month, a second meeting, this time in Sochi, coincided with Touadéra's trip to Russia, in which he met directly with Russia's foreign minister, Sergei Lavrov. These meetings produced an agreement whereby a group of Russian lawyers, geologists and political strategists would go to the CAR, while a Russian mining company would be given a licence to extract gold and diamonds, as well as logging concessions. By the end of the month, Lobaye-Invest, a subsidiary of another new Concord-connected company, M-Finans, was registered by a former cop from St Petersburg affiliated with Prigozhin and Wagner named Yevgeny Khodotov.[5] Later in 2018, Touadéra's government granted more exploratory rights to M-Invest and M-Finans. In return, Wagner provided his government with soldiers, military trainers and advice at a time when rebels were even beginning to attack the capital, Bangui.[6]

Around the same time, a similar scheme was playing out in Sudan. After a high-level meeting between Putin and Sudanese president Omar al-Bashir, M-Invest was awarded a gold-extraction concession in the country. The convenience of this scheme for all parties involved revolved around the fact that in turbulent countries such as Sudan and CAR, Prigozhin was able to provide his own muscle rather than relying on government security, and his forces not only guarded his new interests, they helped train local troops and suppressed opposition to the government. Wagner, after all, was not troubled by the kind of legal constraints placed on Western mercenaries and, even more to the point, did not even have to be paid directly. As part of Prigozhin's wider business empire, there was scope for more creative and long-term payment schemes. Just as the initial payments to set up the mercenary army in 2013–14 seem to have been made by awarding Concord inflated contracts for other government services as well as setting up front companies, so too African governments looking to buy muscle or expertise could do so by granting the appropriate mineral extraction rights to one of his other firms.

The trouble with this scheme, however, was that all parties involved operated outside the legal sphere. Prigozhin had been under American sanctions since 2016 over Wagner's role in eastern Ukraine, and Concord was slapped with US Treasury sanctions in June 2017. This not only limited where he could do business, but necessitated and indeed encouraged him to rely on all sorts of under-the-counter arrangements, dummy companies and illicit financial flows.[7] Gold from Sudan and diamonds from the CAR, for example, would be smuggled to the United Arab Emirates, where they could be converted into cash or otherwise laundered and moved into Russia. Even more importantly, despite his connections to Putin and, indeed, the Kremlin's facilitation of his international projects, Prigozhin was a criminal under Russian law: his PMC, despite some half-hearted lobbying efforts, remained illegal and therefore technically did not exist. This was exactly how the Kremlin wanted things, but it denied Prigozhin the respect and respectability he continued to crave.

Heart of Darkness

A criminalised organization like Wagner not only attracted criminals, but its status encouraged criminal behaviour. From Syria to Sudan to Ukraine, Wagner became synonymous with the most extreme brutality, such as when it beheaded a prisoner-of-war on video in Syria. Indeed, the old ultra-violence would even become part of its brand later on: after a deserter was killed by a sledgehammer blow to the head in Ukraine, this weapon became one of its official logos, proudly displayed on the PMC's merchandise.[8]

Wagner had been a thuggish and even murderous organisation from the first, but arguably it was in the relatively uncontrolled environment of Africa, fighting savage skirmishes against often equally savage insurgents, that it found its true heart of darkness. In the CAR, they have been accused of not just individual rapes, but a systematic campaign of violence and terror in rebel-held areas.[9] In Mali, they helped government forces massacre more than 300 civilians during the five-day siege of Moura in March 2022, described by Human Rights Watch as 'the worst single atrocity reported in Mali's decade-long armed conflict'.[10] Wagner soldiers training locals in counter-insurgency taught interrogation methods that ranged from pulling out victims' nails or cutting off their fingers to dousing them in petrol and threatening to burn them alive.[11]

Prigozhin himself, like Kurtz, the ivory trader turned maniacal warlord from Joseph Conrad's novella *Heart of Darkness* (1899), also seems to have been changed by the experience. He had never minded intimidating or paying off his critics, but had tended to operate within the – admittedly very broad – limits of Russian elite practice. Now, though, the gloves were off. Most notoriously, in the summer of 2018, three Russian journalists investigating Concord's activities in the CAR set out to visit Bambari, site of a goldmine now run by M-Invest. On the way, they were ambushed and killed. Their driver claimed that the attackers were masked rebels speaking Arabic, even though this was far from their usual area of operation.[12] However, it later transpired that the driver had been in regular contact with a CAR police officer who, in turn, was in touch with the local Wagner forces.[13] The strong suspicion that they were murdered by Wagner gunmen was hardly dispelled when Prigozhin, with the kind of brass neck that would become his trademark, offered to pay for headstones for their graves.[14]

He was also becoming, between the actions of his trolls and his mercenaries, an international pariah. He had first been sanctioned in 2016, but in 2019 the US government placed comprehensive sanctions on him and his businesses, with the UK and European Union following suit the next year. Suddenly, he was a public enemy. His assets were, though, pretty safe. The habitual paranoia that had led him to register many under proxies – including his family – and regularly rename, reshuffle and generally reinvent his businesses back in Russia, stood him in good stead. Back in 2016, he had asserted, 'I have no assets abroad, I vacation on Russian territory, I have nothing [that] links me to America and Europe.'[15] Perhaps he should have said that there was nothing traceable, instead. Even the stable of horses owned by Polina and Veronika were hurriedly 'laundered', re-registered to new beneficial owners through the Russian Equestrian Federation, while both daughters continued to ride and compete with them right up to the eve of the February 2022 invasion of Ukraine.[16] All this helped minimise the impact on Prigozhin, his business and his family, but increasingly it meant he was inhabiting the world of the international money launderer, tax fraudster and smuggler.

Indeed, at this time Prigozhin generally seemed more aggressive than had been his previous practice at home, too, perhaps as the result of a toxic combination of arrogance and resentment. On the one hand, he was not only making a great deal of money with his African ventures (even if Concord's domestic operations were the real basis of his finances) but also increasingly famous – or at least infamous – around the world. However, his very status was precisely built on his notional position as the maverick, the outsider. African governments might treat him as a de facto representative of the Kremlin, but the Russian state did not afford him the pomp and courtesy to match. Not for him the televised one-to-one meetings or the invitations to Putin's 'Night League' ice-hockey matches that were the signs of favour at court. Unable to remonstrate with the boss, Prigozhin became increasingly hostile towards lesser figures he felt had wronged him. For example, having swung his media and troll empire behind Alexander Beglov's election campaign for the governorship of St Petersburg in 2019, he felt he was owed some consideration.[17] Beglov not only seemed to think that Prigozhin's support had not been that crucial (he had, after all, enjoyed Putin's endorsement) but also felt that the businessman was getting a little too greedy. Rather than pushing more business his way, notably by approving some major infrastructure projects, Beglov did the opposite, infuriating Prigozhin.[18] The latter's trolls and tame journalists pivoted to a campaign of insults and smears, presenting Beglov as corrupt, incompetent and even of having failed to pay back campaign loans. Later, this rivalry would become even more dangerous, and Beglov would push back, but it speaks to a growing frustration behind Prigozhin's apparent success.

After all, despite the carnage, his continued commitment in Africa was not just lucrative, but increasingly necessary for Prigozhin. He found himself in a bind of his own making. Having based his whole career on doing the Kremlin's bidding, he was quickly learning what many businessmen had found out the hard way: Putin relies on non-state actors to wage his adventures on the cheap, only to discard them when they stop being useful. Prigozhin had founded Wagner because it was useful for the Kremlin at the time, and although it was no longer needed or wanted in either Ukraine or Syria, he was still expected to keep it in the toy box in case Putin wanted to play with it again. A private army is an expensive luxury, and so Prigozhin had to keep finding new ways of making it pay its way. From Syria and Libya to Venezuela, he hustled not only to make a profit, but to show that his forces were indispensable to the Kremlin's agenda – even when it meant inventing that agenda himself.

Illusory Influence

A huge pavilion had been built over an empty lot between the Black Sea and Sochi's green, sloping hills. Inside, 6,000 delegates from Russia and 104 African countries, including 45 heads of state, milled and schmoozed and talked business – a trade convention of global proportions. Russian state arms export monopoly Rosoboronexport and Almaz-Antey Air and Space Defence Corporation held centre stage. Visitors were invited to try out the latest Kalashnikov rifle models and browse the security technologies from laser scanners to facial recognition that Russia was eager to sell.

By October 2019, Prigozhin's meddling in the US elections, and sightings of Wagner from Syria to Venezuela, had created a moral panic in the West, with his hand being seen behind almost every crisis or setback. Western officials scrambled to understand what Moscow was after, particularly in Africa, where so many Russians were engaged in so many seemingly nefarious activities. The Russia–Africa Summit and Economic Conference in Sochi that month was the first of its kind, and it offered the closest to an answer as to what Russian foreign policy was about: a bazaar. Far from the days of imposing any sort of ideology, from communism to anti-colonialism, Moscow seemed to be after one thing only: selling things.

'We do our own thing, and sure, it's in line with what the Foreign Ministry says, but we don't coordinate with them. This is really about business,' a Rosoboronexport official told us. A Russian military expert was even more blunt: 'Rosoboronexport *is* Russia's foreign policy.'[19]

While from abroad the summit was regarded as proof of a Russia resurgent, with a coherent global strategy, at home diplomats and officials, who felt Russia's government was missing out on opportunities on the African continent and simply not doing enough, saw it as more of an afterthought. 'We don't really have a strategy for Africa,' grumbled one diplomat who had lobbied for the summit. 'We still need to overcome our perception of Africa as a black hole where nothing can be done. The last twenty years has seen GDP doubling in countries there. The region is increasingly integrated into global political and economic processes. The consumer market has grown by five times from 1960 to 2000. So we want to be beneficiaries of these processes. We need their markets.'[20]

The Kremlin was taking an especially passive approach. 'We are not going to impose ourselves [in Central Africa],' one senior Russian diplomat said at the time. 'If you need us to come and help, we will. Sudan asked. The Central African Republic asked. We try our best.' On the one hand, this reflected the reduced ambitions of a Foreign Ministry that had been increasingly sidelined when it came to actually shaping Russia's strategic goals abroad. Officials were often visibly frustrated that they were out of the loop. 'The questions of what

Russia is doing in Venezuela,' an irritated Foreign Ministry official in charge of the Venezuela desk told us, 'might be better directed to Sechin. They don't tell us anything, nor are we interested.' Igor Sechin, Putin's former aide when he was deputy mayor in St Petersburg, and now the fearsome head of the Rosneft oil company, had essentially muscled the diplomats aside when it came to setting policy towards impoverished but oil-rich Venezuela. That year, as Caracas descended into a political crisis, Moscow sent a hundred military personnel to support incumbent president Nicolás Maduro, who was in a standoff with Western-backed opposition leader Juan Guaidó. Most were Wagner gunmen – and it was Sechin who had arranged for them to protect Russian assets in-country.[21]

But on the other hand, Russia's passive–aggressive behaviour underscored the lack of specific long-term goals and financial aid or political capital to offer. 'There's this idea: let's buy oil-processing plants just to establish a Russian presence there,' a former Russian minister told us. 'I've been told, "we need to expand our influence, whether or not that's profitable". State corporations are selling Putin the illusion of influence.'[22] Nor was it just state corporations. As the Russia–Africa Summit showed, a whole assortment of private entrepreneurs hustled their wares – from guns to ideas – in the hope that they aligned with what Putin wanted. At one of the summit panels, nationalist billionaire Konstantin Malofeyev – sanctioned by the US for his role turning a pro-Russian insurgency in Ukraine into a proxy war – sat together with Kremlin official Sergei Glazyev and hammered on about protecting the sovereignty of African states, by which he meant separating them from the West. While African officials politely listened to the political rhetoric, they were really looking for Russian trade and investment. 'The way to resolve conflict and improve security,' a senior Sudanese official said, 'is through sustainable energy development and economic cooperation … with Russia.'[23]

Hustlers and Scavengers

What this meant was that, in the name of some quick profits and to troll the West, Moscow was encouraging Russian private and state enterprises alike to take up whatever opportunities they could find in Africa, so long as they weren't expecting the government to bankroll them. Many Russian ventures failed, but this was the kind of freewheeling environment in which a man with an eye for business, a willingness to grease the right palms and his own private army could do well.[24] Governments in Sudan and the CAR got some badly needed military and security support in exchange for letting Concord mine its resources. As the Sudanese official told us with a big grin, 'it's win–win for everybody'.[25] (Except, of course, for those ordinary Sudanese citizens whose resources were being plundered, with some 90 per cent of all the gold leaving the country illegally.[26])

Prigozhin, meanwhile, was not just getting rich in the process, but acquiring the kind of global influence that is normally enjoyed by a transnational CEO or a head of state. Russia, eager to restore some of its Soviet-era status in Africa through military training and advice, in effect outsourced some of its foreign relations mission into private hands. This was, after all, central to Putin's 'adhocracy': Sechin already ran policy towards Venezuela, Syria had become a fiefdom of the Ministry of Defence; why could Prigozhin not affect to speak with Moscow's voice in Africa? He could, after all, be disavowed if he went too far. Yet where the Kremlin lacked a clearcut strategy of how to use private militias to further the interests of its empire in the long-term, Prigozhin, when it came down to the budding empire of his own, did not. As he navigated the marketplace of private deals that Russia's foreign policy had become, Wagner started not only making its own money, but was independently advancing what foreign-policy hawks in Moscow publicly proclaimed should be Russia's foreign goals. Although their deployment to Mozambique's Cabo Delgado province in 2019 to fight the Islamic State proved an embarrassing failure, forcing Wagner to withdraw within a few months, elsewhere from Mali to the CAR, Russian mercenaries often gained a certain popularity among the local population because, in their often rough and ready way, they did provide a kind of order and security.

According to Marat Gabidullin, of all the businessmen trying to capitalise on the Kremlin's growing appetite for PMCs, Prigozhin turned out to be the most farsighted. 'From the beginning, he had a vision of [Wagner] being a global structure,' part of a transnational business empire. Wagner's popularity among the locals wasn't because they were 'good guys', he said. As an integral part of Prigozhin's business empire, it 'was oriented towards capitalising on a huge investment and creating something bigger than diamond and gold traffic. They came [to Africa] to take their business to an industrial level, to create a favourable environment where they could do business. And a favourable environment is – first and foremost – the security of those doing the business.'[27] The Russian government offered a degree of diplomatic support: all of Prigozhin's ventures, whether in the CAR, Sudan or elsewhere, were preceded by agreements reached between local governments and the Russian Foreign Ministry, under the watchful eye of Russia's intelligence agencies. Once those had been achieved, though, the heavy lifting – primarily ensuring security and logistics – fell to Wagner and Prigozhin. 'Prigozhin used the Central African Republic as an advertising poster – see, look what we can create,' Gabidullin said. 'Looking at the CAR, he was hoping other countries would want to live like that too.'[28]

Much like the chartered companies that had spearheaded European imperial expansion, granted the right to explore and exploit, to make deals, war and profit so long as they recognised the sovereign authority of the state, Concord and Wagner occupied that ill-defined space between business and politics, and Prigozhin thrived in the combination of influence and independence it offered him. In Russia, he had built his business empire not just by spotting market opportunities but also by skilful cultivation of the right patrons, an approach that paid dividends in Africa. What did assorted authoritarians and kleptocrats want? He could provide. In Sudan and the CAR, it was gunmen, but elsewhere there were other requests. Zimbabwe wanted some veneer of legitimacy for its rigged elections in 2018; Prigozhin backed a dubious NGO, the Association for Free Research and International Cooperation (AFRIC), which sent election observers who duly reported the vote to be free and fair.[29] AFRIC would go on to give its seal of approval to dodgy elections in the Democratic Republic of Congo (2018) and Mozambique (2019). In South Africa, Prigozhin saw potential work for his trolls and spin doctors, considering plans to try to pitch their assistance to the ruling party, the African National Congress. All the while, he was personally managing a network of contacts, often on the basis of kickbacks and sweetheart deals, and under-the-table financial arrangements to evade Western sanctions and those pesky investigative journalists.

In the process, he was building a powerful brand for himself, both at home and abroad: the can-do merchant-adventurer who could accomplish what no one else could, from rigging an election in the United States to suppressing jihadist rebels in Africa. Wagner itself benefitted from this. Its black-and-red skull-and-crosshairs logo began appearing not just in internet memes but in branded goods for the fanboys, which even began surfacing in some African countries in which it was operating. In due course, Prigozhin's films would also help create what researcher Jack Margolin has called the 'Wagner Cinematic Universe', with recurring characters clearly representing real mercenaries, such as 'Sedmoy' ('Seventh'), whose lanky frame suggests Utkin, and 'Sedoy' ('Grey-hair'), who shares a callsign with the aforementioned Andrei Troshev, Wagner's chief of staff.[30] All of this helped recruitment – one starstruck fan of *The Tourist*, set in the CAR, posted on social media 'What a fantastic movie. How do I join Wagner?' – but more generally contributed to the rise of Prigozhin's own brand, as the man behind the mercenary myth.[31]

He was even freed from much practical dependence on the MoD and the GRU. Although there were intelligence officers embedded within Wagner deployments, whereas in the Donbas Wagner had been directly tasked and overseen by the GRU, on the whole he was now dealing with the civilian bureaucrats of the Presidential Administration. Increasingly constrained by the whims and indecisions of an aging autocrat who had too much on his plate to be particularly interested in forging a coherent Africa strategy, they tended not to care how a businessman conducted his private business, as long as it fell in line with the general idea of establishing a presence.

Prigozhin's status as a deniable privateer might have created the illusion of a formidable Russian presence in Africa, but he was really just looking for new business opportunities and a way of offsetting the cost of maintaining Wagner. Yes, he was making money in his international operations, with a turnover estimated as at least $250 million in the period 2018–22, but essentially he was expanding his own, private, empire – not Russia's.[32] However, while the Kremlin was happy to take advantage of his achievements, it was still unwilling to legitimise Wagner or generally give Prigozhin credit for what he was doing. The maddening irony was that his profile was higher in the West than in Russia. One senior British diplomat considered him 'one of Putin's closest henchmen' but, in reality, Zhenya was still no closer to Vova.[33] In some ways, it was the worst of both worlds, being sanctioned as if he was Putin's right-hand man, yet in practice still being kept below stairs. 'Prigozhin was effective in recreating the kind of system that was imposed on him by the Russian system itself,' Gabidullin said. 'It's a serf economy. They will take care of their serfs, but the serfs always remain serfs.'[34]

CHAPTER 8
Warlord

On 19 March 2022, Yevgeny Prigozhin's phone lit up with a number that couldn't have but put a smile on the increasingly beleaguered businessman's face. It was his old frenemy, Lt General Vladimir Alexeyev, deputy head of military intelligence, and he was calling to ask for a favour.

It was three weeks since Vladimir Putin had launched a full-fledged invasion of Ukraine, dubbing it a 'special military operation' as he expected Kyiv to capitulate within a week. On the morning of 24 February, Russian missiles started hammering Kyiv and other Ukrainian cities, as soldiers and mercenaries – though none of Wagner's – fanned out to Ukraine's north and east. Some drove towards Kyiv, others even engaged in attempts to assassinate Ukraine's president, Volodymyr Zelensky. And it had been three weeks since Alexeyev had indicated to Prigozhin that he was to keep his men out of the special military operation. Wagner was not trusted, nor was it needed because the GRU now had its own mercenary army.

This could not have failed to sting: for months, since mid-2021, Alexeyev, as the GRU's main 'curator' of PMCs, had been reviving a one-time offshoot of Wagner, the Redut (Redoubt) private military company, with funding from Gennady Timchenko, one of Putin's closest allies and a billionaire with resources far beyond Prigozhin's reach.[1] This was just the most recent of the PMCs being spun up by the Defence Ministry, and it was recruiting among Wagner soldiers, particularly those sufficiently disgruntled by Prigozhin's bullying and micromanagement to seek greener pastures. What was more, they were offering better wages and conditions, and their recruiters were being allowed on to bases to pitch to marines, paratroopers and Spetsnaz commandos nearing the end of their service terms. In late January 2022, an enraged Prigozhin had demanded that Alexeyev stop plundering his forces – particularly considering how treacherously the GRU had treated him in the past, and how ineffective it was in the present. Alexeyev invited him to his office at the GRU's headquarters off Moscow's Grizodubovoy Street for a chat. Alexeyev flatly refused to compromise, and made it clear that as far as he was concerned, Anatoly Karazii, the head of Redut, was his go-to mercenary. Karazii, though, had until recently been Wagner's head of intelligence and Prigozhin flew into a rage when the turncoat's name was raised, yelling, 'I'm going to finish him.' Prigozhin's bark was notoriously louder than his bite when dealing with someone other than underlings or prying journalists: when an unperturbed Alexeyev led him to a neighbouring office to confront Karazii in person, Prigozhin backed off.[2] Nor had Prigozhin had any joy trying to go over Alexeyev's head. His direct superiors were Defence Minister Shoigu and Chief of the General Staff Gerasimov, and Prigozhin was hardly going to beg them for favours. As for the commander-in-chief, Putin himself, according to one of Prigozhin's acquaintances, 'they had not communicated personally – not even by video call – for six months'.[3]

Only this time, fate intervened. Ukraine – despite genuine Kremlin expectations that its 'liberators' would be welcomed – struck back. In the first few weeks of the invasion, Russian forces were decimated by an unexpectedly robust Ukrainian defence. Alexeyev's forces were particularly hard hit, and Redut reportedly lost 90 per cent of its soldiers dead or wounded. It turned out that Redut was no more prepared and professional than the rest of the Russian military: 'I want what's owed to me, but now I'm just a poor bastard with no rights! All I've got left to believe in is myself and my AK-47,' one Redut recruit complained.[4] More to the point, for all that they had been deployed around Ukraine's borders for the best part of a year, Russia's generals seemed not to have realised Putin truly intended to invade, and he himself had not ordered a full mobilisation. What this meant was that a peacetime Russian army built for smaller-scale interventions was facing a mobilised Ukraine, and while the former had lots of tanks and artillery, they suffered from a lack of the basic building block of any army: infantry.

Tanks were being sent into battle without infantry support – which is a recipe for disaster – and infantry-fighting vehicles meant to carry a squad of troops into battle were being deployed crewed, but otherwise empty.

It was against this backdrop that Alexeyev made the call. Prigozhin had already used his Vkontakte social media page to demand that Russian cultural figures 'take the right position and speak in a patriotic way about Russia's actions in Ukraine, where Russia is saving the world'.[5] Now, it was time for Prigozhin to do something rather more concrete. It had suddenly become a seller's market for infantry, and by the end of that very day, Wagner's forces were back in action, crossing the border into Ukraine.

The Invasion

To this day, it is impossible to tell when exactly Vladimir Putin made the decision to launch a full-scale invasion of Ukraine and, most of all, why. Through 2021, Russia had amassed over 100,000 troops along the border with Ukraine, a development that signalled to Western intelligence than an invasion was 'imminent'. But for the eight years since 2014, it had been doing much of the same: building up troops on the border to scare Ukraine and its Western allies into a diplomatic concession, retreating, only to rinse and repeat. Was this more of the same, or had something changed?

By all accounts, it had. The Kremlin had grown frustrated with Ukrainian president Volodymyr Zelensky and by summer 2021 Putin had seemingly become convinced – all evidence to the contrary – that, directed from Washington, Kyiv was determined to retake the Crimean Peninsula by force, and that it was just a matter of time before it attacked. Besides, he had convinced himself that the Ukrainians could not or would not resist, and that removing Zelensky and imposing some compliant proxy government would be quick and easy, a nation-scale rerun of the Crimean annexation. Of course, he was catastrophically mistaken, as a country with more than 40 million people, which had spent the past eight years wargaming just such a situation, would soon prove. As the Russians started suffering defeat after defeat, this became a national emergency. Once again, Prigozhin and his men were needed, to help salvage something from the fires of Ukraine. In the process, the man whom one Defence Ministry official described as having 'no morals, no conscience, and no hobbies … He is a machine in the bad sense of the word', would finally find a cause in which he could believe, and yet which would lead to his eventual downfall.[6]

Although some Ukrainian reports said Wagner was involved in early assassination attempts on Zelensky, this seems to have been a misunderstanding based on the fact that they were former *Vagnerovtsy* who had recently been poached by Redut. By the end of March 2022, though, there were almost a thousand Wagner troops in-country, many hurriedly pulled out of African missions. This would quickly grow, though, as Prigozhin demonstrated his entrepreneurial knack for finding new sources of soldiers, and finding them quickly (a friend to some Wagner recruits recalled, 'yesterday they were wandering around, making vacation plans … and now they have already left' for Ukraine).[7] He stripped his African operations, in some cases hiring locals to make up the shortfall. He recruited soldiers from neighbouring Belarus and, through existing Wagner training missions, even Libya and Syria.

By June 2022, there were around 25,000 Wagner fighters in Ukraine, largely in the southeastern Donbas region. They were becoming an army within an army – indeed, more than just an army. In May, for example, a Su-25 ground attack aircraft was shot down during fighting near the town of Popasna, west of Luhansk. The pilot turned out to be Major General Kanamat Botashev, a decorated air force commander who had been cashiered in 2013, only to be hired by Wagner as they suddenly found themselves with an air force of their own.

Wagner forces quickly became a key element of the Russian war effort, especially once Putin had abandoned his early push to take Kyiv and instead began to focus on southern and eastern Ukraine. They helped take Popasna in May, participated in most other local offensives, and in January 2023 seized the salt-mining town of Soledar, against tough Ukrainian resistance. By this time, they were fielding the full panoply of heavy weapons, from T-72B3 tanks and 152mm self-propelled guns, even up to a flight of supersonic Su-24 bombers, all supplied – with varying levels of reluctance – by the MoD. Their numbers also included Prigozhin's son Pavel, who appears to have spent time in Ukraine, although he was also seen partying in St Petersburg, so it seems his service was under rather more permissive terms than the other fighters'.[8] Quite what he was doing is unclear; when Prigozhin senior was asked this question, he replied in a characteristically confrontational way: 'I don't see the need to disclose details of what tasks he performs. Come to the Donbas, ask him yourself.'[9] However, given that Pavel was being groomed to be his father's heir, it was clearly important that he spend time in the 'special military operation', both to distinguish himself from the effete children of most of the elite, and also so that he could develop some kind of a personal relationship with the 'boys'. He was even awarded the Black Cross, one of Wagner's own medals, although it is impossible to know if he genuinely did distinguish himself in action.

The battle with which Wagner became most identified was for Bakhmut, an east Ukrainian city, which was levelled in near-constant back-and-forth struggles for control from August 2022, and which assumed a totemic importance out of proportion with its strategic value. Within a couple of months of their deployment to Ukraine, 5,000 Wagner fighters were dead or wounded according to US estimates, a figure that had risen to almost 15,000 by November. By mid-February 2023, this had doubled, largely because of Bakhmut. It would fall to regular and Wagner forces by May–June 2023, but only to face Ukrainian counter-offensives within a matter of days. At peak, the Wagner forces – which were increasingly concentrated on Bakhmut – numbered 85,000 troops. Only 35,000 of these were what one could call normal mercenary forces, though. The bulk was now drawn from another source: Russia's overcrowded and violent penal system.[10]

The Convict Army

The first videos that emerged showed Prigozhin standing in a circle of *zeks*, Russian penal colony prisoners, in their black and white uniforms. He made no bones about the fact that he was from Wagner, that the war was hard and that he was looking for 'stormtroopers', but he made his pitch based on equal parts patriotism, machismo and self-interest: 'no one falls back, no one retreats, no one surrenders', if need be on pain of a firing squad, but after six months of honourable service, they would be discharged and free. Or dead: 'I take you out of here alive, but don't always bring you back alive.'[11] Admittedly, at least then their families would receive a 5-million-ruble payout (worth some $57,000 at the time). In many ways, this was quintessential Prigozhin. The ever-resourceful businessman had found a new source of manpower for the war, but he could now be out in the open, and talking to the kind of people he had been able to understand and engage in his twenties and still could today. As one prisoner from colony IK-8 Tambov said, 'Prigozhin spoke with a lot of confidence. We all listened when he spoke, and trust me, it is not easy to shut up a good [number] of prisoners. He is one of us in the end, a former inmate. I think many who signed up did so because they trust Prigozhin. They don't trust the authorities, but they believe Prigozhin when he tells them that they will be let free.'[12] Prigozhin had found his people. These men, though looked down upon by everyone, including their government, as the scum of the Russian earth, would show those effete cosmopolitans – who had likewise looked down on Prigozhin as the hired help – who were the real patriots and men of action. 'It's either private military companies and prisoners,' he told his critics, 'or your children – you decide for yourself.'[13]

In June 2022, as a pilot project, Wagner recruited a platoon of prisoners from a couple of high-security prisons in the St Petersburg region. They suffered 15 per cent casualties in a month of hard fighting, but the experiment seems to have been successful enough that, by July, Prigozhin was taking his recruitment show on the road, hopping from prison to prison offering convicts 100,000 rubles a month (more than double the average wage) and amnesty, even though technically this was against the law. Still, as with setting up Wagner in the first place, the law has always taken second place to the needs of Putin's state.

To a large extent, they would be used as poorly armed and poorly trained cannon fodder, deployed in so-called 'meat waves' to wear down or draw out the Ukrainian forces and shield the more experienced Wagner veterans, and their casualties were inevitably frightful. Some units suffered as many as 90 per cent casualties, in operations that often arguably did more to alleviate Russia's prison-overcrowding problem than advance the war. Casualties would be horrific, especially as most of the convicts had been given no more than a week's basic training. Nonetheless, they could prove determined or at least desperate, and did help Wagner achieve successes, not least at Bakhmut.

They also changed the nature of Wagner, accelerating its slide into brutality and depravity. Although German intelligence sources claimed that Wagner mercenaries had been involved in the horrific massacre in the north Ukrainian town of Bucha in March 2022, where at least a couple of hundred civilians and prisoners-of-war were killed, this is unproven, and Bucha was far from the PMC's main area of operation. However, the convicts brought their brutal prison culture with them, and also new challenges in controlling them. Wagner had always been a rough-and-ready force but now, like Stalin's political commissars during the Second World War, its officers would 'zero out', or shoot, anyone who tried to desert or retreat.

Credible allegations of war crimes mounted. Task Force Rusich, an element of Wagner recruited specifically from neo-Nazis, publicly advocated the execution of prisoners-of-war, and Prigozhin reportedly later told prospective recruits at prison colony IK-1 Kopeisk that they were free to treat captured Ukrainians however they liked, even cut their throats.[14] In the culture of the prison system, though, betrayal is the greatest sin – something Prigozhin himself well understood – and perhaps the most graphic and shocking example took place in November 2022. Yevgeny Nuzhin was a convicted murderer who had joined Wagner from IK-3 Ryazan, but then surrendered to the Ukrainians and incautiously gave an interview from captivity in which he claimed that he had only enlisted to get out of prison, and had always planned to desert. His bad fortune was then to be included in a prisoner swap, and he was promptly handed over to Wagner. On 13 November 2022, a video appeared on social media, showing him being executed by a sledgehammer blow to the head.

Far from distancing himself from this murder, Prigozhin approvingly described it as a 'dog's death for a dog', and henceforth, as mentioned, the sledgehammer became incorporated into Wagner's increasingly bloody brand.[15] Prigozhin would send a sledgehammer smeared with – fortunately fake – blood to the European Parliament after legislators called for Wagner to be labelled as a terrorist organisation, and when his home was later raided by police, an oversized example engraved 'for use in important negotiations' was found among the guns, gold, cash and kitsch.[16] By this time, Prigozhin had clearly decided to embrace his dark side.

Finally Unmasked

After all, at last he was now free to boast that he was more than just a catering and real estate magnate. It was not until September 2022 that he formally acknowledged that he was the man behind Wagner – advancing the rather implausible line that he had stayed in the shadows to protect the PMC's reputation – but already for months he had become increasingly open in his role. When the first of his prison-address videos went public, for example, the man who in the past had sued journalists who dared connect him to Wagner, instead had his press service issue a coy admission that 'we can confirm that the person in the video is monstrously similar to Yevgeny Viktorovich. In addition, the person's speech in the video is very well delivered, just like that of Yevgeny Viktorovich.'[17] Short of adding a knowing wink emoji, this was as close to confirmation as could be.

Prigozhin, the thuggish outsider, was suddenly becoming the person to know. In April 2022, the radical conservative parliamentarian Vitaly Milonov posted a picture of himself on social media with him in Donetsk (although Prigozhin tried to deny that he had been there). His every action and utterance became a fixture in the 'milblogger' social media channels obsessively following the war. The first speculation that he might have some kind of a political future began to surface. Indeed, it later emerged that in June, as recognition for his work, Putin had made him a Hero of the Russian Federation, the country's highest award. Something of a cult of Prigozhin began to emerge, as those who had once looked down on him now elevated him as an example of what Russia needed in a time of war, the patriot who was willing to get his hands dirty and do whatever was needed in the defence of the Motherland.

By summer 2022, Prigozhin clearly felt he was riding the wave. He had been made a Hero of the Russian Federation; he was able openly to claim Wagner's victories as his own; and his critics and detractors in the regular military had been forced to come crawling to him to save them from the war into which they had blundered.[18] True to form, he used his new status as the supposed saviour of the war effort to prosecute the personal vendettas that he seems to have nurtured with such passion, from St Petersburg Governor Alexander Beglov to, crucially, Defence Minister Sergei Shoigu. Indeed, his man-of-the-people persona meant that he would increasingly take aim at the whole national elite, seeing them as unwilling to pay the price of the war they had started. In November, while endorsing Nuzhin's execution, he also took aim at other, unnamed traitors, who 'sit in their offices, not thinking about their own people. Some of them fly on their own business jets to countries that still seem neutral to us. They fly away so as not to participate in today's problems.'[19] He made it clear that this included Shoigu and Chief of the General Staff Gerasimov: when the Russians withdrew from the city of Kherson (which was militarily inevitable, as the occupation had become untenable), Prigozhin's internet trolls and tame social media commentators unleashed a barrage of criticism against the high command. The WarGonzo Telegram channel, for example, which was independent but close to Prigozhin (who granted it several exclusive interviews), bemoaned 'a black page in the history of the Russian army. Of the Russian state', without considering that in practice Kherson simply could not have been held.[20]

The Pendulum Swings

Wagner was now able to go public and go corporate, and in November 2022 it acquired shiny new offices in eastern St Petersburg, a 23-floor building emblazoned with its new logo, a simple W rather than the rather more aggressive skull-and-crosshairs still affected by its fighters. However, intoxicated by his new status as the champion of a new, reinvigorated Russia, Prigozhin overplayed his hand.

Putin could hardly allow him to split the elite on which he depended. Although Prigozhin was furious with Beglov for failing to favour him after his media machine had backed him in the 2019 elections, for example, the governor was still a client of Putin's. When Prigozhin claimed that Beglov had been financing Ukrainian nationalists and had his people ask the Prosecutor-General's Office in October to investigate the 'possible fact of the creation by Governor Beglov of an organised criminal network in St Petersburg to plunder the state budget and enrich corrupt officials', he was in effect declaring war.[21] The president could not be seen to not defend his own. Besides, Beglov had leapt on the war bandwagon, pledging funds to rebuild the captured city of Mariupol and echoing Putin's rhetoric at every occasion. Putin stepped in to shield Beglov and the St Petersburg branch of the FSB began investigating some of Concord's businesses. Beglov was signalling that two could play at Prigozhin's game. Indeed, this was also the time when claims from two supposed ex-cons began circulating to the effect that, while in prison, Prigozhin had been 'lowered' and forced sexually to satisfy other inmates. It was clearly meant not only to undermine his tough-guy image but especially his standing with prospective recruits in the labour camps, and bore the hallmarks of an FSB smear operation.[22]

However, the real threat came from the wily Shoigu. According to several accounts, the defence minister had been sceptical of the decision to invade Ukraine in the first place, deeming it unfeasible.[23] Nonetheless, he could not afford to be seen to have lost Putin's war, and in September he had persuaded a reluctant president to launch a partial mobilisation of reservists. Putin, never one quickly or easily to take tough decisions, feared the political fallout, but Shoigu and Gerasimov made it clear that it was necessary if there was to be any hope of successful offensive operations. General Gerasimov was thinking of the military situation, Shoigu of the political one. The mobilisation mustered some 300,000 more soldiers, and in a stark expression of the law of supply and demand, the value of Wagner's soldiers fell dramatically as a result. Meanwhile, Shoigu – who had never trusted or rated him – dismissed General Bulgakov, the head of military logistics who had not only funnelled contracts Prigozhin's way when he could, but also helped keep him up-to-date on the ministry's internal politics. This could easily have been because of the dismal performance of the logistical services during the war, too often failing to keep soldiers properly fed and supplied, but given the circumstances and the bad blood between the two men, Prigozhin inevitably (and quite possibly correctly) interpreted this as just another front in his war with the minister.

So, an angry Prigozhin continued to attack the regular military. When the bastion of Lyman fell to the Ukrainians at the end of September 2022, he said that 'all these bastards' – meaning the generals in charge – 'should be sent barefoot to the front just with assault rifles'.[24] Meanwhile, he did everything he could to talk up Wagner's victories, and to push back against those enemies who, he claimed, 'are constantly trying to steal victory from the Wagner PMC'.[25] When the town of Soledar fell in January 2023, Prigozhin rushed to assert that 'no units besides Wagner took part in the assault', even though a range of other forces had also been active there. Conversely, the official announcement from the Defence Ministry did not even mention Wagner. After a brief behind-the-scenes spat, this was 'clarified' with the addition of an admission that the victory 'was successfully accomplished by the courageous and selfless actions of the volunteers of the Wagner PMC assault detachments'.[26]

On the surface, this may have looked like a win for Prigozhin over those rivals who would steal his thunder. It was a clash of two styles, though: the outspoken populist against the behind-the-scenes operator, and Shoigu was working on a follow-up blow. At the end of the year, he had convinced Putin to allow him to block Wagner from recruiting in the prison camps from February 2023 (ironically, the Defence Ministry would soon instead start to draw on *zeks* for its own Storm-Z assault units). In January, the Wagner 'honorary member' General Surovikin, who had become overall commander of Russian forces in Ukraine in October, was summarily removed from the position, replaced by the self-same General Gerasimov who had been the target of so much of Prigozhin's invective. Meanwhile other mercenary units, not just a revived Redut but even ones being established by local governors and state corporations, also began to appear on the field.

All told, Prigozhin was finding himself no longer so indispensable, and once again reminded that he would be prized and indulged only so long as he was useful. His public attacks on Shoigu and Gerasimov became increasingly serious and scatological: they were fools, incompetents, embezzlers, and worse. He finally acknowledged his role as trollmaster, hoping to leverage this for some credit. On Telegram, he recognised his role 'with pleasure. I've never just been the financier of the Internet Research Agency,' he crowed. 'I invented it,

I created it, I managed it for a long time. It was founded to protect the Russian information space from boorish aggressive propaganda of anti-Russian narrative from the West.'[27] Then, in his desperation to demonstrate his continued value, Prigozhin appears to have promised to deliver the contested city of Bakhmut by 9 May 2023, Victory Day, the high holy day of Putin's nationalist credo. As he failed, he would begin to flail out all the more desperately at the top brass and what he considered a backsliding elite in general. In part, this was to try to escape blame, but it also reflected genuine anger as he felt he and his 'boys' were being scapegoated, abandoned and disdained, all at once.

CHAPTER 9
Rebel

It's 5 May 2023. A bald man with dead eyes stands in the dark; the ground behind him is littered with dozens of corpses. 'These guys are Wagner PMCs that died today,' he says. 'The blood is still fresh.' And then he turns to the camera, his face contorted with rage. 'Now listen to me, you bitches. These are someone's fathers, someone's sons,' he screams. 'And those pieces of shit that don't send ammunition, those bitches will be eating their entrails in hell. We have 70 per cent ammo shortages. Shoigu, Gerasimov, where is the fucking ammo?'[1]

It was as though a mask had been removed from a man who, for eight years, had lied and disavowed 'these guys' ostensibly in the name of protecting them. A man who, for decades, had been discreetly content to serve at Putin's table, to cater to his army, and to keep his mouth shut. Now Yevgeny Prigozhin, who had ten months earlier proudly admitted founding the Wagner Private Military Company, was angry. He was tired of being used. He was, to put it in his own vernacular, tired of being Putin's bitch.

While he didn't know it then, what he was about to start would ultimately cost him his life.

Winning in Bakhmut, Losing in Moscow

Bakhmut would become the rubbled epicentre not just of Russia's war with Ukraine, but Prigozhin's with Shoigu. Although the fighting for this city had begun in May 2022 in the context of a wider Russian offensive meant to encircle a Ukrainian battle group, it had increasingly acquired a symbolic role as a test of respective determination. 'Bakhmut holds!' became a popular meme on Ukrainian social media, and scarcely a day would go by without Russian commentators claiming some advance that, on inspection, would turn out to be a single block or building. By November, the fighting had been stepped up and Russia threw in forces redeployed from the south following their withdrawal from the briefly captured city of Kherson. The battle became a nightmarish combination of First World War-style trench warfare and urban fighting reminiscent of the Second World War struggles for Stalingrad. Wagner increasingly deployed assault groups made up of convicts, whose role was not only to wear down the defenders but also pinpoint their locations for artillery attacks, though usually at terrible cost. By the end of May, Wagner had, by Prigozhin's own accounts, lost an estimated 20,000 men. They slowly made progress through the winter, and although by then they held most of Bakhmut, it became clear that – contrary to promises

Prigozhin had made to Putin – there would be no victory for Victory Day.

Prigozhin was apparently both horrified by the losses being suffered by his 'boys' – even as he maintained the wasteful 'meat wave' assaults – and desperate. According to classified US intelligence reports leaked by an American airman – whose accuracy has, it must be noted, never been confirmed – in January 2023 Prigozhin even made overtures to the Ukrainians, offering them the locations of regular Russian forces in return for their pulling back and allowing him to take Bakhmut.[2] They mistrusted the deal and did not follow through but, if true, it meant that even then, Prigozhin was contemplating what could only be considered treason to get himself and his army out of the hole in which they found themselves.

Instead, all he seemed to feel he could rely upon was his usual staples of bluster and blame. He would regularly claim that Wagner was not getting proper support from the regular military and, above all, being starved of the ammunition it needed. It is questionable whether the mercenaries really were experiencing disproportionate 'shell hunger'. Rather, it was in part the case that it had become accustomed to getting priority for fire support, and resented it when it began to be treated as any regular unit, and in part it was a convenient alibi for not making greater and quicker headway. 'Bakhmut would have been taken before the New Year, if not for our monstrous military bureaucracy,' he claimed in February.[3]

Prigozhin was certainly making all the running in terms of the public game. He was not only increasingly showing himself at the front, in battledress and toting a Kalashnikov – to draw obvious contrasts with the top brass 'fattening yourselves in your mahogany offices' in Moscow – but also expanding the 'Wagner Cinematic Universe' into the real world.[4] Wagner field commanders with callsigns like Lotus and Zombie became mainstays of Prigozhin's public campaign, hyped online almost as if they were top sportsmen by the so-called *voyenkory* social media commentators (a contraction for 'war correspondents', even if many never came anywhere near the fighting). Some of these commentators were backed by Prigozhin's media empire, others wooed by the promise of exclusive access, and yet more simply swept up in the frenzy of 'turbo-patriotism', as it was known.[5] They provided a natural chorus for Prigozhin, seduced by Wagner's macho persona, and happy to follow his lead in blaming the regular military's incompetence, bureaucratism or downright treachery for the disappointing pace of the war. The trouble was that while they had a serious following among the wider 'turbo-patriot' community, it was too easy to confuse public acclaim for political muscle.

Indeed, Prigozhin tried explicitly to enlist the *voyenkory* in his fight. In February, he issued a public appeal for support to get the Defence Ministry to supply more ammunition, using a picture of stacked bodies of Wagner casualties. This was something of a transgression, as the Kremlin was doing everything it could to play down the toll of the war, and he was reportedly summoned to a meeting with Putin and Shoigu that very day. Putin, perennially unwilling to take tough decisions, simply urged the two men to resolve their differences and save their hostility for the enemy. Neither the minister nor the warlord wanted to appear to be the problem, so a hasty deal was cobbled together which saw some extra ammunition released and Prigozhin required to make a public acknowledgement that this had been done. However, whether the shells were never actually provided or whether it was just a one-off consignment, either way Prigozhin was soon again publicly complaining. Even the appointment later of Sergei Surovikin as a liaison between Wagner and the MoD was not enough to resolve these practical issues, largely because they were actually political ones.

Prigozhin might slowly have been winning in Bakhmut, but it was also becoming increasingly clear that Sergei Shoigu was winning their political struggle in Moscow. He had rank, a legal mandate, and sat at the helm of a powerful state institution. He seems to have won the support of another behind-the-scenes operator, Security Council secretary Patrushev. He may not have been a natural ally of Shoigu's, but from October 2022, when he had listened in on a call in which Prigozhin had all but scolded Putin for failing to back him adequately, he had turned against the *condottiere*.[6] More to the point, Shoigu had a personal relationship with Putin – taking the boss on holiday hikes through his native Siberia, skating on his personal ice-hockey team – that Prigozhin, still a private citizen running a business, who had to sing for his supper, could not match.

Gramps

Whether out of habit or desperation, Prigozhin escalated. As well as lacking ammunition, he claimed that recruits who wanted to serve in Wagner were instead being forced to join other units. Perhaps even more seriously, since the February meeting it appears that he no longer had a direct line to Putin. On 5 March 2023, he excused his public campaign by saying that 'they have turned off all special [government] phone lines in all of [Wagner] offices and units' and 'cancelled all my passes to the agencies responsible for making decisions'.[7] This was clearly alarming for him, as it implied that the Kremlin itself did not want to get involved, but also marked a subtle shift in where Prigozhin was placing the blame. However powerful, Shoigu could not cut off his connections to the Kremlin; only the president, the man whom he had served literally and metaphorically for so many years, could do that.

According to the 1 May 2014 Declaration signed by Prigozhin and Wagner's top brass, one of the PMC's commandments was 'do not go against Vladimir Vladimirovich Putin'. But as Prigozhin's criticism of the Defence Ministry mounted, and as it became clear that the reason thousands of Wagnerites were being slaughtered was not just because of his personal rivalry with

Shoigu, sticking to that commandment was becoming increasingly difficult. On 9 May 2023, in lieu of congratulations for Victory Day, Prigozhin recorded a video clearly directed at more than just Defence Minister Shoigu and his alleged refusal to give Wagner the support it needed. 'Our soldiers are being killed, and the happy grandpa thinks that everything's fine,' he said, after railing about Wagner being forced to hold its positions and take the losses, without sufficient backup. 'What should the country do? If it turns out he's right, then good health to everyone. But what should the country do, what should our children, our grandchildren do, and how shall we win the war, if by some accident, I mean hypothetically, it just so happens that this grandpa is a complete asshole?'[8]

It was one thing to play the centuries-old game of absolving the good tsar – or the happy grandfather – by channelling one's anger at his greedy and corrupt boyars, by claiming that it was all Shoigu and Gerasimov's fault as they lied about ammunition, or by saying who was responsible for victories on the ground. It was one thing to cry 'bitch' in the same sentence where you had named your enemies. But in the euphemistic vernacular of a paranoid political culture, 'grandfather' had long come to refer to the aging man in the Kremlin – once Yeltsin, and now Putin. And so it was quite another thing for a powerful businessman with a private army funded by the Kremlin to call this grandfather an asshole. Later, Prigozhin tried to suggest he meant Gerasimov, former chief of military logistics Colonel General Mikhail

Mizintsev or, in a rather bizarre choice for a 'grandpa', a female pro-war blogger by the name of Nataliya Khim.[9] No one believed him.

In that lengthy video address, Prigozhin accused the regular military of abandoning positions around Bakhmut, leaving Wagner's contingent vulnerable, and issued an ultimatum, threatening to withdraw from the city the very next day, unless the Defence Ministry came through with urgently needed ammunition. No one truly expected him to follow through on the threat, even though previously Prigozhin announced that he was already coordinating a withdrawal with Chechen leader Ramzan Kadyrov, whose forces would presumably replace Wagner's. Nevertheless, it was a serious concern for the Kremlin and – almost unforgivably – further tarnished a Victory Day that was already looking pretty lacklustre. The usual phalanx of tanks rolling through Red Square in front of ranks of foreign dignitaries was replaced with a single Second World War vintage T-34, before an audience in which the only heads of state came from post-Soviet countries.

On 20 May 2023, Prigozhin finally could claim that Bakhmut had fallen. It was a moment for satisfaction and revenge: while pointedly thanking his soldiers, Surovikin and Putin, he charged Gerasimov and Shoigu with 'practically assisting the enemy' and threatened that 'someday in history, they will answer for their actions, for their crimes'.[10] However, Wagner was now at a shadow of its former strength, shrunk from 85,000 to perhaps 20,000 exhausted soldiers; and it was getting harder and harder to find new recruits against the competition of the MoD and other mercenary forces. It pulled out of Bakhmut, although not without a further jibe from Prigozhin, the ex-con: in a video talking about his withdrawal, he casually turned to one of his soldiers and ordered them to leave the army some soap.[11] This wasn't to appear magnanimous: the soap was a thinly veiled allusion to prison sodomy.

Beyond Shoigu

That was the end of a scene, maybe even an act, but not the play. There was an intensely personal dimension to Prigozhin's rivalry with Shoigu that could ultimately only be resolved when one or the other was destroyed. There does seem to have been a genuine bond forged at the frontline between Prigozhin and his 'boys', despite his willingness to see them thrown again and again into the meatgrinder (he even called Bakhmut 'Operation Meatgrinder'). Indeed, however much he was undoubtedly a bully, Prigozhin seemed to take the wellbeing of his underlings seriously. 'Wagner is a typical serf–landowner type business, with a diligent overlord who takes care of his peasants,' former Wagner soldier Marat Gabidullin recalled of serving under Prigozhin. 'He always treated mercenaries as instruments, but a good master has to keep his instruments in good condition.'[12] However, there was also the fact that Prigozhin prided himself on being smarter or if need be tougher than any of his rivals. He had seen off business rivals like Mirilashvili and even shrugged off claims of being sexually exploited in prison. It was one thing to be patronised and even discarded by the objectively more powerful Putin, but Shoigu was just another of the tsar's serfs, and was apparently going to beat him on Prigozhin's own terms, at that.

Back in February 2023, Prigozhin had threatened to pressgang the fitness blogger Alexei Stolyarov, who happened to be Shoigu's son-in-law, asking how he could 'go to the United Arab Emirates and shake his bum around?' after he incautiously posted pictures of himself and Ksenia Shoigu on holiday. In May, though, the designer shoe was on the other foot, as videos appeared on social media of Prigozhin's children enjoying a luxury getaway in northern Russia and singing around a campfire, 'you're the cocksucker, and I'm the elite ... you scrub the floor, I eat lobsters'.[13] A furious Prigozhin claimed that the footage had been hacked from their phones by military intelligence. In June, though, matters escalated when risqué videos of Veronika Prigozhina living it up in Dubai were also leaked.[14] Prigozhin's self-righteous attacks on the gilded youth of the Kremlin elite were exposed for the hypocrisy they were. No wonder Prigozhin, the indulgent and jealous head of the household, was exercised.

However, the Shakespearean drama unfolding around Prigozhin and Wagner was becoming about much more than his standoff with Shoigu. His increasingly outspoken interviews reflected his wider grievances about that which no one dared criticise publicly: the war itself. 'We came in boorishly, trampling all over Ukraine's territory in search of Nazis. And while we searched for Nazis, we fucked up everyone we could,' Prigozhin told the pro-war political journalist Konstantin Dolgov in an interview so frank that Dolgov was fired afterwards. 'The special military operation was done for the purpose of "denazification" ... But we ended up legitimising Ukraine. We've made Ukraine into a nation known all over the world. As for demilitarisation ... Fuck knows how, but we've *militarised* Ukraine!'[15]

In the growing paranoia that had enveloped the Kremlin, one couldn't simply say these things – that the invasion was a poorly planned mistake, and that Russia's losses couldn't be explained away by the superiority of the NATO forces backing Ukraine. 'Discrediting the Russian Armed Forces' or simply criticism of the war effort had become a crime punishable by 5 years in prison – 15 if it included disseminating so-called 'fakes'. For months, Prigozhin had railed about Shoigu's alleged incompetence and corruption, but the defence minister had played no real role in the decision to invade, and little in how the war was subsequently waged. The decisions Prigozhin was singling out now were beyond the minister's remit, and he knew it.

It seems as though 'grandpa' was becoming aware of the shifting focus of Prigozhin's wrath, too. For months, he had tried, in his usual fashion, to stay out of the fray and distance himself from the conflict, even to the point of pulling Prigozhin's Kremlin pass. But the increasingly angry and uncontrolled behaviour of the businessman he had charged with running a private army was exposing more than just a rift in his elites – it was, precisely, discrediting decisions and responsibilities that he, Vladimir Putin, had undertaken. There was no mistaking to which 'grandpa' Prigozhin had been referring, and while Putin, whose ego was hardly less fragile than Prigozhin's, would not dare show it publicly – not yet anyway – he was deeply displeased.[16] Something had to be done but, true to form, he let someone else take the lead.

On 10 June 2023, Shoigu issued an order that all 'volunteer groups' – mercenary forces – had to sign official contracts with the MoD by 1 July.[17] For Prigozhin, it would essentially spell the end of his days as a privateer: with his men forced to sign these contracts, he would at best be a subaltern of his bitter rival. He had until 15 June to send the MoD a detailed inventory of his fighters and their materiel – a declaration of capitulation of sorts. Of course, he wasn't going to do it. In his refusal, he carefully noted that while his organisation was fully committed to the interests of the Russian Federation, it was impossible to subordinate oneself to a minister such as Shoigu, who was neither 'honest' nor 'brave' nor 'competent'.[18] Prigozhin had only one hope: that Putin could be prevailed upon to rescind these orders, or at least grant Wagner – which was a rather different force to the scattered other little mercenary companies, and which had delivered victories where the MoD had not – some kind of exemption. He twisted and turned: perhaps Wagner could instead be subordinated to the National Guard? Or made responsible for territorial defence? Anything but submit to the Defence Ministry. Yet in a meeting with war correspondents, Putin backed Shoigu, even if rather half-heartedly, arguing that the official contracts were necessary to ensure that 'volunteers' were entitled to social guarantees. Even then, he could not bring himself to admit that this was about power and control, and instead pretended that it was a minor administrative correction about pensions and bus passes. Once again, Vova had expected Zhenya to do what the Russian state could not, and once again he had failed to back him up.

Slovo i Delo – Word and Deed

In hindsight, US intelligence reports that Wagner forces were beginning to gather near the Russian border may have been indicative, although they could just as easily have been gatherings of depleted units out from the meatgrinder. Nonetheless, it does seem that Prigozhin was at least contemplating some kind of dramatic move for weeks, and maybe even before Shoigu's bombshell of 10 June 2023. He appears to have discussed this with Surovikin, presumably to sound out how the generals would react if he seized Shoigu and Gerasimov when they were visiting the headquarters in the southern Russian city of Rostov-on-Don around 26 June.

Meanwhile, he seemed not just to be preparing the justification for the mutiny he eventually launched, but also stiffening his own sinews, as the serf was about to make a move which, however it was framed, he knew was a challenge to the tsar.

Until the eleventh hour, his preparations – the assembly of forces on the border, conversations with Surovikin and perhaps other generals, a message from 'Sedoy' Troshev telling the authorities in Rostov that they would be passing through on their way to return equipment lent by the MoD – seem to have escaped the attention of the Federal Security Service. Its Military Counter-Intelligence Directorate is, despite its name, first and foremost charged with watching the military and preventing coups. Whether because of the incompetence that it seems to have displayed throughout the war, or because it had not properly expanded its remit to include the mercenaries, it only seems to have cottoned on to what was happening a scant couple of days beforehand, and even then Prigozhin seems to have been alerted to this before the FSB could act.

He had been planning on being a surprise participant at a meeting to consider the progress of the war in the State Duma, the lower legislative chamber, called by Sergei Mironov, head of the nationalist A Just Russia – For Truth party. He suddenly called that off and moved his plans forward. If he could not take Shoigu and Gerasimov in Rostov, he would need to do something else, something equally spectacular. His goal, after all, was not to seize power or topple the regime – neither was anything he could achieve, even if he wanted to – but rather to force Putin to take notice and get him to side with him, rather than Shoigu.

A Presidential Administration insider admitted that they had considered the risk of an armed mutiny but ruled it out, thinking ultimately that 'only a madman would do that'.[19] So how on earth could Prigozhin have thought this possible, let alone wise? In the Middle Ages and the Renaissance, it was quite usual for mercenary armies to practise coercive negotiation, to flex their muscles to persuade their employers to pay more or otherwise rewrite the terms of their relationships. As discussed above, Putin's Russia, or at least Putin's court, owes more to the medieval than we might think. Indeed, Chechen local leader Ramzan Kadyrov had already shown that it was possible to throw your weight around and get away with it. After the Second Chechen War (1999–2009), Chechnya had been pacified at the cost of the installation of a brutal, dynastic regime and constant and massive subsidies from Moscow. Every time those subsidies came into question, Kadyrov would cause trouble, whether threatening to resign or, as he did in 2013, even sending 300 armed policemen in a bid to annex a village in neighbouring Ingushetia. Kadyrov and Prigozhin were both in the private army business (the *Kadyrovtsy*, the 'Kadyrovites', were technically largely part of the National Guard, but swore a personal oath to him), so maybe Prigozhin thought he could also afford a flex.

All this is, of course, entirely speculative. The fundamental truth is probably simpler: he was furious (channelling his anger towards Putin also on to Shoigu) and desperate. True to form, he was lashing out more generally, even picking a fight with Kadyrov, with whom he had an unspoken alliance of sorts in their shared contempt for the MoD. Like Wagner, the Chechen forces tended to consider themselves outside the army's chain of command, and resented attempts to bring them into line. When Prigozhin claimed that Chechen troops would not be able to live up to their promises to be able to hold occupied territories in the Donetsk Region, he was probably speaking the truth, but Kadyrov could not let the slight go unchallenged. His lieutenant, Adam Delimkhanov, denounced him as no more than 'a blogger who screams and shouts at the world', and Prigozhin was forced to make peace.[20] After all, his beef really wasn't with Kadyrov.

Prigozhin had never really outgrown the brutal culture of the prison Zone, in which it was better to take a beating standing up for yourself than meekly to submit and be marked as a victim. Prigozhin's career had been driven by resentment, a stubborn unwillingness to give in. He couldn't let go, but rather had to make one last throw of the dice. And he lost.

The March of Justice

On the night of Friday, 23 June, Wagner forces in Ukraine crossed the border into Russia and quickly seized the military headquarters in Rostov. Although the mutiny had been planned in advance, it sounded as if Prigozhin was still trying to talk himself into rebellion with a series of diatribes. This time, he was hardly pulling his punches. He claimed that the whole invasion of Ukraine had been based on a lie. 'There was nothing extraordinary happening on the eve of 24 February [2022],' he said. Rather, 'the ministry of defence is trying to deceive the public and the president and spin the story that there were insane levels of aggression from the Ukrainian side and that they were going to attack us together with the whole NATO bloc.' There was still the fiction that the good tsar had been deceived by his scheming subordinates, but by this point it was tissue thin. Either the commander-in-chief was complicit in this lie or he was painfully stupid, so blaming the MoD for what was in effect Putin's delusion was a transparent deflection. 'When Zelensky became [Ukrainian] president, he was ready for agreements. All that needed to be done was to get off Mount Olympus and negotiate with him. What was the war for? It was needed so that Shoigu could receive a hero's star. The oligarchic clan that rules Russia needed the war.'[21] His words would hardly have seemed out of place coming from the jailed dissident Alexei Navalny – except that Prigozhin still had an army. Later that day, he issued another rant, this time alleging on the basis of some very dubious footage that Wagner fighters had come under rocket attack by government forces.[22]

As a result, he claimed that 'the Council of Commanders of PMC Wagner has come to a decision. The evil carried out by the country's military leadership must be stopped,' and to this end he was launching a march intended to 'restore justice in the military and after that, justice for all of Russia'.[23] Up until then, the Kremlin had assumed that this was yet another bluff; after all, as one insider source said, 'Prigozhin has been used to getting his way with histrionics.'[24] Putin's ally, Belarusian president Alexander Lukashenko, admitted that they had both 'slept through this situation' and assumed 'it would fizzle out on its own'.[25] As convoys of Wagner fighters, supported by tanks and air-defence systems ironically provided by the MoD, began to pour across the border into Russia, this complacency was shattered. The FSB charged Prigozhin with armed rebellion, and in the early hours of Saturday, 24 June, there was an emergency bulletin on Channel One TV and, following that, both Colonel General Surovikin and GRU deputy chief Lieutenant General Alexeyev – the honorary member of Wagner, and the man who had invited them into the Ukraine war, respectively – released videos appealing to Prigozhin to stop the mutiny. Alexeyev seemed quite natural as he decried this 'stab in the back of the country and the president', but Surovikin appeared much more stilted as he demanded that Prigozhin and the Wagner fighters 'obey the will and orders of the democratically elected president'.[26] It has been likened to a hostage's 'proof of life' video, and certainly Surovikin then disappeared into

FSB detention, suspected of having played a role in the mutiny, and ended up demoted from command of the Aerospace Forces.

It was all much too little, much too late. Wagner forces reached Rostov-on-Don later that morning. There was no resistance: in what turned out to be a harbinger of the response of most of the security forces through this whole crisis, the city's military and National Guard garrisons simply locked themselves up in their barracks, and the police looked on. Wagner fighters took the Southern Military District headquarters, the very complex from which the Ukraine war was coordinated. Shoigu and Gerasimov were not there, but Alexeyev and Deputy Defence Minister Yunus-bek Yevkurov were. There followed a surreal exchange, captured on film, in the HQ's courtyard, as the two men tried unsuccessfully to talk Prigozhin down. He was in bullish mood, even complaining when he felt Yevkurov – a decorated former paratrooper who had fought in two wars and been almost killed in a terrorist bombing – was speaking to him with insufficient respect. Perhaps the most telling moment, though, was when Prigozhin said that they were just after Shoigu and Gerasimov, and Alexeyev, perhaps not realising he was on camera, replied, 'Take them,' with a smirk. It might help explain why Prigozhin may have truly expected he would have the bulk of the army on his side, given just how unpopular those two men had become.

Yet it was Yevkurov, an officer of the old school, who elicited the most telling response. With what seems to have been genuine confusion, he asked, 'You believe everything you're doing now is right. Is that correct?'

'Absolutely correct,' Prigozhin replied. 'We're saving Russia.'[27]

A strange mood descended on Rostov. Much of the city remained closed, but while some left, many locals seemed supportive, chatting with the mercenaries, taking selfies with them, letting their children clamber on to the tanks that took up positions around key junctions. Prigozhin himself settled there, but even as Putin was finally responding directly in a televised address in which, with barely suppressed fury, he denounced the mutiny as treason, the Wagner commander was sending a flying column north. Its aim: Moscow.

Of course, Prigozhin did not think that the couple of thousand men he sent under Utkin would actually take a city of more than 13 million people. Rather, he knew from the first that, as he had missed out on the chance to snatch Shoigu and Gerasimov in Rostov, he needed to keep up the pressure in the hope of pushing the president into backing him. This was again Prigozhin the showman at work, using his soldiers as a political instrument. Ultimately, it didn't work, but what was perhaps more surprising is just how far it got. Instead of rolling in one clumsy and easily tracked convoy – the way Russian forces had tried to take Kyiv – they broke up into a number of fast-moving smaller groups taking a variety of routes, reforming at key waystations then breaking apart for the next leg of the journey. It was unexpected and audacious, and further confused the powerful but ponderous security machine.

Besides, that machine seemed unwilling to move. Prigozhin had hyperbolically claimed that 'half the army' would defect to his side, and this proved a massive over-statement, but the regular military and National Guard seemed equally unwilling to oppose him.[28] Ironically, it would be Surovikin's Aerospace Forces that did the most, and at least three helicopters and an Il-22M command aircraft would be shot down trying to intercept the Wagnerites. Otherwise, National Guard chief General Viktor Zolotov, who had been a drinking buddy of Prigozhin's back when he was Putin's driver-bodyguard in the 1990s, seemed to spend most of that Saturday trying to get through to local commanders in order to organise some kind of defence. They, in turn, did their best to be hard to reach, to avoid being given orders they would have to obey or defy. In the first real test of Putin's authority over the security forces, most seemed willing to sit things out and see what happened.

Wagner's flying column made its way up the M4 motorway, taking the city of Voronezh, then heading through Lipetsk Region, despite some makeshift road-blocks made up of trucks and buses. By late that day, they were at the village of Krasnoye, just over 200 miles south of Moscow. The capital itself was half in a panic, half sticking to business as usual. Mayor Sergei Sobyanin announced an emergency security regime, and extra police appeared at Red Square and other key locations.

There was a rapid exodus of oligarchs and senior officials, with a jet from the Presidential Wing tracked heading for St Petersburg, although Putin's spokesman claimed (not especially convincingly) that the president stayed in the Kremlin. Meanwhile, loyal troops were rushed to the bridges along the Oka River, south of the city, and began digging in for the defence of Moscow.

At the same time, vigorously and performatively closing the stable door after the horse had bolted, the FSB raided Prigozhin's estate and the Wagner headquarters in St Petersburg. As cameras rolled, documents, computers, guns, cash to the value of 10 billion rubles and packs of mysterious white powder were seized.[29] The intent was clearly to suggest some kind of drugs and money conspiracy, although it was later claimed that the powder was planted and, as IRA trolls as well as Wagner fighters and dependents of the fallen were paid in cash, the presence of so much physical money was not quite as suspicious as it may seem. Furthermore, pictures of the expensively trashy inside of Prigozhin's home were also quickly leaked to the press: the marble-walled spa, the icon-bedecked prayer room, the gold bathroom fittings, the study in which hung a uniform jacket encrusted with medals, from Hero of the Russian Federation to Burkina Faso's Grand Cross of the Order of the Stallion. The unsubtle intent was to undermine Prigozhin's status as straight-talking man of the people and scourge of the Moscow kleptocracy. This was made pretty obvious when some of the footage was aired on

TV with the presenter opening with, 'Let's have a look how this fighter for the truth lived, someone who has two criminal convictions and who kept claiming that everyone else was a thief.' 'Fighting for truth costs a lot of money,' another taunted.[30] Most surreal was the closet full of wigs of varying levels of implausibility and a series of photos of Prigozhin in a range of uniforms and disguises, apparently from travels through Africa. In one, with dark glasses, gaudy uniform and expansive beard, he almost seemed to be cosplaying Sacha Baron Cohen's fictional and clueless 'Admiral-General Haffaz Aladeen' from the 2012 black comedy, *The Dictator*. It was not a good look.

As it was, this was all unnecessary. The march on Moscow may have been impressive in its speed and striking for the lack of serious resistance, but it was essentially theatrical. Prigozhin's gambit had depended on presenting Putin with a fait accompli, an excuse to side with him against Shoigu before he had publicly committed himself. From the very moment at 10am, when Putin denounced the mutiny and warned that 'everyone who deliberately took the path of betrayal, who prepared an armed rebellion, took the path of blackmail and terrorist methods, will suffer inevitable punishment – before the law and before the people,' he had known the game was up.[31] The only thing left was to try to cut the best exit deal possible, and by midday he was trying to talk to Putin.

The Deal

Putin didn't want to talk to him. His fury was probably as much an outlet for his fear: a man who had seen not one but two authoritarian regimes crumble around him – East Germany in 1988, the USSR in 1991 – now saw an army marching on his capital, which his own security forces seemed unable or unwilling to resist. Indeed, while dozens of officials had been ordered publicly to denounce Prigozhin, most of them, including Prime Minister Mikhail Mishustin, remained silent. However, once Prigozhin had made it clear he wanted to talk, Putin was glad to take the opportunity of avoiding the humiliating and maybe politically fatal sight of Russian troops shelling a Russian city, and firefights on the outskirts of Moscow.

Nonetheless, he refused to take Prigozhin's repeated calls himself. Instead, as he often does when faced with ultimatums and tough decisions, he shunted the responsibility of talking a way out of a potential civil war to a coterie of Kremlin officials. The main figures involved initially were Nikolai Patrushev, secretary of the Security Council, and Anton Vaino, head of the Presidential Administration. Although he subsequently disclaimed any role, Alexei Dyumin, now governor of Tula but formerly the man who had initially introduced Prigozhin to Utkin, may have been an early mediator.

We know very little about quite how these arm's length talks went; the only person who has discussed them in detail is Belarus's Lukashenko, although to call him an unreliable witness would still be flattery. Nonetheless, it is clear that Prigozhin would not accept talks that did not include the head of state, for fear that any guarantees made would be worthless (little did he know that they would be, anyway). With Vova still unwilling to talk to Zhenya, the decision was made to involve Lukashenko (and Boris Gryzlov, the Russian ambassador to Belarus). He was *a* head of state, within the notional Union State of Russia and Belarus, and he also knew Prigozhin ('I have the best relationship with him. Close'), having first met him when he had dined at New Island with Putin in 2002.[32] As one insider said, 'Prigozhin needed a trusted third party to exit and save face. That's where Lukashenko came in. He enjoys publicity – that's why he agreed.'[33] By his own account, he was the one who took the initiative, who talked Prigozhin down, who arranged a deal, guaranteed it, and in effect forced the Russian security forces to accept it, although he modestly 'told my media not to turn me into a hero in this situation'.[34] Others' recollections differ, including Lukashenko's own as, after Prigozhin's death, he asserted that he hadn't actually given him any guarantees at all. While Lukashenko's account places him rather spuriously at centre stage, nonetheless, it is clear that Prigozhin was looking for an out for himself and his men, and that by late afternoon it had been agreed.

The terms of the deal were, in effect, that an amnestied Prigozhin would be exiled to Belarus, along with whichever of his men wanted to join him; the rest would either stand down, or join the army or a different mercenary unit. It was, frankly, surprisingly generous and showed just how eager Putin was to avoid internal strife: having first called Prigozhin a traitor and vowing to destroy him, the president was apparently willing to let him get away with staging an armed insurrection, calling him a liar and shooting down at least 13 of his pilots. Of course, he tried to spin it as an act of statesmanship. In a televised address on 26 June, Putin reiterated that the organisers of the mutiny had been traitors, but that the majority of Wagnerites were patriots who had been led astray, and that the true enemies were still Russia's external foes: Ukraine and the West. Facing the risk that 'our society would split, would drown in the blood of civil strife … steps were taken on my direct instructions to avoid bloodshed. This took time, including to give those who made the mistake the opportunity to come to their senses, to understand that their actions were decisively rejected by society, and to what tragic, destructive consequences for Russia, for our state, the adventure into which they were dragged would lead.'[35]

However, Prigozhin, while standing down, was not conceding defeat, and like Putin, he tried to turn weakness into a win: 'Our decision to turn back had two factors: we didn't want to spill Russian blood. Secondly, we marched as a demonstration of our protest.' Once that demonstration had been made, there was no need for violence.[36] Whatever each of them said, there was no denying that they had reached a stalemate. For Prigozhin, while Concord would quickly begin to be picked at by rival scavengers, he had retained his life, most of his business empire, and as much of his private army as he could convince to stay with him. Even the billions of rubles confiscated by the FSB would be returned in full. Yet for Putin, he had brought an end to the crisis at the cost of looking weak, indecisive, absent: precisely the failings that, to him, had doomed the East German and Soviet leaderships. Something would have to be done.

CHAPTER 10
Ghost

At 5.46pm on the afternoon of 23 August 2023, the Embraer Legacy 600 executive jet with the tail number RA-02795 lifted off from Moscow's Sheremetyevo airport for St Petersburg. There had been an 'inexplicable delay' for some maintenance work according to one of the three crew, cabin stewardess Kristina Raspopova, in a text message to her family, but now they were off.[1] The plane soon reached its cruising altitude of 28,000 feet, but not long into its journey, at about 6.20pm in the evening, it suddenly went into a steep dive. An eyewitness on the ground reported hearing two explosions in the sky and that the blue-and-white plane started falling, rolling over and trailing smoke, losing one wing and part of its tail. It crashed near the village of Kuzhenkino in Tver Region, just some 60 miles into its flight. The pilots didn't even have the opportunity to issue a mayday, as the plane disintegrated in mid-air, based on the pattern of the wreckage. All ten people on the plane died: the pilot, co-pilot, Raspopova and the passengers: Yevgeny Prigozhin, Dmitry Utkin and Valery 'Rover' Chekalov

– Wagner's head of security and logistics – along with two Wagner soldiers and two of Prigozhin's bodyguards. It was exactly two months since the mutiny.

At once, the rumour mill went into overdrive. It had been shot down by Russian air defence (there is no evidence of this, and the wreckage did not indicate it). It was all a piece of misdirection and Prigozhin was actually alive and well, in Venezuela, or Belarus, or wherever (it wouldn't be the first time Russians put their faith in miraculous escapes, but the DNA tests of the bodies suggest otherwise). Putin himself later implied some kind of drink- or drug-fuelled mid-air shenanigans with explosives, when he claimed that the Investigative Committee had found grenade fragments in the plane, and added his regrets that 'no examination was carried out to determine the presence of alcohol or drugs in the blood of the victims. Although we know that after the well-known events in the company in St Petersburg, the FSB discovered not only 10 billion in cash, but also 5kg of cocaine.'[2] This was, of course, nothing more than a smear: there was no suggestions that any of the people onboard used drugs (and there are widespread suspicions that the white powder found in the search was planted), and Prigozhin was known for treating his many journeys as opportunities to get work done; not only did not drink on them, he ordered the in-flight bar emptied of alcohol before each trip.

Sometimes, things really are as they seem. Prigozhin's security was tight, but to believe that the state could not access the plane while it was sitting at a Moscow airport is naive. Watchers can be distracted or suborned, explosives concealed within innocuous items, equipment sabotaged. It is almost certain that this was just another of the extrajudicial killings with which Putin's political path has been strewn. But why this way, and then? There had been numerous opportunities to arrest or eliminate Prigozhin in the previous two months. Indeed, he had been to a meeting in the Kremlin, and even the most powerful Russian movers and shakers have to leave their bodyguards behind when meeting the president, so he would have been easy pickings. What had changed since the awkward deal that had ended the mutiny?

Dead Man Walking?

All kinds of explanations have been advanced. Of course, the odds that Prigozhin would live a long and happy life after challenging Putin were, to put it mildly, slim. Yet he had made a deal with Putin and been granted an amnesty, and he seemed to be doing what was expected of him. Wagner handed back to the MoD more than 2,000 tanks, artillery pieces and missile launchers. While some of his men opted to transfer to other employers, those who wanted to stay with Prigozhin began relocating to a disused military base at Tsel, in southern Belarus. A video shot from there in July 2023 showed him addressing the first few hundred arrivals, and introducing them to Utkin.[3] Quite what they were going to do there was unclear, whether help train the Belarussian military (in typically bombastic form, Prigozhin said that with their help they could become 'the second-best army in the world' – after Wagner) or be the reserve and logistical base for operations in Africa and elsewhere. In any case, the Molkino base was closed; Wagner's flags were lowered one last time there, and then taken to Tsel.

Meanwhile Prigozhin threw himself into his Africa ventures with renewed vigour. No less a figure than Sergei Lavrov had toured Africa after the mutiny to reassure Wagner's customers that they could expect business as usual. Prigozhin, though, was not looking simply to retain his existing customers, but find more. Following a military coup in Niger, he quickly pitched Wagner to the new regime, promising that 'a thousand Wagner fighters are able to restore order and destroy terrorists'.[4] As so often happened, Western attempts to isolate the new government actually made it more inclined to turn to Prigozhin, and by the time of his death, negotiations were already at an advanced stage. Indeed, he seemed to be showing a renewed enthusiasm for this aspect of his work, and his first video after the mutiny showed him somewhere in Africa (probably Mali), in camouflage and clutching a rifle, saying that even though the temperature out there was more than 50°C, Wagner was there to 'make Russia even greater on all continents, and Africa even more free'.[5]

So far, so loyal, yet things were not quite as amicable as all that may suggest. Zhenya's usual instincts – to push as far as possible, to bargain as hard as he could, and not

to let go of what was his – meant that he was a continued irritant to Vova. On Thursday, 29 June, less than a
week since the mutiny, Putin met with Prigozhin and 35
of Wagner's field commanders to discuss the unit's future.
It was an astonishing mark of Putin's uncertainty as quite
how to handle Wagner – he did not want to lose its veteran
fighters, nor its Africa operation – that he invited these
'traitors' to tea, but nonetheless a three-hour block was
carved out of his schedule for just such a conversation.
By his own account, Putin proposed that Wagner could
continue as before, including its involvement in the 'special
military operation' in Ukraine, but under its current chief
of staff Andrei Troshev, 'Sedoy'. (Troshev had already
begun secret conversations with the MoD and would later
'defect' and become the official coordinator of mercenary
forces in Ukraine.) In other words, nothing would change
– except that Prigozhin and presumably Utkin would be
cut out of the chain of command. According to Putin,
many of the commanders looked happy to go along with
this, but Prigozhin, 'who was sitting in front and did not
see this', flatly rejected the idea, claiming, 'No, the guys
do not agree with this decision.'[6]

It was an amazing admission from the president,
that he was willing to let Prigozhin steamroller over his
own favoured option, just as it was a striking demonstration that the businessman felt emboldened by his survival
and, having challenged the Kremlin to keep control of
his army, was unwilling to hand it over. Indeed, why did
Putin admit to his failure to get his way, considering that

usually his political narrative is as the man who never fails? An interview with correspondents from the newspaper *Kommersant* the following month may well have signalled that he was already beginning to change his mind about the deal and wanted to present Prigozhin as unwilling to meet him halfway. After all, when asked whether Wagner would remain a combat unit, he seems suddenly to have remembered that he never had got round to legalising PMCs: 'There is no such legal entity … The group exists, but legally does not exist!'[7]

Meanwhile, Prigozhin began to regain his confidence. He took to travelling back and forth between Belarus and Russia with increasing frequency, trying to retain and claw back as much of Concord as he could. The Patriot Media group had been officially wound up after the mutiny, and a number of its media outlets as well as the Internet Research Agency were reportedly in the sights of the rival National Media Group. Established by a close friend of Putin's, the billionaire banker Yury Kovalchuk, this was widely seen as a move to bring them more tightly under the control of the Presidential Administration. The status of Concord as a whole was less precarious, but Prigozhin was aware of the risks it faced. Already, some subsidiaries and component companies were facing attempts at 'raiding', a distinctive Russian criminal business tactic involving using the courts and sometimes fictitious loans or title deeds to try to steal assets. More to the point, he was losing state contracts: the MoD ended its final catering deals with Concord, for example, turning back to RBE, the very firm Prigozhin had pushed out ten years earlier, while Moscow Region stopped using it to feed its schoolchildren.

Prigozhin's real focus continued to be Wagner, though. At the end of July 2023, he also turned up on the fringes of the Russia–Africa Summit in St Petersburg. He may have been denied entry to the summit, but the manager of his operations in the Central African Republic posted a picture of him shaking hands with Ambassador Freddy Mapouka, an adviser to the president of the CAR, while he also hobnobbed with representatives of the African media. Putin did not meet him or even acknowledge his presence, and Kremlin officials appeared irked that he was overshadowing the official agenda. The once humble 'chef' seemed no longer to know his place.

Nor had he learned his lesson. In his address to the Wagner fighters in Belarus, Prigozhin praised them for putting up a good fight in Ukraine and doing much for Russia, but could not or would not restrain himself from more digs at the campaign: 'What is currently happening on the frontline is a disgrace that we don't want to have any part in, and we need to wait until we can show our mettle in full.' He made it clear that he thought his and Wagner's time could come again, that while 'the decision has been taken to stay here in Belarus for a certain time', in due course they might return to the war 'when we are sure that we won't be forced to put ourselves and our experience to shame', which presumably meant when Shoigu and Gerasimov were finally gone.[8]

Zhenya for President?

So this was a different Prigozhin, one who had turned. What's more, it was a Prigozhin whose mutiny had elevated him to an unusual public profile well beyond that of any commander, let alone minigarch and restaurateur. When he and his fighters pulled out of Rostov-on-Don, they were cheered and applauded, and locals flocked to get a selfie with the man who had challenged their government. His image as the committed patriot who talked tough but straight and was more committed to his 'boys' at the front than the self-indulgent bureaucrats in Moscow, carefully nurtured by his social media empire and the *voyenkor* fanboys, was a powerful one. In this, Prigozhin was building on an existing political base. In late 2022 and early 2023, the Kremlin's political technologists had even been contemplating co-opting him as a public figure. There was discussion of his setting up his own party or taking over the Just Russia – For Truth party – or even being put forward as a presidential candidate (not to win, of course, but to make Putin look moderate).[9]

They seem to have dropped the idea in spring – but Prigozhin himself seems to have picked it up. In May, he began a campaign called 'Wagner: A Second Front', which saw him touring the country like any politician stumping for votes, holding meetings ranging from big press conferences to motor rallies. In part, they were recruitment events but first and foremost were about himself: his work, his background, his views on the future of the war – and a Russia which, he argued, could be both victorious in Ukraine and also capable of modernisation and prosperity at home. Only with the right leadership, of course. The fact that he explicitly denied he had any political ambitions ('You will not see the Wagner party in the State Duma or presidential candidate Prigozhin') would, to a cynic, confirm that he was toying with the idea.[10]

Of course, he could no more challenge Putin politically than his mutiny could militarily. The intent, rather, was to elevate his status yet further, give him more clout in his struggle against Shoigu, and make him all the more worth the Kremlin co-opting – and more difficult to ignore. Although polling by the Levada Centre only saw his approval ratings reach 4 per cent by June 2023, in a Putin-centric Russia, this was still enough to make him the fifth most recognisable figure in the country, after the president, Prime Minister Mishustin, Foreign Minister Lavrov and, gallingly enough, Defence Minister Shoigu.[11] It also left him alongside former president Dmitry Medvedev and Communist Party leader Gennady Zyuganov. Of course, all this was before the mutiny. More polling from Levada had shown that just before the march on Moscow, 58 per cent of respondents fully or partially approved of him, although this fell to only 29 per cent afterwards.[12] Polling in a police state is always difficult, but a separate survey from Russian Field also found 29 per cent still viewing him in a positive light.[13] In other words, more than a quarter of Russians still supported to some degree a man who had just staged an armed insurrection. This cannot have been reassuring to the Kremlin.

Many explanations have been given for the delay between the mutiny and the response. Was Putin waiting for a proper investigation into who had secretly been supporting it? There certainly was such an inquisition, with figures such as Surovikin dropping from view, but Prigozhin did not need to be alive for that. Was he lulling Prigozhin into a false sense of security, or simply did he not have an opportunity beforehand? Yet Prigozhin was regularly in and out of Russia, and whether in the Kremlin or at an airport would have been easy to arrest or dispose of, as seemed fit. It is at present impossible to know, but the answer may be the simple one that Putin – always slow to take tough decisions – simply did not know at first what to do, or changed his mind. In the height of the crisis, he just wanted the mutiny to go away, as neatly and quickly as possible. He may even have thought – quite possibly rightly – that, without Prigozhin, Wagner's politically useful African operations would wither and die. As it became clear that Prigozhin was becoming cocky again, though, and as his populist style and tough-guy image seemed even sharper a contrast with that of the man opposition leader Alexei Navalny had ridiculed as 'grandpa in his bunker', Putin may have become progressively more angry and concerned.[14] Besides, there was a danger, in hindsight, that the weakness of the deal would be seen by figures within the elite as demonstrating a weakness on the part of the president. It was, in short, a bad deal for Putin, and so it would have to be pyrotechnically revoked.

Life after Zhenya

It was easier to kill Prigozhin than handle the immediate aftermath. According to the *Wall Street Journal*, Nikolai Patrushev had had the intelligence agencies prepare plans for his assassination ahead of time, ready just in case the boss gave the order – and quite possibly in the hope that he would.[15] But what to do after his death? They had to appease his many fans without turning him into a martyr. Putin issued a statement that, even though he would later suggest he was some kind of psychotic alcoholic who might juggle hand grenades on a plane, nonetheless tried to tiptoe through this minefield:

> I knew Prigozhin for a very long time, since the early 90s. He was a man with a difficult fate. He made serious mistakes in his life. And he achieved the results he needed, both for himself and when I asked him about it, for the common cause, as in these last months. He was a talented person, a talented businessman, he worked not only in our country, but also abroad, in Africa in particular, he was involved in oil, gas, precious metals and stones.[16]

Who, hearing that, would even have known he had raised and run a mercenary army, let alone led it against

Moscow? These weasel-words pleased no one, whether those who still considered Prigozhin a traitor or those who held him to be a hero. The Grey Zone, a pro-Wagner social media site, was blunt: 'Prigozhin died as the result of the actions of Russia's traitors. But even in hell, he'll be the best! Glory to Russia!'[17]

The risk that such supporters would turn Prigozhin's funeral into a spectacle meant that great efforts were made to conceal when he and the rest of the dead would be buried, and where. As it was, Prigozhin was interred on 29 August 2023 next to his father in St Petersburg's working-class Porokhovskoye cemetery, behind a cordon of National Guards: none of the pomp that a Hero of the Russian Federation could expect, just the necessary minimum of respect and publicity, and all, the official announcement said, 'at the request of the family'. Since then, though, cards, flowers, even symbolic hammers continue to appear on his grave. The bloody brand remains strong. As Maxim Shugalei, the sociologist-operator Prigozhin immortalised, says, 'Wagner is not just about money, it's a kind of religion. It is unlikely that this structure will completely disappear.'[18]

But his businesses were another matter, not least given the degree to which most were based on government patronage. For all his bullishness, Prigozhin must have realised the continuing risk he was under, even if Putin's amnesty implied he would have maybe a year to demonstrate his continued loyalty and value. Certainly he took the precaution of updating his will, leaving most of his assets – including Wagner, insofar as it could be bequeathed considering its murky legal status – to his 25-year-old son Pavel, with much smaller endowments to his wife and daughters. Pavel had fought in Syria and Ukraine and managed, to a degree, the Lakhta property portfolio in St Petersburg, but his actual experience was irrelevant: he was a man, and to Prigozhin that made him the next head of the household. This was still a business empire of breathtaking scope and reach, including 600 companies, ranging from dozens of hotels and restaurants to major real estate developments, as well as Concord Management and Consulting and Concord Catering. There were the companies exporting gold and diamonds from Africa, and even a 49 per cent stake in Aurum, the film studio that had produced Prigozhin's self-serving action movies.[19] The value of all these assets remains impossible to judge, not least as many depended on state contracts that were quickly being pulled. However, all told they were worth something in the tens of billions of rubles, or hundreds of millions of dollars, in notional value, even as the empire dwindled. No wonder it faced raids by so many predators (including, apparently, Pavel's sisters, as the will was reportedly challenged). Indeed, although the troll farms were reportedly shuttered, by all accounts a number of other players (including former business rivals, the MoD and the Foreign Intelligence Service) hurriedly hired individuals and teams from the Internet Research Agency, as one troll farm spawned many smaller ones.

Pavel was quickly associated with attempts to save Wagner, even if the suspicion is that he is more a figurehead behind such people as Mikhail Vatanin, its head of security. He certainly seems to have inherited his father's capacity to speak before he thinks. In October 2023, he took to Telegram to announce: 'I have taken command of the Wagner PMC, and very soon Wagner fighters will return to the Special Military Operation zone and continue to exterminate the Nazis. There is no one except me to continue my father's work. There is no more time to grieve.'[20] This was definitely not what the Kremlin had in mind, and he quickly deleted it. Subsequently, it emerged that Wagner – or at least its remnants – would be incorporated within the paramilitary National Guard; even as a separate spin-off Wagner would continue to operate abroad, probably outside Pavel's control. It sounds like a clumsy solution, and it is: Wagner's future looks dubious. Prigozhin was not only personally responsible for many of the contracts signed in Africa, but so often they depended on the interconnection between Wagner and the rest of Concord. As the latter is broken apart, then Wagner begins to look just like any other PMC (and the Kremlin's decision to rebrand it as the 'Africa Corps', apparently heedless of the Second World War resonances of the name, is unlikely to help). At home, after Troshev jumped ship, many other mercenaries opted to join the regular military or Redut, and by August 2023, the camp in Belarus was already being dismantled. While the National Guard will retain something called Wagner, this is really just to capitalise on its name and create a vessel for incorporating mercenaries. It will certainly not have anything like the old unit's autonomy.

Of course, Pavel will likely do well enough, so long as he realises that he owns the remnants of his father's mercenary army and business empire alike only so long as the Kremlin allows it. As one British diplomat who had observed him noted, 'he's not his dad. If he's inherited the guts to go against the Kremlin, he's certainly not inherited the wits to get away with it.'[21]

Prigozhin's wife Lyubov took a rather different route, and in September 2023 officially retook her maiden name, Kryazheva. Many companies had passed into and out of her hands as her husband looked for the most tax-efficient and untransparent options, but she still owns a range of properties and companies, including the upmarket Yeliseyevsky delicatessen that made a net profit of 73 million rubles (around a million dollars) in 2022 alone. She is clearly looking to distance herself from her husband's toxic legacy, and her daughters seem – at least as of writing – to be keeping an uncharacteristically low profile, too.

A Portrait in Putinism

Even if the intent of Prigozhin's mutiny had been to compel Putin to sack Shoigu, even if he had no thought of taking power for himself, his rebellion was a challenge to Putin and the Kremlin. As long as he lived afterwards, a spectre of revolution haunted Russia. But what about after 23 August 2023? On the surface, the Kremlin has seemed to learn its lesson of relying on privateers to wage its wars. Prigozhin's Wagner had become the poster child of a 2014 strategy of letting self-motivated volunteers steer a creeping takeover of Ukrainian territory; it got out of hand, and now the government was taking back those roles and perquisites it had handed over to the businessman, reining in his private army under the control of the MoD, and cannibalising his business empire. Putin, too, re-emerged from his increasing seclusion to take a more robust public role, although this may have been as much about his 2024 presidential campaign as it was about ensuring his public absences weren't coming to be filled by someone else.

As of writing, the Kremlin seems to have neutralised the immediate threat of a serious challenge to its hold on power that Prigozhin posed. But rebellions and revolutions are fickle: a spark can ignite the brittle, woodworm-riddled framework of an aging regime; sometimes the spark is put out, and the structure remains intact for a decade more, and sometimes the fire consumes the whole. Prigozhin may be dead, but his rise, rebellion and fall demonstrated, for all to see, a fundamental weakness of the Putin regime.

Prigozhin was unique in having his own private army, but otherwise he was just another of the adhocrats, the scrabbling opportunists – businesspeople or bureaucrats, security officers or scholars, TV personalities or priests – doing whatever the Kremlin wants doing today and trying to predict what it will need tomorrow. These are not Putin's friends, secure in his affection regardless of how much they steal and how bad a job they do. Instead, they have enough profile to play the games of court, enough at stake to be desperate not to lose. And lose they often do, but Putin doesn't care, because he has created a system in which there are always more waiting for their chance. Take, for example, the philosopher Alexander Dugin, a man whose greatest genius may be in self-promotion. For a short while in 2014, his nationalist views aligned with the interests of the Kremlin and he was elevated to scholarly superstar status, his books on every shelf, interviewed on every television channel. Then official policy changed, and Dugin – who for a while was being described as 'Putin's brain' in the West – was no longer needed. The TV appearances dried up, and he even lost his position at Moscow State University. Yet still he stayed loyal – what else was there for him? There were so many others: Vladislav Surkov, the grand choreographer of Russia's sham political system, even former president Dmitry Medvedev, relegated to a busywork position when he was no longer of value. What was different about Prigozhin was his bull-headed unwillingness ultimately to bend the knee – and the fact that he had that army to make resistance just about plausible.

His rebellion was a failure on Putin's part. Central to his political system is the constant competition between rival institutions, factions and individuals. Keeping the adhocrats snapping at each other for assets, status and his favour allows him to maintain his power. However, the corollary is that Putin – and only Putin – is the ring-master. It is he who can ultimately resolve their disputes, elevate one and demean another. Yet at the same time it is he who is expected to be able to see when such struggles risk becoming a threat to the whole system. For months, it was clear that Prigozhin's feud with the MoD was becoming a problem, yet he failed to act. Perhaps he was hoping to protect his friend Shoigu yet retain Prigozhin's services; perhaps, as so often, when he didn't see an easy answer, he prevaricated. Either way, a sharp-toothed and -eyed elite noted that Putin had failed to prevent this crisis. They also noticed that he panicked and gave away too much in his desire to end it. Finally, they were dismayed by the way Putin essentially reneged on that deal: this kind of a system depends on a degree of trust, at least within the 'gang'. Putin may break his word with outsiders, even blithely ignore international law, but this was the first time he had clearly gone against an undertaking made with an insider. They fell in line, of course. After all, the old man had just killed Prigozhin. But the sense that Putin was no longer the Putin of earlier years, the masterful manager of the system, was pervasive – and may yet come to haunt him.

Besides, Putin's chronic propensity to rely on private actors to drive state policy is not just part of a global trend towards the privatisation of the state. It is, at its core, an admission of a moral and ideological vacuum at the heart of 'Putinism'. Elected – or rather, selected

– in 1999–2000 as an effective manager to safeguard the interests of a cabal of corrupt officials and businessmen, Putin emerged at a time when everything, including values, was for sale. At the time, perhaps, he served a certain purpose, providing a sense of stability for a country exhausted by political turmoil. But by 2012 society had started demanding something more from him than just pragmatism. Stability and a small share in national prosperity were no longer enough, they wanted purpose, a faith in something greater.

While he makes much of his Russian Orthodoxy, that kind of faith was precisely what he lacked. In 2014, he had just enough confidence to annex Crimea when the opportunity presented itself, but was too timid to go further and make a decisive commitment: either put a stop to the neo-imperialist volunteers and ambitiously statist security factions he had unleashed, or go all in and invade Ukraine in accordance with their hopes. Putin wanted it both ways: to rely on the vision of his serfs when he himself had none, but still treat them as serfs, even as they came to the brink of realising their vision. When he finally invaded a fully mobilised Ukraine in 2022, he faced a government that seemed outgunned in the purely military–technical sense, but was armed with something the Russian government didn't have: vision and purpose. To compensate for that, he leaned, once again, on Prigozhin's private army.

The trouble was that Prigozhin began to see an actual purpose in the war. His troll farms may have started out as a calculated bid to score points in the changing political climate, but the irony is that, to a degree, he ultimately came to *believe* in their rhetoric. The mercenaries who joined Wagner may have initially done so enticed by a handsome compensation package, but by the time they came to fight in Ukraine, many came to wonder if it was patriotic to be opposed to the official line. Putin's Kremlin wasn't fighting for the Russian-speaking Ukrainians it claimed to be defending, or even for the Russian people as a whole. It was fighting to keep itself in power, to keep stealing from the Russian people, at the cost of thousands of Russian lives, and they could see that, even if they still supported the war itself.

Here is the irony. Prigozhin was no philosopher or moralist, and his men were largely cutthroats and desperados. They were no closet humanitarians, quite the opposite. The vision they had for Russia was often a horrifying one: of a war of conquest to 'reclaim' former Soviet territories, or of a revanchist, neo-Soviet order cleansing itself from the enemy within with Stalinist savagery (Prigozhin himself memorably said that 'Comrade Stalin was absolutely right' about the need to execute those getting in the way of the war effort).[22] Yet there is one common thread that connects all the varied forms of opposition to Putin's regime, from liberal opposition leader Alexei Navalny, through the few within the Communist Party who have not been bought off by the state, to the moderate nationalists and all the way to the 'turbo-patriots': a desire to see greater fairness come to

Russia. It may sound banal, and there is ample room to disagree on what the unfairnesses embodied within Putin's system may be, from economic inequality to the absence of meaningful democracy, yet it stems from a common sense that whatever Putin still offers, it is hollow, and that he has somehow shortchanged the nation.

Prigozhin's 'March of Justice' was many things – but it was also sincere. In his diatribes, Prigozhin may have been lashing out at Shoigu and Gerasimov, but he was more generally giving voice to a mounting sense of injustice, the recognition of a vapid, dishonest system of which Shoigu and Gerasimov were an integral part – a system that claimed to be about justice and values, but which was in reality one in which serfs would always be serfs and masters would aways be masters. Prigozhin used that brutal system to his own advantage, and, indeed, replicated it within his own structures. But what he exposed with his mutiny and his death was the hollowness of an aging regime that didn't believe in anything. Prigozhin and his men were fighting for a vision of Russia that Putin was too old, too tired and too weak to have, and so Prigozhin's ghost will likely haunt him for the rest of his reign.

There was more to Prigozhin than business, guns, money and sledgehammers, even if they came to shape his life and his death. In 2003, long before Prigozhin got anywhere near politics, when his daughter Polina was 11 and his son Pavel was 5, he sat down with them and, with stories about an imaginary world that they invented, created a children's book called *Indraguzik*. It recounts the adventures of Indraguzik, one of a kingdom of tiny people who live in a chandelier. Their king suffers a calamity: for unexplained reasons, he begins to shrink in size. With the help of his friends and a magic flute, Indraguzik saves the king and makes him grow again. But his efforts prove too much: the king gets so large that his head breaks through the roof of his castle. 'Please do something to make me the same king I was! After all, the Indraguziks only need a little king!' the ruler pleads. Indraguzik saves the king and, using the same magic flute, brings him back to his normal size.

Prigozhin could not have known, when he wrote this, that he would end up inflating Putin's actual size so much. Through his interference campaigns, through his projects on the African continent, and through the relative competence of his private army in Ukraine, he made Putin seem more powerful than he actually was, the grandmaster of a global campaign to undermine the West, rather than the ageing autocrat perched atop a rapacious kleptocracy. But his attempt to cut him back down to size showed that, on some level, a man like Prigozhin – a foul-mouthed ex-con who took pride in hounding his detractors and having defectors bludgeoned to death – had more faith in himself than the president of Russia. He may be in hell now, but Prigozhin was never one to aim low, and he may even now be seeking, to echo one of his films, to become 'the best in hell'.

Epilogue

As this book goes to print, it's excruciatingly difficult to imagine Russia's future, leading some to throw up their hands in desperation and assume it doesn't have one at all. They are wrong, of course: every country has a future, and no matter how repressive, how obsessed with war and death its current leaders may be, Russia has survived worse, and it will survive this.

But the despair about its current predicament – whether much will change in our lifetime, and whether things will get worse before they get better – is understandable. Vladimir Putin successfully stifled any opposition to his rule or his political course, winning an entirely predictable and thoroughly stage-managed re-election in 2024, and looks poised to continue his proxy war with the West as long as he is in power. The most prominent opposition leader in Russia, Alexei Navalny, has died in a prison camp, leading many to ask whether his hope for a 'beautiful Russia of the future' had died with it. Nearly a year has passed since Prigozhin's mutiny – a brief period when it looked like Putin's rule balanced on the edge of a precipice – and Russia's future again looks bleak. Yet in his own way, Prigozhin both highlighted and exacerbated growing tensions within Putin's system, which will one day break it apart.

In April 2023, in one of his more prophetic interviews – one, tellingly, scrubbed from sites accessible in Russia – Prigozhin, in signature fashion, railed about saving Russia. Not from Ukraine or from the West, but from itself.

> The issue isn't about conquering the world. Of course we won't. The issue is to not have to tolerate the fucking shame. For the last ten years, I have been fighting tooth and nail for this country so that it at least looks great.[1]

Ten years ago, of course, is when he was first being sounded out as a possible mercenary *condottiere*, but the point is that increasingly he wasn't simply fighting *for* his country, but *with* it. This was the ultimate adhocrat, a man whose willingness to work for Putin and his regime had brought him wealth, fame, and the opportunity to visit his malice on enemies and rivals alike, coming to realise how that very system was not uplifting Russia, but holding it down.

Where was the hope, what was the answer? Some alternative political operator, the liberal metropolitans? Of course not. It was in the 'guys' – not just his guys, but all the guys, the same ordinary Russian people who had toppled tsar and Party general secretary alike. Watching his men dying in droves for Bakhmut, he was clearly thinking about a wider future of the country for which he and they were fighting, and clearly horrified that he couldn't see one.

> Guys, come on, rise up in the trenches with your pitch-forks already!

What could happen if they didn't? Prigozhin was even then, two months before his mutiny, aware of the risks Russia was facing – and that he was taking by publicly acknowledging them:

> It's better if you kill me, but I cannot lie. Russia stands on the threshold of a catastrophe. If you don't tighten the bolts, the airplane will crumble in mid-air.

Of course, it is possible to read too much in one angry interview. This was no political manifesto for reform, any more than he predicted his own death in an airplane crumbling in mid-air. Nonetheless, it is striking how this crude, grasping and vindictive man still came to understand and despise so many of the weaknesses and injustices of the system which had elevated him from ex-con to magnate: the lies, the contempt of the rulers for the ruled.

It is impossible to know how far he ended up truly motivated by a sense of dismay and anger at what he saw happening to Russia, but it is undeniable that this became an increasingly central element of his public statements. His sense that it was the people – and the guys at the front, in particular – who represented the best of Russian society, even as they brutalised the Ukrainians and each other, mirrors the views of many 'turbo-patriots', who combine ultra-nationalist views with contempt for Putin and his circle. They did not have a problem with the invasion of Ukraine so much as the incompetence, corruption, and amateurishness with which it was conducted. Though still a small minority, they are disproportionately represented within the military and security apparatus. The arrest and conviction after the mutiny of one of the most prominent 'turbo-patriots', Igor 'Strelkov' Girkin – even though he was no friend of Prigozhin's, whom he called a liar and a psychopath – was a sign of mounting Kremlin concern about the threat they could pose.

Besides, Prigozhin's apparent belief that it was the 'guys' who could save Russia reflects a deep historical trope. From the popular militias who helped drive invading Poles out of Moscow in the seventeenth century (known as *opolchentsy*, the very term later used in 2014 for the Donbas fighters) to the nineteenth-century Populists who believed they could stir up revolution in the countryside, to Putin's own appeal to the supposed 'silent majority' during the 2011–12 Bolotnaya protests, there has been a strong and sentimental tradition of the virtue in the masses – and their capacity to reshape the world once their long-suffering patience was exhausted.

One thing Putin's regime has not faced is a serious and unified blue-collar challenge. The thought that Navalny could extend his crusade beyond the middle classes was one reason why the Kremlin decided it had to eliminate him. Prigozhin likewise was a threat precisely because he highlighted the regime's betrayal of the 'guys' on whom it depended, and who could talk to them in their own language.

And, indeed, even of so many within the elite. Putin's system has been designed to feed and protect himself and his friends, yet depends on the officials', entrepreneurs' and adhocrats' willingness to continue to squabble for the relative crumbs falling from their table. What does it say, when even someone like Prigozhin finds himself questioning this system, and when his mutiny demonstrates how many within both the security forces and the political elite were unwilling to stand up for it?

Prigozhin was no revolutionary, let alone a liberal. He was driven largely by self-interest, desperation, and a bloody-minded refusal to admit defeat. Nonetheless, his rise and fall demonstrates not just how the Putin system works, but how it is beginning to fail. The monarch no longer seems so capable of overseeing his feuding court: he failed to appreciate the danger in Prigozhin's feud with Shoigu and put off dealing with it for too long. Yet this was not just about a clash between two warlords. The adhocrats more generally are getting frustrated paying the price to protect and serve Putin's closest cronies; as Western sanctions bite, it is the latter whose fortunes are being protected, often at the expense of the former. The security forces, once Putin's final backstop of power, are discontent, and were not even eager to resist the mutiny. The Russian people, facing worsening standards of living and the threat of being drafted to Putin's bloody war in Ukraine, are restive. This is not a recipe for imminent revolution, necessarily, but rather the signs of weakness in a regime which has been holding back the pressures for change for twenty-four years now.

In what appears an odd comparison, Prigozhin and Navalny had very little in common in their respective rebellions – one sudden and violent while the other constructive, protracted, and long-term – but they shared a belief in Russia's future. If, unlike Navalny, he had no clear vision, Prigozhin had at least articulated the right question to ask: what are we fighting for?

Democratic institutions arise when the classes and factions battling for security and resources become tired of the fight, and recognise that the state power on which they rely to protect them and resolve their squabbles no longer does its job. They recognise the need for impartial rules to protect them from each other, and articulate those rules based on the years of vicious conflict that preceded. They have different visions for the future of their country, but they all believe it exists, and have the will to build those visions. It may take years or generations, but the conversation has already started.

There are reasons why so many Russians believe Prigozhin faked his own death (he is in Cuba! In Venezuela!

In Africa!) and, as the nationalist Orthodox media outlet *Tsargrad* coyly put it, 'at a critical moment will come to the rescue and "settle" problems in his signature style'.[2] It is not that they truly see him as their saviour, but that they recognise his scathing assessment of the system he knew so well, and they are starved of hope. Nonetheless, someday, democracy will be coming to Russia, and although he is hardly a suitable banner-bearer for reform, Prigozhin's disruptive mutiny and critique will have played its part in that process.

Notes

Chapter 1: Thug

1 All this is according to the court documents for Case No. I-I75 in the Leningrad City Court Judicial Collegium for Criminal Cases of the Leningrad City Court of 17 December 1981, the unsuccessful appeal by Prigozhin and Alexei Bushman against their conviction on 6 October 1981.

2 Ilya Davlyatchin, «Бурная молодость "кремлевского ресторатора"», *Rosbalt*, 21 September 2018, https://www.rosbalt.ru/piter/2018/09/21/1733712.html.

3 «Биография членов семьи Евгения Пригожина», *Stories of Success*, https://stories-of-success.ru/statyi/chlenov-semi-evgeniya-prigozhina.

4 Yevgeny Vyshenkov, «Евгений Пригожин: "Я пошел к Беглову, он к Медведеву, тот к Путину"», *Gorod 812*, 20 February 2018 (reprint of interview published in 2011), https://gorod-812.ru/evgeniy-prigozhin-ya-poshel-k-beglovu-k-medvedevu-tot-k-putinu/.

5 Maya Novik, «Зарплата как у министров: Когда и кто из обычных людей в СССР получал зарплаты министров», *Life*, 19 February 2022, https://life.ru/p/1472180.

6 Conversation with Anna Arutunyan, August 2023.

7 «Кто такой Евгений Пригожин и чем он запомнился. Только важное и интересное», *Sekret Firmy*, 23 August 2023, https://secretmag.ru/enciklopediya/evgenii-prigozhin.htm.

8 Andrei Zakharov, Katya Arenina, Yekaterina Reznikova and Mikhail Rubin, «Шеф и повар. Часть 5. Портрет Евгения Пригожина, персонального садиста при президенте России», *Proyekt*, 13 July 2013, https://www.proekt.media/portrait/evgeniy-prigozhin/.

9 Ilya Davlyatchin, «Бурная молодость «кремлевского ресторатора», *Rosbalt*, 21 September 2018, https://www.rosbalt.ru/piter/2018/09/21/1733712.html.

10 «Последние дни СССР глазами журналистов», *Voice of*

America, 23 November 2011, https://www.golosameriki.com/a/fall-of-the-soviet-union-panel-2011-11-23-134433033/248708.html.

11 Mark Galeotti, *The Vory: Russia's Super Mafia* (Yale, 2018).

12 Julian O'Shaughnessy, 'Smear campaign exposes sordid past of Wagner Group boss Yevgeny Prigozhin', *The Times*, 23 December 2022, https://www.thetimes.co.uk/article/wagner-group-boss-yevgeny-prigozhin-putin-russia-infighting-kznb69dfq.

13 Andrei Zakharov, Katya Arenina, Yekaterina Reznikova and Mikhail Rubin, «Шеф и повар. Часть 5. Портрет Евгения Пригожина, персонального садиста при президенте России», *Proyekt*, 13 July 2013, https://www.proekt.media/portrait/evgeniy-prigozhin/.

14 «Кто такой Евгений Пригожин и чем он запомнился. Только важное и интересное», *Sekret Firmy*, 23 August 2023, https://secretmag.ru/enciklopediya/evgenii-prigozhin.htm.

15 Shaun Walker and Pjotr Sauer, 'Yevgeny Prigozhin: the hotdog seller who rose to the top of Putin's war machine', *Guardian*, 24 January 2023, https://www.theguardian.com/world/2023/jan/24/yevgeny-prigozhin-the-hotdog-seller-who-rose-to-the-top-of-putin-war-machine-wagner-group.

Chapter 2: Entrepreneur

1 Yevgeny Vyshenkov, «Евгений Пригожин: "Я пошел к Беглову, он к Медведеву, тот к Путину"», *Gorod 812*, 20 February 2018 (reprint of interview published in 2011), https://gorod-812.ru/evgeniy-prigozhin-ya-poshel-k-beglovu-k-medvedevu-tot-k-putinu/.

2 Ibid.

3 Andrei Zakharov, Katya Arenina, Yekaterina Reznikova and Mikhail Rubin, «Шеф и повар. Часть 5. Портрет Евгения Пригожина, персонального садиста при президенте России», *Proyekt*, 13 July 2013, https://www.proekt.media/portrait/evgeniy-prigozhin/.

4 Oleg Blotsky, Владимир Путин: история жизни, vol. 1 (Izdatelstvo Mezhdunarodnie Otnosheniya, 2001), p. 68.

5 Irina Ivoilova, Sergei Mikheyev and Aleksandr Shanskov, «Николай Кропачев: Владимир Путин диплом защитил

на "отлично"», *Rossiiskaya Gazeta*, 18 June 2014, https://rg.ru/2014/06/18/kropachev-dz.html.

6   Conversation with Arutunyan, Moscow, 2019.

7   According to a friend who recalled how Putin would talk about dissidents and Solzhenitsyn in particular. Yuri Felshtynsky and Vladimir Pribylovsky, *The Corporation: Russia and the KGB in the Age of President Putin* (Encounter Books, 2008), p. 41.

8   Masha Gessen, *The Man Without a Face: The Unlikely Rise of Vladimir Putin* (Granta, 2013).

9   Anna Arutunyan, *The Putin Mystique: Inside Putin's Power Cult* (Skyscraper, 2014), p. 87.

10 Ibid., p. 91.

11 This and subsequent quotations come from a series of interviews Putin gave in 2000 to Andrei Kolesnikov, Natalia Timakova and Natalia Gevorkyan. *От первого лица. Разговоры с Владимиром Путиным* (Vagrius, 2000), http://archive.kremlin.ru/articles/bookchapter6.shtml.

12 Karen Dawisha, *Putin's Kleptocracy: Who Owns Russia?* (Simon & Schuster, 2015), pp. 21–4.

13 Yevgeny Vyshenkov, «Евгений Пригожин: "Я пошел к Беглову, он к Медведеву, тот к Путину"», *Gorod 812*, 20 February 2018 (reprint of interview published in 2011), https://gorod-812.ru/evgeniy-prigozhin-ya-poshel-k-beglovu-k-medvedevu-tot-k-putinu/.

14 Nina Petlyanova, «Рецепт успеха личного повара Путина», *Novaya Gazeta*, 14 October 2011, https://novayagazeta.ru/articles/2011/10/14/46298-retsept-uspeha-lichnogo-povara-putina.

15 Andrei Zakharov, Katya Arenina, Yekaterina Reznikova and Mikhail Rubin, «Шеф и повар. Часть 5. Портрет Евгения Пригожина, персонального садиста при президенте России», *Proyekt*, 13 July 2013, https://www.proekt.media/portrait/evgeniy-prigozhin/.

16 «Расследование: как личный кулинар Путина накормит армию за 92 млрд рублей», *Forbes*, 17 March 2013, https://www.forbes.ru/kompanii/potrebitelskii-rynok/235779-rassledovanie-kak-lichnyi-kulinar-putina-nakor-mit-rossiiskuyu-a?page=0,2.

17 «Внимание к мелочам: ресторатор Тони Гир рассказал, как Пригожин создал "Старую таможню"» ('Attention to

detail: restaurateur Tony Gear on how Prigozhin created "Staraya Tamozhnya"'), *Argumenty Nedeli*, 5 December 2022, https://argumenti.ru/society/2022/12/802433.

18 Ilya Zhegulyov, «Расследование: как личный кулинар Путина накормит армию за 92 млрд рублей», *Forbes*, 17 March 2013, https://www.forbes.ru/kompanii/potrebitelskii-rynok/235779-rassledovanie-kak-lichnyi-kulinar-putina-nakormit-rossiiskuyu-a.

19 Maxim Leonov, «Яд для "охранника Путина"», *Novaya Gazeta*, 31 August 2020, https://novayagazeta.ru/articles/2020/08/31/86901-yad-dlya-ohrannika-putina.

20 As of writing, Kumarin (also known as Barsukov) is in prison, having been sentenced to 24 years, in 2019, for his role in founding and heading the Tambov group.

21 «С кем враждует, "повар Путина"», *Vazhnye istorii*, 28 December 2022, https://istories.media/opinions/2022/12/28/s-kem-vrazhduet-povar-putina/.

22 Andrei Zakharov, Katya Arenina, Yekaterina Reznikova and Mikhail Rubin, «Шеф и повар. Часть 5. Портрет Евгения Пригожина, персонального садиста при президенте России», *Proyekt*, 13 July 2013. https://www.proekt.media/portrait/evgeniy-prigozhin/.

Chapter 3: Chef

1 Alexander Herzen, Былое и думы, Collected Works, vol. 4 (Goslitizdat, 1975), pp. 41–2.

2 Yevgeny Vyshenkov, «Евгений Пригожин: "Я пошел к Беглову, он к Медведеву, тот к Путину"», *Gorod 812*, 20 February 2018 (reprint of interview published in 2011). https://gorod-812.ru/evgeniy-prigozhin-ya-poshel-k-beglovu-k-medvedevu-tot-k-putinu/.

3 Illya Zhegulyov, «Кормилец президента», *Forbes*, 1 March 2012, https://www.forbes.ru/forbes/issue/2012-03-1/234794-kormilets-prezidenta.

4 «Внимание к мелочам: ресторатор Тони Гир рассказал, как Пригожин создал "Старую таможню"», *Argumenty Nedeli*, 5 December 2022, https://argumenti.ru/society/2022/12/802433.

5 Ibid.

6   Ilya Zhegulyov, «Кормилец президента», *Forbes*, 1 March 2012, https://www.forbes.ru/forbes/issue/2012-03-1/234794-kormilets-prezidenta.

7   «От элитных ресторанов до ЧВК: Евгений Пригожин в 15 фотографиях», *RBC*, 24 August 2023, https://www.rbc.ru/photoreport/24/08/2023/64e643779a79471f13817f22.

8   «Внимание к мелочам: ресторатор Тони Гир рассказал, как Пригожин создал "Старую таможню"», *Argumenty Nedeli*, 5 December 2022, https://argumenti.ru/society/2022/12/802433.

9   According to the journalist Andrei Zakharov, who took a picture of the painting. https://t.me/zakharovchannel/1017.

10 «Внимание к мелочам: ресторатор Тони Гир рассказал, как Пригожин создал "Старую таможню"», *Argumenty Nedeli*, 5 December 2022, https://argumenti.ru/society/2022/12/802433.

11 Yevgeny Vyshenkov, «Евгений Пригожин: "Я пошел к Беглову, он к Медведеву, тот к Путину"», *Gorod 812*, 20 February 2018 (reprint of interview published in 2011), https://gorod-812.ru/evgeniy-prigozhin-ya-poshel-k-beglovu-k-medvedevu-tot-k-putinu/.

12 Irina Tumakova, «Обед молчания», *Novaya Gazeta*, 26 November 2019, https://novayagazeta.ru/articles/2019/11/26/82879-obed-molchaniya.

13 Alice Speri, 'Hacked Resume Gives Inside Look at Wagner Group Founder Yevgeny Prigozhin', *The Intercept*, 2 March 2023, https://theintercept.com/2023/03/02/yevgeny-prigozhin-hacked-resume/.

14 Shaun Walker and Pjotr Sauer, 'Yevgeny Prigozhin: the hotdog seller who rose to the top of Putin's war machine', *Guardian*, 24 January 2023, https://www.theguardian.com/world/2023/jan/24/yevgeny-prigozhin-the-hotdog-seller-who-rose-to-the-top-of-putin-war-machine-wagner-group.

15 Yevgeny Vyshenkov, «Евгений Пригожин: "Я пошел к Беглову, он к Медведеву, тот к Путину"», *Gorod 812*, 20 February 2018 (reprint of interview published in 2011), https://gorod-812.ru/evgeniy-prigozhin-ya-poshel-k-beglovu-k-medvedevu-tot-k-putinu/.

16 Khodorkovsky, speaking of Putin, then prime minister, in 1998, called him his boss, and joked about his assets: 'I don't

own anything, I rent it' from the state, even though legally he owned it. Steve Liesman and Andrew Higgins, 'Some Astonishing Missteps Helped Grease the Slope', *Wall Street Journal*, 23 September 1998, https://www.wsj.com/articles/SB906436850722683000.

17 Yuri Lvov and Konstantin Smirnov, «Тридцать три путинских богатыря», *Kommersant Vlast*, 13 November 2001, https://www.kommersant.ru/doc/290986.

18 «Юмашев рассказал, благодаря кому Путин оказался в администрации президента», *Vedomosti*, 22 November 2019, https://www.vedomosti.ru/politics/news/2019/11/22/816968-kak-putin-prishel.

19 In a leaked telephone call, Prigozhin referred to Sechin and Zolotov as ready to rise up against Defence Minister Sergei Shoigu in March 2022. «Предполагаемый разговор между Пригожиным и Ахмедовым с критикой войны: как развивались события», *Voice of American Russian Service*, 27 March 2023, https://www.golosameriki.com/a/prigozhin-akhmedov-razgovor-utechka/7024121.html.

Chapter 4: Minigarch

1 Yevgeny Vyshenkov, «Евгений Пригожин: "Я пошел к Беглову, он к Медведеву, тот к Путину"», *Gorod 812*, 20 February 2018 (reprint of interview published in 2011), https://gorod-812.ru/evgeniy-prigozhin-ya-poshel-k-beglovu-k-medvedevu-tot-k-putinu/.

2 Anastasia Savinykh, «Солдат и школьников накормят из пакета», *Izvestia*, 21 September 2010, https://iz.ru/news/366135.

3 Greg Rosalsky, 'How Putin Conquered Russia's Oligarchy', NPR, 29 March 2022, https://www.npr.org/sections/money/2022/03/29/1088886554/how-putin-conquered-russias-oligarchy.

4 Sabrina Tavernise, 'Putin exerting his authority meets with Russia's tycoons', *New York Times*, 29 July 2000, https://www.nytimes.com/2000/07/29/world/putin-exerting-his-authority-meets-with-russia-s-tycoons.html.

5 «Пригожин Евгений Викторович Основатель Конкорд

Кейтеринг», *Delovoi Peterburg*, https://whoiswho.dp.ru/cart/person/93639.

6   Conversation with Mark Galeotti, Moscow, April 2017.

7   «От элитных ресторанов до ЧВК: Евгений Пригожин в 15 фотографиях», *RBC*, 24 August 2023, https://www.rbc.ru/photoreport/24/08/2023/64e643779a79471f13817f22.

8   Yevgeny Vyshenkov, «Евгений Пригожин: "Я пошел к Беглову, он к Медведеву, тот к Путину"», *Gorod 812*, 20 February 2018 (reprint of interview published in 2011), https://gorod-812.ru/evgeniy-prigozhin-ya-poshel-k-beglovu-k-medvedevu-tot-k-putinu/.

9   'Vladimir Putin and Bill Clinton had their first meeting as the US president visited Moscow', Official Site of the President of Russia, 3 June 2000, http://en.kremlin.ru/events/president/news/38511. See also Patrick Tyler, 'Clinton and Putin meet at Kremlin with wide agenda', *New York Times*, 4 June 2000, https://www.nytimes.com/2000/06/04/world/clinton-and-putin-meet-at-kremlin-with-wide-agenda.html.

10 «Где отмечал день рождения Владимир Путин», *Kommersant*, 8 October 2003, https://www.kommersant.ru/doc/417825.

11 Yevgeny Vyshenkov, «Евгений Пригожин: "Я пошел к Беглову, он к Медведеву, тот к Путину"», *Gorod 812*, 20 February 2018 (reprint of interview published in 2011), https://gorod-812.ru/evgeniy-prigozhin-ya-poshel-k-beglovu-k-medvedevu-tot-k-putinu/.

12 Anna Arutunyan was at one of these meetings, Moscow, spring 2008.

13 'V. Putin and Mechel steel – В.Путин о Мечеле и докторах', https://www.youtube.com/watch?v=y2SEXLQFuak.

14 Catherine Belton, Rachel Morarjee and Charles Clover, 'Steel group dives after Putin attack', *Financial Times*, 29 July 2008, https://www.ft.com/content/88f6033e-5d94-11dd-8129-000077b07658.

15 See a video of the televised meeting, https://www.youtube.com/watch?v=48Kk7kobMQY.

16 Stephen Grey, Jason Bush and Roman Anin, 'Special Report: Billion-dollar medical project helped fund "Putin's palace"', Reuters, 21 May 2014, https://www.reuters.

com/article/us-russia-capitalism-health-special-repo-idINBREA4K0D220140521.

17 Yevgeny Vyshenkov, «Евгений Пригожин: "Я пошел к Беглову, он к Медведеву, тот к Путину"», *Gorod 812*, 20 February 2018 (reprint of interview published in 2011), https://gorod-812.ru/evgeniy-prigozhin-ya-poshel-k-beglovu-k-medvedevu-tot-k-putinu/.

18 Ilya Zhegulyov, «Кормилец президента», *Forbes*, 1 March 2012, https://www.forbes.ru/forbes/issue/2012-03-1/234794-kormilets-prezidenta.

19 US Department of the Treasury, 'Treasury Targets Financier's Illicit Sanctions Evasion Activity', press release, 15 July 2020, https://home.treasury.gov/news/press-releases/sm1058.

20 «Несовершеннолетняя дочь Пригожина стала владелицей отеля в Петербурге – "Можем объяснить"», *The Insider*, 9 November 2022, https://theins.ru/news/256832.

21 The Russian press at the time and since included numerous claims as to Mirilashvili's alleged gangster connections. See, for example, Maxim Maximov, «За кого сидите, Михал Михалыч?», Fontanka, 26 February 2001, https://www.fontanka.ru/2001/02/26/60872/; Кто такой МММ «Ловушка для олигарха», *Novaya Gazeta*, 2 April 2001, https://novayagazeta.ru/articles/2001/04/02/11991-lovushka-dlya-oligarha; and Yevgenii Kolesnikov, «МММ не про Мавроди», Versiya, 17 April 2023, https://versia.ru/pochemu-avtoritetnyj-biznesmen-mixail-mirilashvili-brosil-svoi-torgovo-razvlekatelnye-aktivy. He himself has firmly and consistently denied them, and the one conviction against him, on kidnapping charges in 2003, was subsequently characterised by the European Court of Human Rights as unsafe as 'the proceedings in question, taken as a whole, had not satisfied the requirements of a 'fair hearing''.

22 Ilya Zhegulev, «Кормилец президента», *Forbes*, 1 March 2012, https://www.forbes.ru/forbes/issue/2012-03-1/234794-kormilets-prezidenta.

23 Ilya Davlyatchin and Maria Ilyina, «Повар не для всех», *Verstka*, 7 February 2023, https://verstka.media/povar-ne-dlia-vseh.

24 Yevgeny Vyshenkov, «Евгений Пригожин: "Я пошел к Беглову, он к Медведеву, тот к Путину"», *Gorod 812*, 20 February 2018 (reprint of interview published in 2011),

https://gorod-812.ru/evgeniy-prigozhin-ya-poshel-k-beglovu-k-medvedevu-tot-k-putinu/.

25 Ilya Zhegulyov, «Кормилец президента», *Forbes*, 1 March 2012, https://www.forbes.ru/forbes/issue/2012-03-1/234794-kormilets-prezidenta.

26 Denis Korotkov, «Пригожин подобрал остатки оборонного госзаказа», *Fontanka*, 22 August 2016, https://www.fontanka.ru/2016/08/17/153/.

27 Mikhail Maglov, Timur Olevskiy and Dmitry Treshchagin , 'Part 2. Patties for the dogs of war', *Scanner*, 10 May 2019, https://munscanner.com/2019/05/prigozhin2-en/.

28 Paul Roderick Gregory, ;What the Mueller report tells us about Putin, Russia and Trump's election', *The Hill*, 21 May 2019, https://thehill.com/opinion/white-house/444673-what-the-mueller-report-tells-us-about-putin-russia-and-trumps-election/.

29 Andrei Zakharov, Katya Arenina, Yekaterina Reznikova and Mikhail Rubin, «Шеф и повар. Часть 5. Портрет Евгения Пригожина, персонального садиста при президенте России», *Proyekt*, 13 July 2013, https://www.proekt.media/portrait/evgeniy-prigozhin/.

30 «Кортеж Пригожина взяли со спецназом», *Fontanka*, 30 May 2016, https://www.fontanka.ru/2016/05/30/024/.

31 «ФСБ не простила охране Пригожина сплетение рук», *Fontanka*, 8 September 2016, https://www.fontanka.ru/2016/09/08/101/.

32 Isabel van Brugen, '"Putin's Chef" Sued 560 Times for Supplying Russian Army with Rotten Food', *Newsweek*, 24 January 2023, https://www.newsweek.com/putins-chef-wagner-group-yevgeny-prigozhin-sued-rotten-food-1776138.

Chapter 5: Trollmaster

1 «Оппозиционеры в Москве встали в "Большой белый круг"», BBC Russian Service, 26 February 2012, https://www.bbc.com/russian/russia/2012/02/120226_big_white_circle.

2 Anna Arutunyan reported on the flashmob from the scene.

3 Nikita Girin and Diana Khachatryan, «Анатомия про тесто», *Novaya Gazeta*, 9 April 2012, https://novayagazeta.ru/articles/2012/04/08/49159-anatomiya-pro-testo.

4   'Medvedev backs Putin for president in 2012 election', Agence France-Presse, 24 September 2011, https://www.france24.com/en/20110924-medvedev-supports-putin-president-elections-russia.

5   Conversation with Arutunyan, Moscow, spring 2012.

6   Anastasia Strelkovskaya, «"Если люди приходят на митинги, власти нужно думать не о том, кто кого финансирует"», *Kommersant*, 15 December 2011, https://www.kommersant.ru/doc/1838828.

7   Guy Faulconbridge, 'Analysis: Russia's Putin risks losing touch amid protests', Reuters, 25 December 2011, https://jp.reuters.com/article/us-russia-putin/analysis-russias-putin-risks-losing-touch-amid-protests-idUKTRE7BO03K20111225.

8   Anna Arutunyan, *The Putin Mystique: Inside Russia's Power Cult* (Skyscraper Press, 2014), p. 228.

9   Nina Petlyanova, «Пищевая цепь Пригожиных», *Novaya Gazeta*, 26 October 2011, https://novayagazeta.ru/articles/2011/10/26/46491-pischevaya-tsep-prigozhinyh.

10 Nikita Girin and Diana Khachatryan, «Анатомия про тесто», *Novaya Gazeta*, 9 April 2012, https://novayagazeta.ru/articles/2012/04/08/49159-anatomiya-pro-testo.

11 Andrei Zakharov, Katya Arenina, Yekaterina Reznikova and Mikhail Rubin, «Шеф и повар. Часть 5. Портрет Евгения Пригожина, персонального садиста при президенте России», *Proyekt*, 13 July 2013, https://www.proekt.media/portrait/evgeniy-prigozhin/.

12 Nina Petlyanova, «Старо, как КГБ», *Novaya Gazeta*, 19 June 2013, https://novayagazeta.ru/articles/2013/06/19/55155-staro-kak-kgb.

13 «Маша Хари. Кто шпионит в российских СМИ», *Novaya Gazeta*, 26 June 2013, https://novayagazeta.ru/articles/2013/06/26/55249-kto-shpionit-v-rossiyskih-smi.

14 'Novaya Gazeta Report: "Putin's Chef" Involved in Attacks, Killing', RFE/RL, 22 October 2018, https://www.rferl.org/a/novaya-gazeta-reports-claims-of-putin-s-chef-involved-in-attacks-killing/29557806.html.

15 Irina Tumakova, «Обед молчания», *Novaya Gazeta*, 26 November 2019, https://novayagazeta.ru/articles/2019/11/26/82879-obed-molchaniya.

16 Denis Korotkov, «Повар со своими тараканами», *Novaya*

Gazeta, 8 November 2018, https://novayagazeta.ru/articles/2018/11/08/78496-provokatsii-prigozhina?utm_source=push.

17 «От первых комментаторов до гигантской сети. В медиагруппе "Патриот" рассказали, как зарождалась "фабрика троллей"», *Fontanka*, 30 June 2023, https://www.fontanka.ru/2023/06/30/72452711/.

18 Andrei Zakharov, Katya Arenina, Yekaterina Reznikova and Mikhail Rubin, «Шеф и повар. Часть 5. Портрет Евгения Пригожина, персонального садиста при президенте России», *Proyekt*, 13 July 2013, https://www.proekt.media/portrait/evgeniy-prigozhin/.

19 Alexandra Garmadzhapova, «Где живут тролли. И кто их кормит», *Novaya Gazeta*, 7 September 2013, https://novayagazeta.ru/articles/2013/09/07/56253-gde-zhivut-trolli-i-kto-ih-kormit.

20 «Красавицы ЧВК "Вагнер", кто они, дочери Евгения Пригожина, чем занимаются и как выглядят? Рассказываем, показываем», *Dzen*, 27 August 2022, https://dzen.ru/a/ZOsTJJNoLClpbXn9.

21 'What's next for Wagner chief Prigozhin's hydra-headed media empire?', *Politico*, 18 July 2023, https://www.politico.eu/article/whats-next-for-yevgeny-prigozhin-wagner-chief-media-empire-patriot/.

22 Ibid.

23 Denis Korotkov, «Повар со своими тараканами», *Novaya Gazeta*, 8 November 2018, https://novayagazeta.ru/articles/2018/11/08/78496-provokatsii-prigozhina.

24 Vladimir Isachenkov, 'Charged "Putin's chef" runs news sites along with troll army', Associated Press, 24 February 2018, https://apnews.com/article/e36c5768bbfe4f30916b46da3b3d0a6f.

25 Nick Penzenstadler, Brad Heath and Jessica Guynn, 'We read every one of the 3,517 Facebook ads bought by Russians. Here's what we found', *USA Today*, 11 May 2018, https://eu.usatoday.com/story/news/2018/05/11/what-we-found-facebook-ads-russians-accused-election-meddling/602319002/.

26 Emily Tamkin, 'This Is What $1.25 Million Dollars a Month Bought the Russians', *Foreign Policy*, 16 February 2018,

https://foreignpolicy.com/2018/02/16/this-is-what-1-25-million-dollars-a-month-bought-the-russians/.

27 Christopher Ingraham, 'Somebody just put a price tag on the 2016 election. It's a doozy', *Washington Post*, 14 April 2017, https://www.washingtonpost.com/news/wonk/wp/2017/04/14/somebody-just-put-a-price-tag-on-the-2016-election-its-a-doozy/.

28 Polina Rustaeva and Andrei Zakharov, «Расследование РБК: как "фабрика троллей" поработала на выборах в США», *RBC*, 17 October 2017, https://www.rbc.ru/magazine/2017/11/59e0c17d9a79470e05a9e6c1.

29 Conversation with Galeotti, Moscow, summer 2016.

30 Conversation with Arutunyan, Moscow, summer 2020.

31 Max Seddon, '"Putin's chef" who trolled the US election', *Financial Times*, 16 February 2018, https://www.ft.com/content/978b7c3a-1351-11e8-8cb6-b9ccc4c4dbbb.

32 Sergei Yarkovskii, «Вклад в сохранение памяти: фильм "Ржев" Евгения Пригожина и молодежные проекты помогают увековечивать имена героических предков», *FederalCity*, 7 September 2022, https://federalcity.ru/14469-vklad-v-sohranenie-pamjati-film-rzhev-evgenija-prigozhina-i-molodezhnye-proekty-pomogajut-uvekovechivat-imena-geroicheskih-predkov.html.

33 Scott Johnson, 'Before He Turned on Putin, Yevgeny Prigozhin Made Hollywood-Style Propaganda Films to Sell His War', *Hollywood Reporter*, 23 August 2023, https://www.hollywoodreporter.com/news/general-news/russia-wagner-group-prigozhin-propaganda-movies-1235507691/.

34 Under the terms of Ukrainian Presidential Decree No. 116/2023, 26 February 2023. The Foundation for the Defence of National Values is also sanctioned by the USA.

35 'Fake Film Critic "Anton Dolin" Praises Russian War Films', *Moscow Times*, 19 July 2021, https://www.themoscowtimes.com/2021/07/19/fake-film-critic-anton-dolin-praises-russian-war-films-a74553.

36 Dean Sterling Jones, 'How Russia's Top Propagandist Foretold Putin's Justification for the Ukraine Invasion Through this Dramatic Film', *BuzzFeed*, 11 March 2022, https://www.buzzfeednews.com/article/deansterlingjones/russia-yevgeny-prigozhin-ukraine-trump-giuliani-films.

Chapter 6: Condottiere

1   Gennady Zubov and German Petelin, «Вагнера ищет боевая подруга», *Gazeta*, 16 December 2016, https://www.gazeta.ru/social/2016/12/16/10431467.shtml.

2   Irek Murtazin, «Задачи ставили генералы», *Novaya Gazeta*, 29 June 2023, https://novayagazeta.ru/articles/2023/06/29/zadachi-stavili-generaly.

3   Technically, since 2010 the GRU (Main Intelligence Directorate of the General Staff) has simply been known as the GU (Main Directorate), but its older acronym is pretty much universally still used, even by Putin.

4   Anna Arutunyan's interview with Marat Gabidullin, 2023.

5   Yevgeny Prigozhin's post, 26 September 2022, https://vk.com/concordgroup_official?w=wall-177427428_1194.

6   This and following quotes from Arutunyan's interview with Marat Gabidullin, 2023.

7   Conversations, Moscow, February 2020.

8   See interviews in Anna Arutunyan, *Hybrid Warriors: Proxies, Freelancers and Russia's Struggle for Ukraine* (Hurst, 2022).

9   «Прошлое и будущее Пригожина», *Dossier Center*, 6 July 2023, https://dossier.center/wagner-fall/.

10 'Putin Chef's Kisses of Death: Russia's Shadow Army's State-Run Structure Exposed', *Bellingcat*, 14 August 2020, https://www.bellingcat.com/news/uk-and-europe/2020/08/14/pmc-structure-exposed/.

11 «Частная армия для президента: история самого деликатного поручения Евгения Пригожина», *The Bell*, 29 January 2019, https://thebell.io/41889-2.

12 Valery Gerasimov, «Ценность науки в предвидении», *Voyenno-promyshlennyi kurer*, 27 February 2013; see: https://inmoscowsshadows.wordpress.com/2014/07/06/the-gerasimov-doctrine-and-russian-non-linear-war/.

13 «Путин поддержал идею создания в России частных военных компаний», *Kommersant*, 11 April 2011, https://www.kommersant.ru/doc/1913423.

14 Moran is not a mercenary force but an established and reputable Russian private security company that does everything from mine clearing in Libya to providing armed guards for commercial shipping heading through pirate-infested waters.

15 «Последний бой "Славянского корпуса"», *Fontanka*, 14 November 2013, https://www.fontanka.ru/2013/11/14/060/.

16 Irina Malkova and Anton Bayev, «Частная армия для президента: история самого деликатного поручения Евгения Пригожина», *The Bell*, 29 January 2019, https://thebell.io/41889-2. Malkova and Bayev say that recruitment started in late 2013, but other sources place this later, in spring 2014.

17 «Прошлое и будущее Пригожина», *Dossier Center*, 6 July 2023, https://dossier.center/wagner-fall/.

18 This and subsequent quotes from interview with Anna Arutunyan, 2023.

19 'Putin Chef's Kisses of Death: Russia's Shadow Army's State-Run Structure Exposed', *Bellingcat*, 14 August 2020, https://www.bellingcat.com/news/uk-and-europe/2020/08/14/pmc-structure-exposed/.

20 «Частная армия для президента: история самого деликатного поручения Евгения Пригожина», *The Bell*, 29 January 2019. https://thebell.io/41889-2.

21 Telegram post by @NeogicialniyBeZsonoV, 9 July 2023, https://t.me/s/NeoficialniyBeZsonoV?before=28247.

22 Mark Galeotti, *We Need to Talk about Putin* (Ebury Press, 2019).

23 «'Славянский корпус' возвращается в Сирию», *Fontanka*, 16 October 2015, https://www.fontanka.ru/2015/10/16/118/.

24 Khazov-Kassia, «Проект "Мясорубка". Рассказывают три командира "ЧВК Вагнера"», Svoboda, 7 March 2018, https://www.svoboda.org/a/29084090.html.

25 «Последний бой "Славянского корпуса"», *Fontanka*, 14 November 2013, https://www.fontanka.ru/2013/11/14/060/.

26 Khazov-Kassia, «Проект "Мясорубка". Рассказывают три командира "ЧВК Вагнера"», Svoboda, 7 March 2018, https://www.svoboda.org/a/29084090.html.

27 «Они сражались за Пальмиру», *Fontanka*, 29 March 2016, https://www.fontanka.ru/2016/03/28/171/.

28 Ibid.

29 «Кухня частной армии», *Fontanka*, 9 June 2016, https://www.fontanka.ru/2016/06/09/070/.

30 «Россиянин из ЧВК "Вагнер" рассказал, как готовят

боевиков для Луганска и Донецка, – Путину лучше не слышать», *Dialog*, 17 May 2018, https://www.dialog.ua/war/151765_1526538145.

31 Claire Bigg, 'Vostok Battalion, a Powerful New Player in Eastern Ukraine', RFE/RL, 30 May 2014, https://www.rferl.org/a/vostok-battalion-a-powerful-new-player-in-eastern-ukraine/25404785.html.

32 «Полевой командир Мозговой убит под Луганском», *BBC News*, 24 May 2015, https://www.bbc.com/russian/international/2015/05/150524_ukraine_mozgovoi_killed.

33 «Батю подорвали Кто ликвидировал ехавшего на свою свадьбу казачьего атамана в ЛНР», *Lenta*, 14 December 2015, https://lenta.ru/articles/2015/12/14/batya/.

34 «Убит герой обороны Луганска – начштаба 4-й бригады ЛНР Александр Беднов, позывной "Бэтмен"», *Russkaya Vesna*, 2 January 2015, https://rusvesna.su/news/1420125547.

35 Yevgeny Norin, «Полевой командир года: "Вагнер"», *Sputnik I Pogrom*, 2015, https://sputnikipogrom.com/2015-in-review/48899/warlord-of-2015/. See also: «"Славянский корпус" возвращается в Сирию», *Fontanka*, 16 October 2015, https://www.fontanka.ru/2015/10/16/118/. See also Girkin's Telegram post from 6 March 2023, https://t.me/strelkovii/4129.

36 Conversations with Anna Arutunyan: Russian volunteer, pro-Novorossia political activist, Moscow, March 2018; Wagner fighter, Moscow, April 2018; Wagner fighter, Moscow, March 2020.

37 Vladimir Dergachev, «Российские наемники в боях за Пальмиру», *Gazeta*, 24 March 2016, https://www.gazeta.ru/politics/2016/03/22_a_8137565.shtml.

38 Denis Korotkov, «Вагнер в Кремле», *Fontanka*, 12 December 2016, https://www.fontanka.ru/2016/12/12/064/.

39 Conversation with Arutunyan, Moscow, February 2020.

40 'Statement by the President on Actions in Response to Russian Malicious Cyber Activity and Harassment', White House, 29 December 2016, https://obamawhitehouse.archives.gov/the-press-office/2016/12/29/statement-president-actions-response-russian-malicious-cyber-activity; Mike Eckel, 'Coup Plots, Poison, Hacking, Sabotage:

What Is The GRU's Unit 29155?', RFE/RL, 24 April 2021, https://www.rferl.org/a/gru-unit-29155-russian-military-intelligence/31220707.html.

41 Roland Oliphant, 'Inside ambitious mercenary outfit Redut, the Wagner rival linked to the Russian spy services', *Telegraph*, 24 August 2023, https://www.telegraph.co.uk/world-news/2023/08/24/redut-russia-yevgeny-prigozhin-plane-crash-rival/.

42 «Призраки войны: как в Сирии появилась российская частная армия», *RBC*, 25 August 2016, https://www.rbc.ru/magazine/2016/09/57bac4309a79476d978e850d.

43 «Командующий группировкой войск РФ в Сирии дал первое интервью – "РГ"», *Rossiiskaya Gazeta*, 23 March 2016, https://rg.ru/2016/03/23/aleksandr-dvornikov-dejstviia-rf-v-korne-perelomili-situaciiu-v-sirii.html.

44 Ilya Rozhdestvensky, Anton Baev and Polina Rusyaeva, «Призраки войны: как в Сирии появилась российская частная армия», *RBC*, 25 August 2016, https://www.rbc.ru/magazine/2016/09/57bac4309a79476d978e850d.

45 Conversation with Galeotti, Washington, DC, 2022.

46 «В Екатеринбурге полковник застрелился на учениях на глазах у командования, не выдержав критики», *News.ru*, 22 April 2004, https://www.newsru.com/arch/russia/22apr2004/colonel.html.

47 «Центр "Досье": генерал Суровикин был почетным членом ЧВК "Вагнер" с 2017 года», *Nastoyashchee Vremya*, 28 June 2023, https://www.currenttime.tv/a/surovikin-vagner/32480673.html.

48 Ilya Barabanov, «"Гопники не могут войти в историю". Краткая история взаимоотношений Пригожина и Суровикина», *LRT*, 6 June 2023, https://www.lrt.lt/ru/novosti/17/2029105/gopniki-ne-mogut-voiti-v-istoriiu-kratkaia-istoriia-vzaimootnoshenii-prigozhina-i-surovikina.

49 «Евгений Пригожин назвал генерала Суровикина легендарной личностью», *Argumenty i Fakty*, 8 October 2022, https://aif.ru/society/evgeniy_prigozhin_nazval_generala_surovikina_legendarnoy_lichnostyu.

50 Ilya Rozhdestvensky, Anton Baev and Polina Rusyaeva, «Призраки войны: как в Сирии появилась российская

частная армия», *RBC*, 25 August 2016, https://www.rbc.ru/magazine/2016/09/57bac4309a79476d978e850d.

51 Ilya Barabanov, «"Гопники не могут войти в историю". Краткая история взаимоотношений Пригожина и Суровикина», *LRT*, 6 June 2023, https://www.lrt.lt/ru/novosti/17/2029105/gopniki-ne-mogut-voiti-v-istoriiu-kratkaia-istoriia-vzaimootnoshenii-prigozhina-i-surovikina.

52 Andrei Guselnikov, «Боец ЧВК Вагнера: "Лафа закончилась после ссоры Шойгу и Пригожина"», 19 October 2018, https://ura.news/articles/1036276546.

53 Ilya Barabanov, «"Гопники не могут войти в историю". Краткая история взаимоотношений Пригожина и Суровикина», *LRT*, 6 June 2023, https://www.lrt.lt/ru/novosti/17/2029105/gopniki-ne-mogut-voiti-v-istoriiu-kratkaia-istoriia-vzaimootnoshenii-prigozhina-i-surovikina.

54 Khazov-Kassia, «Проект "Мясорубка". Рассказывают три командира "ЧВК Вагнера"», Svoboda, 7 March, 2018, https://www.svoboda.org/a/29084090.htmlhttps.

55 Anastasia Yakoreva and Svetlana Reiter, «"Ресторатор Путина" перестал быть любимым подрядчиком Минобороны», *The Bell*, 2 March 2018, https://thebell.io/restorator-putina-perestal-byt-lyubimym-podryadchikom-minoborony.

56 «Немного бизнеса в сирийской войне», *Fontanka*, 26 June 2017, https://www.fontanka.ru/2017/06/26/084/?ref=en.thebell.io.

57 'Russian mercenary army financier made an oil deal with Syria just before clash with US troops', *The Bell*, 27 February 2018, https://en.thebell.io/russian-mercenary-army-financier-made-oil-deal-syria-just-clash-u-s-troops/.

58 Kimberly Marten, 'The Puzzle of Russian Behavior in Deir Al-Zour', *War on the Rocks*, 5 July 2018, https://warontherocks.com/2018/07/the-puzzle-of-russian-behavior-in-deir-al-zour/.

59 'How a 4-Hour Battle Between Russian Mercenaries and US Commandos Unfolded in Syria', *New York Times*, 24 May 2018, https://www.nytimes.com/2018/05/24/world/middleeast/american-commandos-russian-mercenaries-syria.html.

60 «От 13 до 200 погибших. Что известно о гибели

российских бойцов в Сирии», *The Bell*, 13 February 2018, https://thebell.io/ot-13-do-200-pogibshih-chto-izvestno-o-gibeli-rossijskih-bojtsov-v-sirii.

61 'Russian mercenary army financier made an oil deal with Syria just before clash with US troops', *The Bell*, 27 February 2018, https://en.thebell.io/russian-mercenary-army-financier-made-oil-deal-syria-just-clash-u-s-troops/.

62 Ellen Nakashima, Karen DeYoung and Liz Sly, 'Putin ally said to be in touch with Kremlin, Assad before his mercenaries attacked US troops', *Washington Post*, 22 February 2018, https://www.washingtonpost.com/world/national-security/putin-ally-said-to-be-in-touch-with-kremlin-assad-before-his-mercenaries-attacked-us-troops/2018/02/22/f4ef050c-1781-11e8-8b08-027a6ccb38eb_story.html?ref=en.thebell.io.

63 Irina Malkova and Anton Baev, «Частная армия для президента: история самого деликатного поручения Евгения Пригожина», *The Bell*, 29 January 2019, https://thebell.io/41889-2.

64 Yevgeny Prigozhin's Telegram channel, 12 June 2023, https://telegra.ph/Evgenij-Prigozhin-o-tragedii-8-fevralya-2018-v-Hshame-06-12.

Chapter 7: Scavenger

1 Christophe Châtelot, Isabelle Mandraud and Marie Bourreau, 'La Centrafrique, un pion sur l'échiquier russe', *Le Monde*, 7 December 2018, https://www.lemonde.fr/international/article/2018/12/07/la-centrafrique-un-pion-sur-l-echiquier-russe_5394051_3210.html.

2 «О переговорах в Хартуме по урегулированию в Центральноафриканской Республике», Russian MFA statement, 31 August 2018, https://archive.mid.ru/web/guest/maps/cf/-/asset_publisher/obfEMxF2i9RB/content/id/3334252.

3 Irek Murtazin, «На этой кухне что-то готовится», *Novaya Gazeta*, 9 November 2018, https://novayagazeta.ru/articles/2018/11/09/78517-na-etoy-kuhne-chto-to-gotovitsya?utm_medium=desktop&utm_source=yxnews.

4 «СМИ объяснили участие Пригожина во встрече Шойгу

с ливийским маршалом», *RBC*, 9 November 2018, https://www.rbc.ru/rbcfreenews/5be5ddc09a7947e17d8f7d7a.

5 'Final Report on the Murder of Orkhan Dzhemal, Aleksandr Rastogruev and Kirill Radchenko in the Central African Republic', *Dossier Center*, 25 October 2019, https://dossier-center.appspot.com/car-en/.

6 'Putin's Private Army', CNN Special Report, August 2019, https://edition.cnn.com/interactive/2019/08/africa/putins-private-army-car-intl/.

7 David Lewis and Tena Prelec, 'New Dynamics in Illicit Finance and Russian Foreign Policy', SOC ACE Research Paper No. 17, University of Birmingham, 2022, https://news.exeter.ac.uk/wp-content/uploads/2023/08/SOCACE-RP17-NewDynamics-Aug23-avedit.pdf.

8 Murtaza Hussain, 'The Grisly Cult of the Wagner Group's Sledgehammer', *The Intercept*, 2 February 2023, https://theintercept.com/2023/02/02/wagner-group-violence-sledgehammer/

9 Catrina Doxsee and Jared Thompson, 'Massacres, Executions, and Falsified Graves: The Wagner Group's Mounting Humanitarian Cost in Mali', CSIS, 11 May 2022, https://www.csis.org/analysis/massacres-executions-and-falsified-graves-wagner-groups-mounting-humanitarian-cost-mali.

10 'Mali: Massacre by Army, Foreign Soldiers', Human Rights Watch, 5 April 2022, https://www.hrw.org/news/2022/04/05/mali-massacre-army-foreign-soldiers.

11 'Architects of Terror. The Wagner Group's Blueprint for State Capture in the Central African Republic', The Sentry, 2023, https://thesentry.org/wp-content/uploads/2023/06/ArchitectsTerror-TheSentry-June2023.pdf.

12 'Final Report on the Murder of Orkhan Dzhemal, Aleksandr Rastogruev and Kirill Radchenko in the Central African Republic', *Dossier Center*, 25 October 2019, https://dossier-center.appspot.com/car-en/.

13 Tim Lister and Sebastian Shukla, 'Murdered journalists were tracked by police with shadowy Russian links, evidence shows', CNN, 10 January 2019, https://edition.cnn.com/2019/01/10/africa/russian-journalists-car-ambush-intl/index.html.

14 'Russian Tycoon Prigozhin Offers Tombstone for Journalists Killed in Central Africa', *Moscow Times*, 15 January 2021, https://www.themoscowtimes.com/2021/01/15/russian-tycoon-prigozhin-offers-tombstone-for-journalists-killed-in-central-africa-a72622.

15 '"Putin's Chef" Has Sanctioned Jets Flying to Strange Destinations', *Hromadske*, 29 October 2019, https://hromadske.ua/en/posts/putins-chef-has-sanctioned-jets-flying-to-strange-destinations.

16 Miles Johnson, 'Horses, art and private jets: the charmed life of Russian warlord's family', *Financial Times*, 26 April 2023, https://www.ft.com/content/03137d7f-6ea0-45eb-9284-d8957a650ba4.

17 Evgeny Antonov, «Кто помогает Беглову стать следующим губернатором Петербурга и что будет, если он победит», *Bumaga*, 17 July 2019, https://paperpaper.io/kto-pomogaet-beglovu-stat-sleduyushim/.

18 Anton Mukhin, 'Prigozhin vs. Petersburg Governor: What a Feud Reveals about Russia's Power Vertical', *Carnegie Politika*, 6 December 2022, https://carnegieendowment.org/politika/88572.

19 Conversations with Arutunyan, Moscow and Sochi, October 2019.

20 This and following quotes from conversation with Arutunyan, Moscow, 2019.

21 US State Department official, conversation with Galeotti, Washington, DC, 2022.

22 Conversation with Arutunyan, Moscow, 2020.

23 Conversation with Arutunyan, Sochi, 2019.

24 «"Повар Путина" отправился добывать золото в Африку», *The Bell*, 4 June 2018, https://thebell.io/povar-putina-otpravilsya-dobyvat-zoloto-v-afriku.

25 Conversation with Arutunyan, Sochi, October 2019.

26 Nima Elbagir et al., 'Russia is plundering gold in Sudan to boost Putin's war effort in Ukraine', CNN, 29 July 2022, https://edition.cnn.com/2022/07/29/africa/sudan-russia-gold-investigation-cmd-intl/index.html.

27 Arutunyan's interview with Marat Gabidullin, 2023.

28 Conversation with Arutunyan, 2023.

29 Anton Shekhovtsov, 'The Globalisation of Pro-Kremlin

Networks of Politically Biased Election Observation: The Cases of Cambodia and Zimbabwe', European Platform for Democratic Elections, 2018, https://www.epde.org/en/news/details/the-globalisation-of-pro-kremlin-networks-of-politicallybiased-election-observation-the-cases-of-cambodia-and-zimbabwe-1686.html.

30 Jack Margolin, *The Wagner Group: Inside Russia's Mercenary Army* (Reaktion, 2024), n.p.

31 Pjotr Sauer, 'New Movie Depicting Heroic Russian Instructors in Central African Republic Linked to "Putin's Chef"', *Moscow Times*, 21 May 2021, https://www.themoscowtimes.com/2021/05/21/new-movie-depicting-heroic-russian-instructors-in-central-african-republic-linked-to-putins-chef-a73973.

32 Miles Johnson, 'Wagner leader generated $250mn from sanctioned empire', *Financial Times*, 21 February 2023, https://www.ft.com/content/98e478b5-c0d4-48a3-bcf7-e334a4ea0aca.

33 Conversation with Galeotti, London, 2019.

34 Conversation with Arutunyan, 2023.

Chapter 8: Warlord

1 Danila Galperovich, «Будущее наемников Пригожина: "Вагнер 2.0" или "ронины" в поисках заработка?», VOA, 1 September 2023, https://www.golosameriki.com/a/group-wagner-without-prigozhin-future/7250127.html.

2 «Жаба и Минобороны. Как поссорились Евгений Викторович с Сергеем Кужугетовичем», *The Insider*, 12 May 2023, https://theins.ru/politika/261683.

3 Lilia Yapparova, «Грубо говоря, мы начали войну», *Meduza*, 13 June 2022, https://meduza.io/feature/2022/07/13/grubo-govorya-my-nachali-voynu.

4 Lilia Yapparova, 'A mercenaries' war: How Russia's invasion of Ukraine led to a "secret mobilization" that allowed oligarch Evgeny Prigozhin to win back Putin's favor', *Meduza*, 14 July 2022, https://meduza.io/en/feature/2022/07/14/a-mercenaries-war.

5 Dean Sterling Jones, 'How Russia's Top Propagandist Foretold Putin's Justification for the Ukraine Invasion Through this Dramatic Film', *BuzzFeed*, 11 March 2022,

https://www.buzzfeednews.com/article/deansterlingjones/russia-yevgeny-prigozhin-ukraine-trump-giuliani-films.

6 Pjotr Sauer and Andrew Roth, '"Someone will fall victim": insiders reveal elite anguish as Russia's war falters', *Guardian*, 7 October 2022, https://www.theguardian.com/world/2022/oct/07/intense-dread-and-infighting-among-russian-elites-as-putins-war-falters.

7 Lilia Yapparova, «Грубо говоря, мы начали войну», *Meduza*, 13 June 2022, https://meduza.io/feature/2022/07/13/grubo-govorya-my-nachali-voynu.

8 «Кто такой Павел Пригожин и как он стал главой нашумевшей ЧВК "Вагнер"», *Sekret Firmy*, 1 November 2023, https://secretmag.ru/enciklopediya/kto-takoi-pavel-prigozhin.htm.

9 Kseniya Askerova, «Пригожин подтвердил участие сына в боевых действиях на Украине», RTVI, 24 September 2022, https://rtvi.com/news/prigozhin-podtverdil-uchastie-syna-v-boevyh-dejstviyah-na-ukraine/.

10 Grigorii Leiba, «Пригожин: в боях за Бахмут погибли 20 тыс. бойцов ЧВК "Вагнер"», *Kommersant*, 24 May 2023, https://www.kommersant.ru/doc/6001275.

11 SOTA's Telegram channel, 14 September 2022, https://t.me/sotaproject/46171.

12 Pjotr Sauer and Andrew Roth, '"Someone will fall victim": insiders reveal elite anguish as Russia's war falters', *Guardian*, 7 October 2022, https://www.theguardian.com/world/2022/oct/07/intense-dread-and-infighting-among-russian-elites-as-putins-war-falters.

13 «"Не нравится, детей своих на фронт отправьте." Пригожин прокомментировал сообщения о вербовке заключенных на войну», *The Insider*, 15 September 2022, https://theins.ru/news/255097.

14 Yuliya Krasnikov, «"Пытайте, издевайтесь, хоть горло перережайте". Как Евгений Пригожин вербует заключенных», *Vazhnye istorii*, 14 November 2022, https://istories.media/news/2022/11/14/pitaite-izdevaites-khot-gorlo-pererezaite-kak-yevgenii-prigozhin-verbuet-zaklyuchennikh/.

15 Guy Faulconbridge, 'Video shows sledgehammer execution of Russian mercenary'. Reuters, 13 November 2022, https://www.reuters.com/world/europe/sledgehammer-

execution-russian-mercenary-who-defected-ukraine-shown-video-2022-11-13/.

16 Kira Chernykh, «'Фонтанка' узнала, когда Евгений Пригожин стал Героем России», *Fontanka*, 5 July 2023, https://www.fontanka.ru/2023/07/05/72467339/.

17 Sebastian Shukla and Anna Chernova, 'Putin's "chef" Prigozhin admits creating Wagner mercenary outfit in 2014', CNN, 26 September 2022, https://edition.cnn.com/2022/09/26/europe/yevgeny-prigozhin-wagner-russia-intl/index.html.

18 «Глава ЧВК "Вагнер" рассказал, за что получил звания Героя России, ДНР и ЛНР», *62info*, 21 June 2023, https://62info.ru/news/russian/110425-glava-chvk-vagner-rasskazal-za-chto-poluchil-zvaniya-geroya-rossii-dnr-i-lnr/.

19 Concord Group Telegram post, 13 November 2022, https://t.me/concordgroup_official/27.

20 Peter Dickinson, 'Putin suffers humiliating defeat as Russia announces Kherson retreat', *UkraineAlert*, 19 November 2022, https://www.atlanticcouncil.org/blogs/ukrainealert/putin-faces-humiliating-defeat-as-russia-announces-kherson-retreat/.

21 Mike Eckel, 'The Rise of Prigozhin: "Putin's Chef" Steps Further into the Limelight', RFE/RL, 2 November 2022, https://www.rferl.org/a/russia-prigozhin-putin-chef-vagner-limelight-ukraine-war/32112554.html.

22 «С кем враждует "повар Путина"», *Vazhnye istorii*, 28 December 2022, https://istories.media/opinions/2022/12/28/s-kem-vrazhduet-povar-putina/.

23 «Прошлое и будущее Пригожина», *Dossier Center*, 6 July 2023, https://dossier.center/wagner-fall/.

24 «Кадыров и Пригожин регулярно (и подозрительно синхронно) критикуют российскую армию. Чего они добиваются?», *Meduza*, 4 October 2022, https://meduza.io/feature/2022/10/04/kadyrov-i-prigozhin-regulyarno-i-podozritelno-sinhronno-kritikuyut-rossiyskuyu-armiyu-chego-oni-dobivayutsya.

25 On Concord's Vkontakte page (now closed), 13 January 2023.

26 «Минобороны РФ сообщило об успешном штурме кварталов Соледара добровольцами ЧВК "Вагнер"», TASS, 13 January 2023, https://tass.ru/armiya-i-opk/16796997.

27 Mick Krever and Anna Chernova, 'Wagner chief admits to founding Russian troll farm sanctioned for meddling in US elections', CNN, 14 February 2023, https://edition. cnn.com/2023/02/14/europe/russia-yevgeny-prigozhin-internet-research-agency-intl/index.html.

Chapter 9: Rebel

1 https://www.youtube.com/watch?v=dIbJuJbR5_E.

2 Shane Harris and Isabelle Khurshudyan, 'Wagner Chief offered to give Russian troop locations to Ukraine, leak says', *Washington Post*, 14 May 2023, https://www. washingtonpost.com/national-security/2023/05/14/ prigozhin-wagner-ukraine-leaked-documents/.

3 Concord Group Telegram post, 15 February 2023, @ concordgroup_official.

4 Matt Murphy, 'Wagner, Prigozhin, Putin and Shoigu: Bitter rivalries that led to a rebellion', *BBC News*, 25 June 2023, https://www.bbc.co.uk/news/world-europe-66013532.

5 Morgan Meaker, 'Wagner Mutiny Puts Russia's Military Bloggers on a Razor's Edge', *Wired*, 29 June 2023, https://www.wired.co.uk/article/wagner-mutiny-russia-military-telegram-bloggers.

6 Thomas Grove, Alan Cullison and Bojan Pancevski, 'How Putin's Right-Hand Man Took Out Prigozhin,' *Wall Street Journal*, 22 December 2023, https://www.wsj.com/ world/russia/putin-patrushev-plan-prigozhin-assassina-tion-428d5ed8.

7 Telegram post, 9 March 2023, https://t.me/Prigozhin_ hat/2817.

8 «Пригожин записал видео к 9 мая – про "победу дедов" и какого-то "счастливого дедушку", который может оказаться "законченным мудаком"», *Meduza*, 9 May 2023, https://meduza.io/video/2023/05/09/ prigozhin-zapisal-video-k-9-maya-pro-pobedu-dedov-i-ka-kogo-to-schastlivogo-dedushku-kotoryy-mozhet-okazatsya-zakonchennym-mudakom.

9 «Какого "дедушку" оскорбляет Пригожин? Отвечает сам основатель ЧВК Вагнера», *Meduza*, 10 May 2023, https://meduza.io/feature/2023/05/10/kakogo-dedushku-

oskorblyaet-prigozhin-otvechaet-sam-osnovatel-chvk-vagnera.

10   Concord Group Telegram post, 20 May 2023, https://t.me/concordgroup_official/1002.

11   Concord Group Telegram post, 25 May 2023, https://t.me/concordgroup_official/1040.

12   Arutunyan's interview with Marat Gabidullin, 2023.

13   Anton Gerashchenko, Twitter post of video originally on Telegram channels, 23 May 2023, https://x.com/Gerashchenko_en/status/1663918446365626369?s=20.

14   «"Шлюха я или не шлюха" – дочь Пригожина о своей жизни в Дубае», *Ekho Moskvy*, 13 June 2023, https://arbatmedia.kz/exo-moskvy/slyuxa-ya-ili-ne-slyuxa-doc-prigozina-o-svoei-zizni-v-dubae-3711.

15   '"We need to take a page from North Korea's book"', *Meduza*, 24 May 2023, https://amp.meduza.io/en/feature/2023/05/24/we-need-to-take-a-page-from-north-korea-s-book

16   «Вхожий в Кремль военкор описал мнение Путина о конфликте Пригожина с Минобороны», *Lenta*, 14 June 2023, https://lenta.ru/news/2023/06/14/sladkov/.

17   «Заместитель Министра обороны России Николай Панков провел селекторное совещание по вопросам комплектования ВС РФ военнослужащими по контракту», Russian MoD, 10 June 2023, https://function.mil.ru/news_page/person/more.htm?id=12470053@egNews.

18   Georgy Alexandrov, «Кто не под нами, тот против нас», *Novaya Gazeta*, 12 June 2023, https://novayagazeta.eu/articles/2023/06/12/kto-ne-pod-nami-tot-protiv-nas.

19   Andrey Pertsev, 'They thought the risk was nil', *Meduza*, 24 June 2023, https://meduza.io/en/feature/2023/06/24/they-thought-the-risk-was-nil.

20   «Соратник Кадырова обратился к Пригожину и назвал его блогером», *Lenta*, 1 June 2023, https://lenta.ru/news/2023/06/01/delimkhanov/.

21   Pjotr Sauer, 'Wagner chief accuses Moscow of lying to public about Ukraine', *Guardian*, 23 June 2023, https://www.theguardian.com/world/2023/jun/23/wagner-chief-accuses-moscow-of-lying-to-public-about-ukraine-yevgeny-prigozhin.

22 «Пригожин заявил, что Минобороны РФ ударило по позициям ЧВК Вагнера. "Эта тварь будет остановлена", – сказал Пригожин о Шойгу», *Meduza*, 23 June 2023, https://meduza.io/news/2023/06/23/prigozhin-zayavil-ob-udare-minoborony-rf-po-pozitsiyam-chvk-vagnera-sleduyuschiy-shag-za-nami-zayavil-biznesmen.

23 «"Нас 25 тысяч, и мы идем разбираться, почему в стране творится беспредел". Пригожин заявил, что собирается "восстановить справедливость" в России», *Meduza*, 23 June 2023, https://meduza.io/news/2023/06/23/nas-25-tysyach-i-my-idem-razbiratsya-pochemu-v-strane-tvoritsya-bespredel-prigozhin-zayavil-chto-sobiraetsya-vosstanovit-spravedlivost-v-rossii.

24 Andrey Pertsev, 'They thought the risk was nil', *Meduza*, 24 June 2023, https://meduza.io/en/feature/2023/06/24/they-thought-the-risk-was-nil.

25 '"They'll squash you like a bug": How Alexander Lukashenko "negotiated" with Yevgeny Prigozhin, in his own words', *Meduza*, 27 June 2023, https://meduza.io/en/feature/2023/06/28/they-ll-squash-you-like-a-bedbug.

26 «"Пока не поздно, нужно остановить колонны и подчиниться воле президента". Генерал Суровикин призвал бойцов ЧВК Вагнера "решить вопросы мирным путем"», *Meduza*, 23 June 2023, https://meduza.io/news/2023/06/24/poka-ne-pozdno-nuzhno-ostanovit-kolonny-i-podchinitsya-vole-prezidenta-general-surovikin-prizval-boytsov-chvk-vagnera-reshit-voprosy-mirnym-putem.

27 '"We're saving Russia": In a meeting with military leaders, Yevgeny Prigozhin demanded respect. Read the transcript', *Meduza*, 24 June 2023, https://meduza.io/en/feature/2023/06/24/we-re-saving-russia.

28 Lilia Yapparova, '"There's nobody on earth who can stop them': What Wagner Group veterans have to say about Yevgeny Prigozhin's armed rebellion', *Meduza*, 24 June 2023, https://meduza.io/en/feature/2023/06/25/there-s-nobody-on-earth-who-can-stop-them.

29 Evgeny Vyshenkov, «Евгению Пригожину вернули 10 миллиардов рублей», *Fontanka*, 4 July 2023, https://www.fontanka.ru/2023/07/04/72460373/.

30 Vitaly Shevchenko, 'Wagner Group: Russian state media takes aim at Prigozhin', *BBC News*, 6 July 2023, https://www.bbc.co.uk/news/world-europe-66127952.

31 «Обращение к гражданам России», 24 June 2023, http://kremlin.ru/events/president/news/71496.

32 «"Я называю его Женя." История знакомства Лукашенко и Пригожина», Svoboda, 27 June 2023, https://www.svoboda.org/a/ya-nazyvayu-ngo-zhenya-istoriya-znakomstva-lukashenko-i-prigozhina/32477806.html.

33 Andrey Pertsev, «Путина не было нигде», *Meduza*, 25 June 2023, https://meduza.io/feature/2023/06/25/putina-ne-bylo-nigde.

34 '"They'll squash you like a bug": How Alexander Lukashenko "negotiated" with Yevgeny Prigozhin, in his own words', *Meduza*, 27 June 2023, https://meduza.io/en/feature/2023/06/28/they-ll-squash-you-like-a-bedbug.

35 «Обращение к гражданам России», 26 June 2023, http://kremlin.ru/events/president/news/71528.

36 Andrew Roth and Pjotr Sauer, 'Vladimir Putin says enemies wanted Russia to "choke on civil strife"', *Guardian*, 26 June 2023, https://www.theguardian.com/world/2023/jun/26/yevgeny-prigozhin-breaks-silence-after-armed-mutiny-russia.

Chapter 10: Ghost

1 VChK-OGPU Telegram channel, 23 August 2023, https://t.me/vchkogpu/41193.

2 Inna Greseva, «Что Путин рассказал о крушении самолета Пригожина», *Vedomosti*, 5 October 2023, https://www.vedomosti.ru/society/articles/2023/10/05/999080-putin-rasskazal-krushenii-samoleta-prigozhina.

3 Razgruzka Wagnera Telegram channel, 19 July 2023, https://t.me/razgruzka_vagnera/238.

4 Vera Bergengruen, 'Despite Rift with Putin, the Wagner Group's Global Reach is Growing', *Time*, 2 August 2023, https://time.com/6300145/wagner-group-niger-future/.

5 «Появилось полное видео из последней поездки Пригожина в Африку», *Lenta*, 1 October 2023, https://lenta.ru/news/2023/10/01/afrique/.

6   Andrei Kolesnikov, «ЧВК "Вагнер" не существует», *Kommersant*, 13 July 2023, https://www.kommersant.ru/doc/6098488.

7   Ibid.

8   Razgruzka Wagnera Telegram channel, 19 July 2023, https://t.me/razgruzka_vagnera/238.

9   Andrey Pertsev, 'He wants his own deputies', *Meduza*, 11 April 2023, https://meduza.io/en/feature/2023/04/11/he-wants-his-own-deputies.

10 «Если мы воюем дальше, надо объявлять мобилизацию уже сейчас», *Meduza*, 31 May 2023, https://meduza.io/feature/2023/05/31/esli-my-voyuem-dalshe-nado-ob-yavlyat-mobilizatsiyu-uzhe-seychas.

11 Andrei Kolesnikov, «Блеск и нищета Евгения Пригожина. Есть ли у него политическое будущее», *Carnegie Politika*, 6 June 2023, https://carnegieendowment.org/politika/89884.

12 «"Левада-центр": после мятежа почти 30% россиян заявили, что одобряют деятельность Евгения Пригожина. Неделей ранее таких людей было в два раза больше», *Meduza*, 29 June 2023, https://meduza.io/news/2023/06/29/levada-tsentr-posle-myatezha-pochti-30-rossiyan-zayavili-chto-odobryayut-deyatelnost-evgeniya-prigozhina-nedeley-ranee-takih-lyudey-bylo-v-dva-raza-bolshe.

13 Anatoly Kurmanaev, 'Prigozhin's public support remains significant despite Russian propaganda efforts, polls show', *New York Times*, 3 July 2023, https://www.nytimes.com/2023/07/03/world/europe/prigozhin-ukraine-war-poll.html.

14 Mikhail Savelyev, «Так можно с президентом? Навальный жестко потроллил "бункерного дедушку" Владимира Путина», *Sobesednik*, 30 October 2020, https://sobesednik.ru/obshchestvo/20201030-tak-mozhno-s-prezidentom-naval.

15 Thomas Grove, Alan Cullison and Bojan Pancevski, 'How Putin's Right-Hand Man Took Out Prigozhin,' *Wall Street Journal*, 22 December 2023, https://www.wsj.com/world/russia/putin-patrushev-plan-prigozhin-assassination-428d5ed8.

16 Yuliya Kotova, «"Человек сложной судьбы": Путин впервые прокомментировал крушение самолета Пригожина», *Forbes*, 24 August 2023, https://www.forbes.

ru/society/495127-celovek-sloznoj-sud-by-putin-vpervye-prokommentiroval-krusenie-samoleta-prigozina.

17 Andrew Roth, 'Is Yevgeny Prigozhin really dead? Not everyone is convinced', *Guardian*, 24 August 2023, https://www.theguardian.com/world/2023/aug/24/is-yevgeny-prigozhin-really-dead-not-everyone-is-convinced.

18 Andrey Suvorov, «Началась борьба за наследство Пригожина. Кто на него претендует», RTVI, 9 September 2023, https://rtvi.com/news/nachalas-borba-za-nasledstvo-prigozhina-kto-na-nego-pretenduet/.

19 Denis Lebedev, Nikolay Kudin and Ksenia Klochkova, «Бизнес Пригожина. Что принадлежит самому известному в мире российскому бизнесмену», *Fontanka*, 24 August 2023, https://www.fontanka.ru/2023/08/24/72633500/.

20 «Павел Пригожин возглавил подразделение Росгвардии, куда вошла ЧВК "Вагнер"», *Kommersant*, 1 November 2023, https://www.kommersant.ru/doc/6312235.

21 Conversation with Galeotti, December 2023.

22 «"Надо объявить мобилизацию уже сейчас". Пригожин объяснил, как и когда можно закончить СВО», *V1*, 31 May 2023, https://v1.ru/text/politics/2023/05/31/72353648/.

Epilogue

1 «Пригожин дал интервью, где рассказал что Россия стоит на грани катастрофы», Politkremru, 30 April 2023, TikTok, https://www.tiktok.com/@politkremru/video/7227943535700348187.

2 «Пригожин не просто жив. Глава Чвк "Вагнер" жжёт на всю катушку и взрывает сеть», *Tsargrad*, 9 February 2024, https://tsargrad.tv/news/prigozhin-ne-prosto-zhiv-glava-chvk-vagner-zhzhjot-na-vsju-katushku-i-vzyvaet-set_957882.

Index

A Just Russia – For Truth,
  party 178
Abramovich, Roman 71
actors, reliance on 210–1
adhocracy viii, 111–13, 142
administrative
  entrepreneurship 26–9
advertising notices 87–8
Aerospace Forces 121, 183,
  185
AFRIC (Association for Free
  Research and International
  Cooperation) 144
Africa
  illusory influence in 138–41;
  pivot to 130–2; and post-
  Zhenya life 205; Prigozhin
  commitment in 137–8;
  touring 196
African National Congress 144
AK-47s 124
akademiya (prison) 18
Alexei, ex-convict 1–2
Alexeyev, Vladimir 118,
  147–50, 182–3
Almaz-Antey Air 138
Amelchenko, Valery 85
Anatomy of a Protest 84, 87
Angelika Film Center 98
Apraksin Dvor (Aprashka)
  19–20
Argumenty i Fakty 83
Article 359, Criminal Code
  103

Assad, Bashar 119
Association for Free Research
  and International
  Cooperation (AFRIC) 144
Aurum 97
Aven, Piotr 71
Averianov, Andrei 119

Bakhmut, Ukraine 151–4,
  166–70
  fall of 172–3
bas cuisine 41–4
Bashir, Omar al- 132
Batman Battalion 116
Bednov, Alexander 116
Beglov, Alexander 136–7, 159,
  160–1
Belarus, exile to 188–91
Bell, The 126
Berezovsky Boris, 55
Berlusconi, Silvio 46
betrayal, condottiere and
  123–7
Black Cross 153
Black Lives Matter 93
black market 7, 15, 21–2
Blair, Tony 46
blat (economy of favours) 3,
  22–3
BlinDonald's, establishing
  41–4, 58
bloggers 87–8
Bogatov, Andrei 117
Bolotnaya protests 218

Bolotnaya Square, Moscow
80–1
Bulgakov, Dmitry 106
Bush, George W. 60
Bushman, Alexei 7
Business Project 71
byudzhetniki 81

Cabo Delgado, Mozambique
142
Cape Idokopas 64
Capital Legal Services 46
CAR (Central African
Republic) 129–32, 134–5,
141, 143
Central African Republic
(CAR) 129–32, 134–5,
141, 143
Chávez, Hugo 46
chef, Yevgeny Prigozhin as
35–7
haute and bas cuisine
41–4; opening Staraya
Tamozhnya 37–40; salon of
Prigozhin 44–8; *tusokva* rise
48–52
Chekalov, Valery 'Rover' 193
Chemezov, Sergei 56
Chirac, Jacques 59–60
Chubais, Anatoly 50
City Hall 29, 31–3, 40, 48–51
Clinton, Bill 58
Clinton, Hillary 80, 82, 90–5
Cohen, Sacha Baron 187
commentators 88, 93, 160,
166, 168
Communist Party 3–4, 8, 23,
28
compromising materials
(kompromat) 45–6

Concord Catering, 57, 76,
83–4, 205
Concord Management and
Consulting, 15, 66, 131,
205
condottiere, Prigozhin as
101–3
adhocracy 111–13; betrayal
123–7; covert war 105–11;
establishing Wagner 113–15;
rival narratives 103–5; Syria
events 118–23; Wagner in
Donbas 115–17
Congo, Democratic Republic
of 144
contracts, padding of 73–4
Contrast Ltd 30–1
convicts, army of 154–7
cooperatives *(kooperativy)* 10
covert war 105–11
Crimea, annexation of, 119
Crimean Peninsula 105, 151
criminal behaviour
encouraging, 133–8
Criminal Code 103

dark side, embracing 154–7
Day of Heroes of the
Fatherland 117
deal, Prigozhin-Putin 188–91
death (of Prigozhin)
aftermath of 203–7;
delay between mutiny
and response 202–3;
explanations of 195–9;
overview 193–5; portrait
in Putinism 207–14; public
profile elevation 200–3
Defence Ministry 70, 73, 105
Deir ez-Zor, province 125

Democratic Republic of
    Congo 144
Deripaska, Oleg 62
diamonds, collecting 130–3
Dictator, The (film) 187
Dolgov, Konstantin 175
Donbas 145, 153, 218, 118
    defending 112; deployment
    in 110; establishing army
    in 113–5; forces emerging
    in 105; scouting for
    opportunities in 102–3;
    Wagner in 115–17
Donetsk Region 180
Dremov, Pavel 'Batya' 116
Dresden, East Germany 24–5
Dugin, Alexander 209
Dvor, Stroganovsky 41
Dvornikov, Alexander 120
Dyumin, Alexei 102, 111, 188

Embraer Legacy 600, shooting
    down 193–5
entrepreneur, Yevgeny
    Prigozhin as 17–18
    administrative
    entrepreneurship 26–9; fresh
    out of prison 18–21; Putin
    beginnings 21–6; Zhenya
    meeting Vova 29–34
Executive Outcomes 106
External Affairs Committee
    25

fast food, sector 41–4
favours *(blat)* 22–3
Federal Protection Service 69
Federal Security Service (FSB)
    26–7, 178
folklore 36

Fontanka (news outlet) 114
Forbes Russia 82–3
Frunze Embankment 106
FSB (Federal Security Service)
    26–7, 186

Gabidullin, Marat 102–3,
    110–12, 122, 142–3, 173
gambling 27–30
Gazeta o Gazetakh (Newspaper
    about Newspapers) 83–4,
    86
Gazprom 49
Gear, Tony 38, 44, 57
General Staff 106–7, 121, 149,
    159
Gerasimov, Valery 107, 149,
    159, 178–9
    and March of Justice 180–7;
    and swinging pendulum
    161–4
Ghost brigade 116
Girkin, Igor 116, 218
glasnost (speaking up) 8–10
Glazyev, Sergei 141
going national 69–74
gopniks 122
Gorbachev, Mikhail 24
    on *glasnost* 8–10; liberals
    working under 22–3; on
    perestroika 8–10
Gorbenko, Igor 29
grandfather, absolving 170–3
Granit (film) 96–7
Grey Zone, The (website) 204
Grom, Federal Security
    Service 73
GRU 103, 115, 145, 148
    Syria and, 118–20
Gryzlov, Boris 189

Guaidó, Juan 140
Gudkov, Gennady 79
Gulyayev, Yevgeny 86, 111–12
Gusev, Vadim 108
Gusinsky, Vladimir 55

Haftar, Khalifa 129–30
haute cuisine 41–4
Health National Project 64
Heart of Darkness (Conrad) 134–5
Hero of the Russian Federation (medal) 117, 186, 204
Herzen, Alexander 35–6
hot-dog stand, making money off of 18–21
Human Rights Watch 134
hustlers 141–6

IK-1 Kopeisk, prison colony 157
Indraguzik (book) 213–4
influence, illusion of 138–41
Ingushetia 179
intelligentsia 2, 4–5
Internet Research Agency (IRA) 86–7, 88, 89, 91–2, 95, 163, 198, 205
IRA (Internet Research Agency) 86–7, 88, 89, 91–2, 95, 163, 198, 205
Islamic State 142

Jacko (Progozhin) 6–7. *See* also Prigozhin, Yevgeny
journalists 46, 64, 83–4, 88–9, 91, 135, 137, 144, 148, 158
Just Russia – For Truth 200

Kadyrov, Ramzan 33–4, 172, 179
Kadyrovites 179
KGB (Committee for State Security)
  administrative entrepreneurship and 26–9; joining 23–4; officers 16, 26–8, 48–9, 56
Khim, Nataliya 172
Khodorkovsky, Mikhail 5, 47
Khodotov, Yevgeny 132
khozyayin 62
Kitch, Russky 41
kolshchik (pricker) 12–13
Kommersant (newspaper) 198
kompromat (compromising materials) 45–6
Komsomol (Young Communist League) 81
Konstantinovsky Hall, St Petersburg 88
Konstantinovsky Palace 72
kooperativ (cooperatives) 10–11, 19
laws of pay for 20–1; restaurant as 40
Korotkov, Denis 85
Koshara, Dmitry 76, 84
Kremlin 105
  diamonds and 130–3; friends of 87–90; paranoia in 175; passive approach 139–4; Prigozhin specter haunting 207–14; and Syria 118–23; taking advantage of Prigozhin achievements 146
Kruchina, Nikolai 28
Kryazheva, Lyubov 18, 30, 57, 67, 70, 207

krysha (roof) 40
KSSO (Special Operations Forces Command) 102–3, 111
Kudrin, Alexei 49
Kuibyshev District Court 6
Kumarin, Vladimir 32–3
Kunstkamera (museum) 37
Kuprashevich, Maria 85
Kurara, Sasha 12
Kuzhenkino, Tver Region 193
Kyiv 90, 103, 105, 109, 147, 151–2, 184

Lake Komsomolskoye 51
Lavrov, Sergei 131, 201
Law on Cooperatives 11
Lenin, Vladimir 36
Leningrad (St Petersburg) 19
Leningrad Chemical and Pharmaceutical College 18
Leningrad Sports Boarding School No. 62 4
Leningrad State University 21, 48
liberalisation, campaign 60–5, 78–9
Libyan National Army 129–30
Lipetsk Region 185
Litvinenko, Aleksander 32
LNR (Luhansk) 116
Lobaye-Invest 132
London Symphony Orchestra 46
lowered, risk of being 12
Luhansk (LNR) 116
Lukashenko, Alexander 182, 189
Lyakhta Plaza 70

M-Finans 132
M-Invest 131–2, 135
M-Invest and Meroe Gold 67
Maduro, Nicolás 140, 142
Makarov, Nikolai 107
Mali, Wagner in 134, 142, 196
Malofeyev, Konstantin 140–1
Malyshevskaya gang 20
Mapouka, Freddy 199
March of Justice 180–7, 213
May 2014 Declaration 170
McDonald's. *See* BlinDonald's, establishing
meat waves 155–6, 167
Mechel 62
MedStroi 83–4
Medvedev, Dmitry 49, 61–2, 64, 76, 201, 209
Megaline (company) 70–1
mercenary captain. *See* condottiere, Prigozhin as
Mikhailov, Andrei 85
Military Counter-Intelligence Directorate 178
military intelligence. *See* GRU
militsia (Societ police) 2
Miller, Alexei 49
minigarchs
  expansion of ambitions 65–8; feeding nation 60–5; going national 69–74; overview 53–4; partying like Russians 57–60; rise of 54–7
Ministry of Defence (MoD) 103, 176–7
Mirilashvili, Mikhail 29, 37, 67–8
Mironov, Sergei 178
Mishustin, Mikhail 188
Mizintsev, Mikhail 171–2

MoD (Ministry of Defence) 103, 176–7
Moran Security Group 108
Mori, Yoshiro 29, 45
Moscow State University 209
Moscow, losing in 166–70
Moskovsky Komsomolets 83
Moskovsky, Grisha 12
Moskva-177 (party boat) 42
'Most Favoured Nation Principle in International Law, The' 22–3
Moura, siege of 134
movies, financially backing 96–9
Mozgovoi, Alexei 116
Mueller, Robert 91–2
mutiny, speculation of 177–8

na levo (to the left) 22
Naryshkin, Sergei 61
Nashi ('Ours'), 81, 88
nation, feeding 60–5
National Guard 32, 177, 179, 183, 185, 204, 206
National Media Group 198
National Priority Projects 64
Navalny, Alexei 79–80, 181, 202–3, 212, 215
Neva-Chance 31, 33
New Island (boat restaurant) 42–3, 45, 48, 50, 59–60, 69, 189
New Russians 43
Niger, military coup in 196
Night League 71, 136
nomenklatura 23
Novaya Gazeta 74, 83–86
Novgorod 6

obshchak 28
Oka River 186
oladyi 39
oligarchs 49, 54–5, 62–4, 71–2, 131, 186
Onishchenko, Gennady 53, 70
Operation Meatgrinder. *See* Bakhmut, Ukraine
opolchentsy 218
Order of Courage 117
outsider, Yevgeny Prigozhin as 2–8

pariah, becoming 135–6
Party Central Committee 28
Patriot Media 90, 198
Patrushev, Nikolai 49, 112, 169, 188, 203
penal military unit 154–7
pendulum, swing of 160–4
perestroika (rebuilding) 8–10, 16
permissions 57–60
petukhi (roosters) 12
Pikalyovo Cement Factory 54
PMC (Private Military Company) 103, 107–11, 148, 165, 198
ponyatiya 47–8
Porokhovskoye cemetery 204
post-Zhenya life 203–7
Presidential Administration 49–50, 111, 145, 179
Presidential Property Management Department 49
Presidential Security Service 102
pricker *(kolshchik)* 12–13
Prigozhin, Lyubov 207
Prigozhin, Pavel 153, 205

Prigozhin, Violetta 2, 57–8, 66, 71, 84

Prigozhin, Yevgeny Ilyich vii–x, 96, 215–21
adhocracy and 111–13; as administrative entrepreneur 26–9; ambitions of 65–8; becoming international pariah 135–6; betraying 123–7; building brand of 143–6; as chef 35–52; as condottiere 101–27; convict army of 154–7; curating image of 95–9; death of 193–5; education of 4–6; embracing dark side 154–7; encouraging criminal behaviour 33–8; as entrepreneur 17–34; going beyond St Petersburg 69–74; illusory influence of 138–41; as Jacko 6–8; legacy of 193–214; life after 203–7; making Hillary squirm 90–5; and March of Justice 180–7; meeting Putin 29–34; minigarchs and 53–74; moniker of 'Putin's chef' 35–7; partying like Russians 57–60; path of self-realisation 76–82; as rebel 165–91; rival narratives of 103–5; and rivalry with Shoigu 173–7; as scavenger 129–46; seeing purpose in war 211–4; standing down 188–91; and swinging pendulum 160–4; as thug 1–16; as trollmaster 75–99; uniqueness of 208–9;
unmasking 158–60; as warlord 147–64; wealth of 56–7; Zone life 11–16

Prigozhina, Veronika 174

prison *(akademiya)* 18

prison system 13

Private Military Company (PMC) 103, 107–11, 148, 165, 198

Prizrak 116

propiska 2

Prospekt Energetikov 18

provocations, tit for tat 82–7

proxy war 119, 140, 215

public profile, elevation of 200–3

Putin, Vladimir 75, 215–21, vii–x
actor reliance of 210–1; adhocracy and 111–13; beginnings of 21–6; betraying Prigozhin 123–7; challenge facing 219–20; covert war of 105–11; creating National Priority Projects 64; deciding to invade Ukraine 150–4; defending thesis 22–3; delay between mutiny and response 202–3; in Dresden, East Germany 24–5; ego of 77–8; favour as currency of success 57–60; first two presidential terms of 77; as grandfather 170–3, 175–6; leaving KGB 25–6; liberalisation 60–5; making Hillary squirm 90–5; man-of-the-people performances of 63–4; and

March of Justice 180–7; and Medvedev liberalisation campaign 78–9; meeting Prigozhin 29–34; minigarchs and 53–74; missing out on *perestroika* 16; political machine of 80; portrait in Putinism 207–14; and post-Zhenya life 203–7; and Prigozhin standing down 188–91; Prigozhin steamrolling favoured opinion 197–9; rebellion failure on part of 209–10; and rise of *tusovka* 48–52; and swinging pendulum 160–4; word and deed 177–80

Putinism, portrait in 207–14

Raspopova, Kristina 193
rebellion
absolving happy grandfather 170–3; beyond Shoigu 173–7; losing in Moscow 166–70; March of Justice 180–7; overview 165–6; standing down 188–91; winning in Bakhmut 166–70; word and deed 177–80
rebuilding *(perestroika)* 8–10, 16
Red Army 70
Red Stars Hotel 67
Redut (Redoubt) 148, 151, 206
reform, Soviet Union 8–10
Republic of Komi 13
restaurateur, work as. *See* Staraya Tamozhnya
Revolution of Dignity 90, 109
rival narratives 103–5

roof *(krysha)* 40
roosters *(petukhi)* 12
Rosoboronexport 138–9
Rostov-on-Don, city 177, 183–4, 200
Rostropovich, Mstisla 46
Rotenberg brothers 56, 71
ruble, market value of 19–20
Russia
passive-aggressive behaviour of 138–41; Prigozhin spectre haunting 207–14
Russia-Africa Summit and Economic Conference 138, 140, 199
Russian Energy Ministry 125
Russian Equestrian Federation 136
Russian Field 21
Russian Foreign Ministry 129, 143
Russian Orthodoxy 211
Russian, party like 57–60
Rzhev (film) 96

Salman, king 46
salon (of Progozhin) 44–8
sanctions 58, 67, 97, 119, 133, 135, 144
scavengers 141–6
scavenging
encouraging criminal behaviour 133–8; hustles and 141–6; illusory influence 138–41; overview 129–30; pivot to Africa 130–2; Sudan scheme 132–3
Sechin, Igor 48, 55, 140
Second Chechen War 179
2nd Special Forces Brigade 10

Second World War 22, 96, 156, 172
Serdyukov, Anatoly 106, 110
Shamalov, Nikolai 49, 64
shell hunger 167
shestyorka (gangster's runner) 20–1
Shkolnik, Moskovsky 66–7
Shoigu, Ksenia 174
Shoigu, Sergei 51, 71, 122, 125, 149, 159, 178–9, 201
beyond 173–7; and March of Justice 180–7; relationship with Putin 169; and swinging pendulum 161–4
Shugalei, Maxim 204
Sidorov, Yevgeny 108
16-i (16th) (film) 98
Sklyarov, Alexander 88
Slavonic Corps 108, 114
slovo i delo (word and deed) 177–80
Smirnov, Vladimir 50
Sobchak, Anatoly 25, 31, 48
Sobyanin, Sergei 70, 185
Sochi Winter Olympics 56
social media 12, 87, 89, 91, 93, 96, 98, 114, 145, 157–8, 160, 166, 168, 174, 200, 204
Society of Blue Buckets 72
Solntsepyok (Blazing Sun) (film) 96–7
Solzhenitsyn, Alexander 24
Soviet Union
authorities in 6–7; average salary 20; citizen life in 2–5; collapse of 14–16; cooperative movement in 10; reform of 8–10; social safety net of 63–4; unspoken rule of 15
Space Defence Corporation 138
speaking up *(glasnost)* 8–10
Special Operations Forces Command (KSSO) 102–3, 111
Spektor, Boris 29, 37
Spektr Joint Stock Company and Contrast Consulting 29–30
Spetsnaz,Brigade 101, 113, 117–8, 123, 148
Spiridon 36. *See also* Putin, Vladimir
St Petersburg, Russia
Economic Forum 106; experiment in 65–6; positions of power in 41–2; Prosecutor's Office 68; Staraya Tamozhnya in 37–40
Stalin, Joseph 36
Staraya Tamozhnya (Old Customs House) 30–1
Staraya Tamozhnya (restaurant) 37–40
State Duma 178
Steel, youth organisation 82
Stolyarov, Alexei 174
Sudan, scheme in 132–3, 141
Supervisory Council for Casinos and Gambling 25, 31
Surkov, Vladislav 77, 80–1
Surovikin, Sergei 121–2, 169, 177–8, 182
Syria, Russian forces in 118–23

Tamozhnya, Staraya 8, 44–45, 69

10th Spetsnaz Brigade 113

thieves' world (vorovskoi mir) 11–13

thug, Yevgeny Prigozhin as 1–2
    getting mixed up with wrong crowd 2–8; life in Zone 11–16; reform 8–10

tit for tat 82–7

Tkachev, Gennady 59

to the left (na levo) 22

Touadéra, Faustin-Archange 131

transparency 55

troll farm 88, 205, 211

trolls
    image curation 95–9; Kremlin friends 87–90; making Hillary squirm 90–5; overview 75–6; revenge of 'best and the most productive' 76–82; tit for tat 82–7

Troshev, Andrei 117, 178, 197

Trump, Donald 71, 82, 91–2

tsar, absolving 170–3

Tsargrad 221

Tsepov, Roman 32–3

turbo-patriots 168, 212–3, 218

Turist (The Tourist) (film) 96

tusovka, rise of 48–52

2008 financial crisis 107

Ukraine ix, 95, 102, 136, 215–21
    Bakhmut battle 153–4; convict army in 154–7; fall of Bakhmut 172–3; invasion of 150–4; and March of Justice 180–7; overview of 147–9; and Prigozhin spectre 207–14; Revolution of Dignity 109; striking back 149–50; and swinging pendulum 160–4; Wagner in 151–4; winning in Bakhmut 66–70

United Russia 76–9, 81, 88

United States 138

Unknown Battle (film) 96

unmasking 158–60

UralVagonZavod, 81

US Treasury 133

Utkin, Dmitry 101, 111–15, 193

Vagnerovtsy 151

Vaino, Anton 188

Valentina, ex-convict 1–2

Venezuela 45, 137–8, 140, 142, 194

Victory Day 164, 167, 171

Viktorovich, Yevgeny 158

Vladislav, Teraway 1–2

Vneshtorgbank 60

Volodin, Vyacheslav 81, 87

vorovskoi mir (thieves' world) 11–13

Vostok Battalion 115

Vova. See Putin, Vladimir

voyenkor 200

voyenkory 168–9

VTB. See Vneshtorgbank

Wagner 132, 138, 145, 177, 205
    addressing Belarus fighters 199; Bakhmut battle

153–4; becoming shadow of former strength 170–3; changing nature of 156; Chechen forces and 180; and condottiere betrayal 123–7; convict army and 154–7; in the Donbas 115–17; encouraging criminal behaviour 133–8; establishing 113–15; independence of 142; March of Justice 180–7; and May 2014 Declaration 170–1; and pivot to Africa 130–3; popularity of 143–4; Prigozhin unmasking 158–60; reassuring customers of 196; retaining 206–7; and Shoigu rivalry 173–7; and swinging pendulum 160–4; in Syria 118–23; in Ukraine 151–4; 'Wagner: A Second Front' campaign 200–2; Zelensky assassination attempts 151–2

Wagner Cinematic Universe 145, 168

Wagner Private Military Company 165

'Wagner: A Second Front', campaign 200–2

Wall Street Journal 203

war crimes, allegations of 156–7

WarGonzo Telegram 160

warlord, Prigozhin as 147–50. See also Ukraine

West, moral panic in 138–9

Wine Club 37

word and deed (slovo i delo) 177–80

World Trade Organization (WTO) 23, 61

WTO (World Trade Organization) 23

Yakovlev, Vladimir 42

Yanukovych, Viktor 102, 109

Yeltsin era 54

Yeltsin, Boris 22, 54, 63–4

Yevkurov, Yunus-bek 183–4

YMCA 81

youth movements 81–2

Yukos 55

zeks 154

Zelensky, Volodymyr 147 and invasion of Ukraine 150–4

Zhenya. See Prigozhin, Yevgeny

Zhigulis (car) 18, 20

Zhuravlyov, Alexander 123–4

Ziminov, Kirill 37, 68

Zolotov, Viktor 31–2, 185

Zone, living inside 11–16

Zubarev, Yevgeny 89

Zyuganov, Gennady 201